Jack Orchard's book, *A Handbook for Improving Student Achievement in Secondary Schools,* is a functional work centered on democratic citizenship, student ownership, and collaborative learning. An outgrowth of his experience, research, and reflection as a parent, teacher, department head, principal, secondary school district consultant, superintendent of schools, and provincial education facilitator.

His book distinguishes a series of clusters—interrelated factors contributing to high school reform. As we advance, we need practitioners supplementing university-based change research through books and articles describing first-hand secondary school observations, appreciations, concerns, failures, successes, reflections, understandings, interventions, and conclusions. This is one of them.

My children—Kevin, Cheri, Brent, and Donna—I have so much respect for their resilience, learning capacity, and concern for others.

Jack Orchard

A Handbook for Improving Student Achievement in Secondary Schools

Democratic Citizenship, Student Ownership, and Collaborative Learning

Austin Macauley Publishers
LONDON · CAMBRIDGE · NEW YORK · SHARJAH

Copyright © Jack Orchard 2025

All rights reserved. No part of this publication may be reproduced, distributed, or transmitted in any form or by any means, including photocopying, recording, or other electronic or mechanical methods, without the prior written permission of the publisher, except in the case of brief quotations embodied in critical reviews and certain other non-commercial uses permitted by copyright law. For permission requests, write to the publisher.

Any person who commits any unauthorized act in relation to this publication may be liable to criminal prosecution and civil claims for damages.

Ordering Information
Quantity sales: Special discounts are available on quantity purchases by corporations, associations, and others. For details, contact the publisher at the address below.

Publisher's Cataloging-in-Publication data
Orchard, Jack
A Handbook for Improving Student Achievement in Secondary Schools

ISBN 9798891554191 (Paperback)
ISBN 9798891554207 (Hardback)
ISBN 9798891554221 (ePub e-book)
ISBN 9798891554214 (Audiobook)

Library of Congress Control Number: 2024910659

www.austinmacauley.com/us

First Published 2025
Austin Macauley Publishers LLC
40 Wall Street, 33rd Floor, Suite 3302
New York, NY 10005
USA

mail-usa@austinmacauley.com
+1 (646) 5125767

Rea Taylor Gill for her editing, encouragement, and honesty.

Anthony Riffel for his sage advice, personal and professional.

Message to Readers:

December 11, 2024

I invite your contributions to the website: "Improving Student Achievement in Secondary Schools." Sharing concerns, questions, suggestions, achievements, and reflections while collaborating with other contributors works toward needed change. This give and take important for achieving such goals as democratic citizenship, distributed leadership, improved student thinking, student learning ownership, enhanced school and community supports, and finding common ground for progressives and conservatives.

At the heart of pragmatic reform are seven theorems—a "compelling roadmap" for change as described by John Hattie. Collaborative learning is critical for determining superordinate goals, democratic leadership in classrooms, schools, districts, and communities; deeper thinking, student self-regulation, parents and students as partners, building social capital, and both individual and group accountability.

Mutual learning depends on small and large groups (direct or virtual) of teachers, students, parents, administrators and community members (bottom up and top-down) fulfilling and consolidating student-centered change.

Please send contributions by clicking "Contact Jack" at *http://jackorchard.ca*

Thank you,
Jack Orchard

Table of Contents

Introduction	11
Chapter 1: Past Performance: Stuck in Neutral	49
Chapter 2: Change Leadership: Distributed Ownership	73
Chapter 3: Working Together: Alignment for Success	106
Chapter 4: Cognitive Acceleration: Deeper Thinking	130
Chapter 5: Self-Regulation: Students as Independent Learners	155
Chapter 6: Activating Allies: Parents and Students as Partners	196
Chapter 7: Building Social Capital: Team Building	220
Chapter 8: The Distributive Property: Student Achievement/ Accountability	256
References	303

Introduction

Democratic Citizenship, Student Ownership, and Collaborative Learning

"We now accept the fact that learning is a lifelong process of keeping abreast of change. And the most pressing task is to teach people how to learn": Peter Drucke, June 25, 2019

Concept Map 1

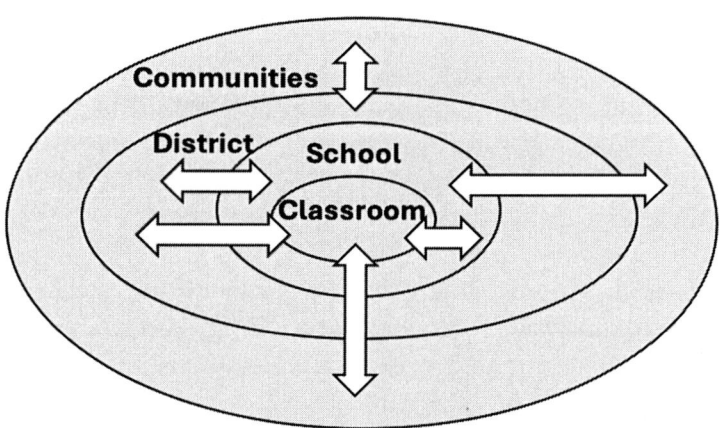

The interdependence of democracy and education is undervalued; our form of government assumes well educated citizens while education systems require fully functioning democracies—the arrows representing pressure and support both ways. When schools, districts, communities, and nations invest in students, their achievements both sustain and enhance democratic ideals.

George H. Wood in *Time To Learn: How to Create High Schools That Serve All Students* 2nd edition (2005) connects a healthy democracy with self-directed learning capacity currently missing in secondary schools:

> Passivity and low expectations are not only the enemies of learning, they are also enemies of democratic life. A democracy requires that its citizens be engaged, think for themselves, be willing to take action, and tolerate ambiguity. When the final part of a young person's public education is to passively consume sometimes trivial information, they are not learning what it means to be a self-directed thinker and citizen. (p. 18)

Dominici P. (2023) from his Prospects article, "The weak link of democracy and the challenges of educating toward global citizenship":

> The correlations between education and inclusion, between education and citizenship, and between education and democracy have never been clearer. A shared ethics and a cultural model based on legality, civic-mindedness, and a full awareness of the rights and duties of citizenship are the building blocks and essential mechanisms for the very survival of any social or organizational system, not to mention one that aspires to form a global network. It is of paramount importance that decision-makers in this environment realize that ethics and morals cannot be imposed but must develop through real-life experiences and processes.
>
> Instead, schools should have the function of awakening and stimulating these passions, of guiding students on pathways capable of merging reason and imagination and of linking thought, action, and emotion—factors that are all but neglected in our current school and university curricula.

The need to be unequivocal in growing democratic values in public schools is referenced by Crowther et al. (2009):

> While Western democracies tend to have explicit national statements that affirm the importance of their schools in nurturing democratic processes and institutions, it is difficult to see mature manifestations of 'deep' democracy in the workings of their schools. Mulford (2004, pp. 635–636).

> Among Mulford's conclusions is that if schools are in fact to nurture 'deep' democracy, they must become professional learning organizations with students, teachers, and leaders bound by relationships that are grounded on trust, collaboration, shared mission, risk taking, and ongoing professional learning. (p. 33)

From the United States, Ken Jones in his book, *Democratic School Accountability: A Model for School Improvement* (2006), helps define shared mission:

> Perhaps the most basic notion of democracy is the idea of participatory decision making in an open society. And perhaps the most basic ideals associated with democracy are that the government should promote freedom, justice, and equity for all of its citizens. We hold these ideals high as a nation, despite the cruel realities that exist for many of our citizens. (p. 7)

Bickmore [Abstract], Citizenship Education in Canada: 'Democratic' Engagement with Differences, Conflicts, and Equity Issues? September 1, 2014:

> Implicit citizenship education is embedded in day-to-day school-related activities and relationships: patterns of discipline and conflict management, community service activities, and student voice and leadership roles. Thus active, engaged citizenship, attentive to multicultural diversity, is a prominent goal in recent Canadian citizenship education policy and programming—yet in practice, Canadian students (especially those from less privileged backgrounds) have few opportunities to practice democratically-relevant citizenship learning in school. (p. 1)

Hinchey P. H. and Konkol P.J. (2018) in *Getting to Where We Meant to Be: Working Toward the Educational World We Imagined*:

> Rather than avoiding political issues related to social problems that plague individual communities as well as the nation as a whole, the justice-oriented perspective encourages

student analysis of structural causes of the problems and efforts to provoke change in them. Citizenship in this case involves ongoing critical analysis to determine where tenets of democracy seem to have been violated or abandoned and working to get things back on course. (p. 106)

Joe L. Kincheloe and Shirley R. Steinberg in their introduction to "Thirteen Questions: Reframing Education's Conversation" 2nd edition (1996) on the need for a guiding vision:

> Any social or education reform demands the creation of a guiding vision, a purpose that helps individuals make meaning. Indeed, the malformations of Western culture will never be addressed until a vision is formulated. Students drift through school with little understanding of the meaning of education that goes beyond 'it's in the curriculum' or 'look in the textbook'. Teacher education often ignores questions of educational meaning, focusing its attention on techniques of delivering information.
> … As dramatic as it may seem, many argue that not only does educational reform rest on the creation of a system of meaning, but human survival itself may be at stake. Short-term technicist thinking has allowed the world's eco-system to be threatened, justified the spending of unfathomable monies on weapons, and ignored the needs of the poor and dispossessed. Education, operating with the blinders of such thinking, has accepted and even promoted such cognitive pathology. The idea that school may need to help students make meaning in a time of informational chaos has never been high on education's list of priorities. A critical system of meaning can be used to help us define school purpose, the nature of education and what it means to be a smart learner and teacher. (p. 3)

Democratic citizenship is a superordinate goal: a composite of communicative abilities, freedom with responsibility, career preparation, community mindfulness, collective ownership, distributed leadership, and direct or indirect support for those in need. Responsible citizens require the same learning abilities/attitudes as for careers: ask thoughtful questions, communicate and collaborate effectively with others, see beyond themselves, analyze information, and form independent opinions.

As stated above, such results should not be taken for granted. One example is a town deciding only parents should bear the cost of public education. They passed a law to that effect; only possible because a majority of its citizens had, for some time, failed to participate in democratic decision making.

One reader's response: [name of person], referring to one of the law's supporters, "thinks 'freedom' is looking out for himself alone. How wrong he is. What's more important than supporting our children's education? And our aging community's health? He'd rather not be taxed. His view doesn't represent freedom, but meanness fueled by a careless disregard for others." New York Times, August 10, 2022

From Michael Fullan's introduction to the report, *How the world's most improved school systems keep getting better* (2010) by Mourshed, Chigiuke, and Barlow:

> For a long time, there has been the realization that better education is the key to societal and global productivity and personal and social well-being. Only recently are we beginning to see that interest turn into specific questions about how you actually go about whole system reform. (p. 1)

The report summarizes how change occurs:

> The *first* aspect is the status quo, called here the performance stage, which identifies the point where the system currently stands according to student outcomes. The *second* is the set of interventions necessary to make the desired improvements in student outcomes, here called the intervention cluster. The *third* is the system's adaptation of the intervention cluster to the prevailing context: taking into account the history, culture, politics, and structure of the school system and the nation. (p. 18)

Functional change interventions/strategies are set out in this book: chapters describing the system according to student outcomes, changes necessary for improving those outcomes, and interventions based on locally determined perceptions/starting points—the shared history, culture, politics, and structures within classrooms, schools, districts, provinces, counties, parishes, states, local governments, territories, and countries. The sequence is prescribed through chapter topics: purpose, distributed leadership, collaborative learning, teaching/ learning expertise, extended social capital, and collective accountability.

There are two kinds of goals: performance goals (ones that focus on results) and learning goals (those that improve ongoing capabilities); both exist within high school course outcomes, mechanisms for parent involvement in schools, alignment of goals and resources within school districts, collaborative partnerships with other districts, higher levels of cooperation with local communities, and national responses to internal and external threats to democracy.

Missing in this reform, according to Roland S. Barth in *Improving Schools from Within: Teachers, parents, and principals can make the difference* (1990), is practitioners studying and writing about schools:

> "Paradoxically, those who systematically examine and write about schools come, for the most part, not from the school community itself but from higher education." (pp. 86–87)

He goes on:

> It would seem that writing about schools as an 'insider looking in' offers unusual opportunity for insight into public education. Obviously, teachers and principals have constant access to classrooms and a school setting, not to mention their own ideas, motives, satisfactions, and methods. And the practitioner-author acquainted as colleague or trusted friend with parents, administrators, and teachers would be assured of a sympathetic, even grateful audience. (p. 8)

He sees, however, the opposite as true. One reason being "the problem of generalization" where successful change strategies in a particular school/district may not be applicable to other settings:

> The university researcher may study one classroom or school at a time but usually bases conclusions on larger samples, thereby gaining credibility and perhaps the capacity to generalize. But many school practitioners have never worked in more than one school. (p. 91)

The question is whether observations, understandings, and conclusions from other schools/districts can provide answers to local concerns. One difficulty, as stated, is that some practitioner-authors' time in education may not be indicative of deeper understandings; often doing the same work, in the same way, in the same school or district for their entire careers.

Barth sees other obstacles:

> The school practitioner who writes, then, can expect little support and recognition from others in the building. The culture of schools places little positive value—and often places negative value—on teachers and principals using their positions as participant-observers to write about practice. To write is to reveal oneself. So, many school people do not write for the same reason they construct walls in open spaces: in order to conceal themselves. (pp. 92–93)

While my experience as a teacher, department head, vice-principal, principal, high school district consultant, superintendent of schools, and provincial education facilitator is widespread, determining relevance to other contexts remains. There are at least two categories: roles and settings. Broad experience in both, along with pertinent research and reflection, I believe, are important for appreciating both the complexity and commonality of secondary schools.

Accompanying this journey were bookmarks:

Bruner J. *The Process of Education* (1960) as mathematics/physics teacher at Minitonas High School, Manitoba

Holt J. *How Children Fail* (1964) while department head of mathematics at Stratford Junior High School in Edmonton, Alberta

Cardinal H. *The Unjust Society—the Tragedy of Canada's Indians* (1969) as principal at Frontier Collegiate Institute in Cranberry Portage, Manitoba

Brown G. *Human Teaching for Human Learning: An Introduction to Confluent Education* (1971) while part of a Manitoba ministry of education contingent of districts observing secondary school classes in Santa Barbara, California

Castillo. G. A. *Left-Handed Teaching* (1974) as vice-principal, mathematics department head within Assiniboine South School Division No. 3, Winnipeg, MB

Sarason S. *The Culture of the School and the Problem of Change* (1971) as support for my master's degree in administrative studies at the University of Manitoba

French W. L. and Bell C.H. Jr: *Organization Development: behavioral interventions for organization improvement* (1973) along with Schmuck R. and Runkel P. *Handbook of Organization Development in Schools* (1972) as a Manitoba ministry of education consultant serving school districts across the province.

Good T.L. and Brophy J. E. *Looking in Classrooms* (1978) during tenure as principal of Grand Rapids School (K-12), Frontier School Division #48, Manitoba

Hunter M. *Mastery Teaching: Increasing Instructional Effectiveness in Elementary and Secondary Schools* (1982) while English/ mathematics/ physics teacher at Frontier Collegiate Institute in Cranberry Portage, MB

Fullan M. *The Meaning of Educational Change* (1982) as principal of Margaret Barbour Collegiate Institute in The Pas, Manitoba

Vacca R. Vacca J. and Mraz M. *Content Area Reading: Literacy and Learning across the Curriculum* 1st edition (1979) as consultant to eight high schools within Frontier School Division #48, Manitoba

Atwell N. *In The Middle: Writing, Reading, and Learning with Adolescents* (1987) as teacher in R. B. Russell Vocational School, Winnipeg School Division #1

Coleman P. and Larocque L. *Struggling to be Good Enough: Administrative Practices & School District Ethos* (1990) as superintendent of schools for the South Slave Divisional Board in the NWT

Fullan M. *Leading In a Culture of Change* (2001) while principal of Horsefly Elementary/Junior Secondary School in Horsefly, BC, Cariboo-Chilcotin School District #27

Clay M. *Becoming Literate: The Construction of Inner Control* (1994) as a certified Later Literacy teacher in Horsefly, BC

Hattie J. *Visible Learning: A Synthesis of Over 800 Meta-Analyses Related to Achievement* (2009) as principal of BC High School SUIS, in Shanghai, China

Brownlie F. and Schnellert L. *It's all about thinking: Collaborating to Support All Learners* (2009) also as principal in Shanghai, China

To be explicit, my view is that secondary schools are largely disconnected from goals described in this book: democratic citizenship, student learning ownership, quality student achievement, and improved classroom, school, district, and community supports. Substantive changes then, along with how these changes can happen, are the topics discussed.

There are seven intersecting and overarching theorems. Theorem: "an idea accepted or proposed as a demonstrable truth, often as a part of a general theory."

Theorem 1: We learn how to begin

It's not one size fits all. As stated, the first step in any learning process is gathering information specific to the setting. Just as teachers appraise students' prior knowledge/thinking skills within classrooms, internal and external facilitators supporting school/district change require context knowledge: history of change, immediate concerns, strengths, trust levels, role expectations, leadership efforts in the past, and widespread contributions and suggestions.

This assessment process mirrors the "personal mastery" discipline presented by P. Senge et al. in *Schools That Learn* (2012) — "a realistic assessment of the current reality" as compared to 'the results you most want to create' (p. 7); just as relevant to schools, districts, states, provinces, and nations as it is to individuals.

Students and parents front and centre. All in an effort to find the right starting points based on teacher/student readiness for added responsibilities and new freedoms. There is not much a school can't do if they do it together. Not so much top-down planning although it frequently requires top-down support.

Foundations: shared vision, collaborative goal setting, relationships, democratic initiatives, deep thinking, accountability (individually and collectively), trust, internally negotiated role expectations, distributed leadership/ownership, team building, communication skills, integrity, public commitment from leaders, group learning processes, metacognition, conflict resolution attitudes/skills, ongoing support, choice, and gradual release of responsibility.

This is where organizational development and current educational change efforts converge: scrutinizing concerns, strengths, suggestions, and prior knowledge of individuals/groups as the starting point. Michael Fullan (2011): "You can't find answers outside yourself—you have to start inside and look for the best external connections to further develop your own thinking and action." (p. xii)

The rules for teachers are these: 1) start with what you know; become the best professional teacher/learning community member you can be 2) seek allies with an open arms approach—students, parents, and the public 3) look upward and collaborate with principals and district personnel as part of the team 4) use student success as your prime aim/proof for change, and 5) view school and community as opportunities for student ownership/leadership.

Guy Claxton et al. (2013) reinforce the need for students as allies:

> In our experience, students are usually highly astute observers of learning—both their own and others'—and know quite clearly how and when they learn best, and what kinds of help they need from teachers. In traditional schools, this capacity to be their own and others' teachers, and to contribute responsibly to the improvement of teaching and learning in the whole school, is often grievously underestimated. (p. 140)

Gradually releasing responsibility can result in self-regulated learning for students *and* teachers. More options for both. For students this means *learning to learn principles* of determining and choosing (with teacher help) what is to be learned, connecting prior knowledge with the task at hand, and filling in gaps using collaborative efforts with others through memorization, deliberate practice, visualization, new vocabulary, summarizing the basics, transferring understandings from one situation to another through comparison and contrast, practicing thinking routines, reading for a purpose, writing to learn, improved questioning, guided inquiry, and gathering and appreciating perspectives from other people.

Theorem 2: We learn what we teach

Teaching accelerates *teachers' own thinking and learning capabilities*. Split screen lesson plans link learning/thinking strategies with content outcomes, model deeper thinking, build student independence, and enhance teacher efficacy. They also include self-provided feedback that allows students to gain ownership of their learning while teachers improve their teaching. Helping students learn to think better is the goal—an increase in intelligence for both students and teachers.

Claxton et al. (2013): "Learning involves the active habits of noticing, questioning, experimenting, reflecting, and discussing. In the process of becoming learning-power coaches, teachers very often find that they are developing their own learning power." (p. 205)

Students also teach. An example is reciprocal teaching, a learning comprehension strategy focused on summarizing, questioning, clarifying, and predicting abilities. Reciprocal teaching, according to John Hattie (2012), has an effect size of 0.74. His research provides evidence of its effectiveness with second language learners, bilingual students, and those with disabilities.

Groups of four students (1) summarize the first passage of a piece of text in terms of key information/themes (2) question the meaning of words/phrases, notice organizational patterns, and determine inferences (3) clarify information through discussion, and (4) predict, based on the first passage, the content of the next passage. Discussion amongst the group after each passage is the key to improving comprehension abilities.

More evidence of teachers as learners: Goodlad S. & Hirst B. in *Peer Tutoring: A Guide to Learning by Teaching* (1989): "Research shows that not only can peer tutoring make learning more efficient and pleasurable for those who are taught *(tutees)*, it can also increase significantly the learning of the *tutors*" (p. 13).

Starr Sackstein (2015) believes efforts to quantify a particular task or curriculum outcome should be replaced with demonstration of proficiency in different settings, along with *the ability to teach it to a peer.* That would be evidence of mastery. Teachers to spend less time on calculators and more on observing student behaviour.

Same goals for teachers as for students. Throughout this book I have reinforced one basic principle: What is good for students is good for teachers. The same improved relationships, democratic decision making, focus on personal inquiry through widespread questioning, freedom of choice with responsibility, clarity of outcomes, creative opportunities, and employment of language, deeper thinking, and reflection on how to learn are as critical for teacher satisfaction and success as they are for students.

Successful school improvement requires time. Time for teachers to observe others teach, time for students to pursue learning goals at their own pace, time for professional learning communities of teachers to learn from each other, time for principals to go beyond administrative responsibilities and provide learning leadership, and time for teachers, students, parents, and communities to build relationships.

In Chapter 7: "Building Social Capital: Team Building", I suggest a high school timetable that provides much of the above. Assumptions: that shortening classes to an average of sixty-six minutes is compensated through a combination of forty minutes per day of small group social/academic support in advisories, extended school assemblies that teach, a daily activities/learning period for student choice, and three guaranteed hours of PLC (Professional Learning Community) action research each week.

Moreover, PLC planning time not at the expense of individual teachers' daily one-hour preparation. Also, students not confined to the subject timetable. This freedom of choice, over time, is essential for promoting student ownership and maturity—students deciding *what, where, how, who with, and when* they will be learning.

In their book, *Rethinking High School: Best Practice in Teaching, Learning, and Leadership* by Harvey Daniels et al. (2001), the forward-thinking Best Practice High School in Chicago also determined a timetable (set out in Chapter 7) for supporting learning to learn, democratic citizenship, student learning independence, collaborative learning, and parent/community partnerships. A major opportunity to collaborate with the local community laid out in their internships program for a half-day each week.

Theorem 3: We teach the whole person

George Kelly's Construct Theory (1963) from *Guided Inquiry: Learning in the 21st Century* by Kuhlthau et al. (2007) recognizes fundamental connections between social-emotional learning and academic achievement:

> Theorists agree that emotions play a significant role in directing thinking and action throughout the constructive process of learning. Recent brain research in neuroscience further supports the holistic view of learning that the brain runs on emotions that drive thoughts and actions to seek meaning through patterns and connections. (pp. 15–16)

Emotions underline one's experience when working with others; deeper thinking is often laced with positive feelings/emotions, while attitudes based on emotions are strong predictors of future action. Helping students become more aware of emotions can complement and reinforce their learning. Informed decision making, whether individual or group, often comes down to considerations based on the head *and* heart. Both unremittingly present in learning whether the initial purpose is cognitive, affective, or learning how to learn.

An online post regarding exercise commitment during the recent pandemic: "More than anything, it's about nourishing your mind. It's the feeling of accomplishment when you finish something hard. It's the commitment that comes from sticking with something that requires you to step out of your comfort zone. It's knowing that there are other people out there with similar struggles who are getting on that bike and pushing through" (Westover, 2021).

What we want is students (and teachers within *their* learning opportunities) to self-regulate in various ways. In the most basic sense, it involves monitoring one's behaviour, emotions, and thoughts in the pursuit of long-term goals. This is the definition of personal mastery. Self-regulation refers to the ability to manage disruptive emotions and impulses—to think before acting, be resilient, and be positive after disappointments. And while feelings influence behaviour, the opposite is also true. Getting started is a powerful way of generating attitudes and emotions that motivate ourselves and others.

Theorem 4: We learn by doing

You have to go get it; it won't come to you. Richard DuFour et al. (2006) refers to Robert Evans in *"The Human Side of School Change: Reform, Resistance, and the Real-Life Problems of Innovation"* (1996) where changes in belief, such as all students being capable of learning, while supportive, are deemed insufficient for achieving behavioural change. It is by considered action that we learn.

Claxton (2015) accentuates the point: "we are fundamentally built for action, not for thinking or understanding, and that, as a consequence, our intelligence is deeply oriented towards the construction of effective and appropriate behaviour" (p. 5).

Learning by doing is learning from mistakes. John Holt in his book, *How Children Fail* (1964), got it right. He pointed out that when a student makes an error, teachers rarely make an effort to find out why. The thinking that led the student astray is never determined. Instead, the student is simply told the correct response. Unless erroneous thinking is addressed, the same error will be repeated. And even if it isn't, it will be the result of memorization, not understanding.

Presently, high schools ignore mistakes and reward right answers. Exactly the wrong approach; discussion of wrong answers leads to exploring a number of paths to both correct and incorrect solutions, all leading to resilience for future success.

Why was the error made? While reading error-filled writing can be disconcerting, errors help us identify cognitive strategies the learner is using to process information. As Ellis' book, *Understanding Second Language Acquisition* 2nd edition (2015) explains, analyzing learner errors elevates them from undesirability to guiding our understanding of the inner working of language learning/thinking processes.

Effective professional learning communities learn by doing: teachers examining data/information, recognizing that attitudes are the result of practice, not the reverse; visiting each other's classrooms, supporting each other, sharing research in pursuit of student learning solutions, developing common formative assessments, setting a limited number of SMART (Specific, Measurable, Ambitious, Relevant, and Time-Bound) goals, taking considered risks/learning from mistakes, and, when appropriate, requesting additional expertise.

"Why We Should Embrace Mistakes in School" (2017), an article by Amy L. Eva, focuses on learnable skills/strategies. Her cited research compared a "direct instruction" group, where students learned step by step how to solve mathematical problems with a second group called 'productive failures'.

"Productive failures" struggled alone until the teacher intervened, helped analyze mistakes with the students, and then, together, they determined the correct solution. In the final test, common for both, the productive failures did better for both simple and complex problems. The difference is palpable: ownership is critical for building confidence and success. Productive failures were taking charge of their learning, *albeit with some help*, whereas the direct instruction group was copying ideas.

The learning suggested here emphasizes a corollary: gradual release of responsibility. Faye Brownlie and Leyton Schnellert (2009), in their analysis/summary of lesson planning advocate lessons that promote self-regulated learning based on the gradual release of responsibility for individual students, collaborative groups, and the entire class founded on transparent outcomes, assessed readiness, potential learning sequences, and teacher support.

Teachers to: (1) connect success with effort rather than innate capabilities, (2) include students in the planning, (3) encourage student initiative in seeking help, (4) assist students in the use of feedback, and (5) reflect on cognitive processes and products.

Theorem 5: We learn how to lead

Leading from within, we demonstrate and encourage change leadership by modeling the other six theorems: supportive beginnings, learning what we teach, whole person teaching, observable doing, collaborative expertise, and personal/group accountability.

As recognized in Chapter 2 of this book, leadership within any role is *affiliative* as valuing personal relations, *democratic* as inviting participation with the goal of consensus, *authoritative* based on the leader's knowledge/moral values, *pacesetting* as modeling commitment, and *coaching* through observation. All existing to one degree or another in every school and school district; each founded on different motivational assumptions.

Peter Cuttance (2001) believes leadership requires cooperation amongst different roles with different functions. This cooperation based on differences in expertise, not on authority; improved culture, then, sees questioning, dialogue, and debate while reducing or eliminating status differences with distributed leadership across the board.

Superordinate goals are impossible to attach numbers to, but they, not content objectives, are what stimulate teachers to transform the system. Concerns from Charles Naylor, a professional development consultant for the British Columbia Teachers' Federation: "The worst proponents of Professional Learning Communities avoid connecting them to innovative and ambitious learning goals but stick to the technicalities of specifying narrow performance goals, defining a focus, examining data, and establishing teams." Hargreaves, in his paper, "Push, Pull and Nudge: The Future of Teaching and Educational Change" (2013, p. 134).

Distributed leadership taps into the potential of individuals *and* groups. Participation through district committees, principals' professional communities, and school-based learning communities improves the learning capabilities of both. Often we think of individuals, especially those with titles, as the only leaders. But interlocking communities of all types, each with their own collaborative style, accomplishments, and creative thinking also have leadership responsibilities.

This applies to students. Student leadership, including school research (their own school and others) not only benefits the school generally but prepares high school students for freedom, responsibilities, and opportunities as democratic citizens. Their leadership to work collaboratively with teachers, administrators, school boards, and local communities in school/district decision making.

Some might disparage the ability of high school students to take on more responsibility. Claxton et al. (2013) in *The Learning Powered School: Pioneering 21st Century Education* disagree:

> "In some cases, teachers are nervous allowing students to work in such ways since they fear a loss of control. They may be concerned that students will abuse the apparent freedom and lose focus and commitment. But in our experience, provided teachers introduce changes in ways *that are gradual and cumulative*, and do not create too much anxiety or disruption, their *fears that students will abuse the responsibility they are being offered are rarely realized*. On the contrary, we hear time and again from schools who took small steps in this direction, and were astonished by the levels of maturity and responsibility which their students showed— *especially those who were lower achievers or who had histories of disaffection.*" (p. 105, [emphasis added])

There are secondary teachers who feel they don't have time to foster student ownership/deep thinking and also drill enough into students for success on external examinations. They are wrong: students remember more, not less information through connections/visualizations after deeper thinking. Such thinking increases capacity to remember through those connections. When students are successful in taking charge of their learning, including in-depth thinking, the by-product is improved exam scores.

A study described in *Building A Better Teacher* (2014) by Elizabeth Green, emphasizes the point. Noticing that which doesn't fit with one's prior knowledge/ experience captures our attention. We form generalizations, patterns, and systemic information throughout our lives. Such noticing/ evidence, then, where the patterns are violated, is part of remembering experiences that, in themselves, would otherwise be forgotten.

School-wide discipline planning supports and includes students. It has little to do with writing one-sided contracts for students listing ways to suspend/expel. Quality leadership recognizes social and emotional skills students are lacking, then addresses them as with any other learning through clear expectations, collaborative planning, direct instruction, deliberate practice, cooperative thinking, teacher modeling, and gradual release of responsibility.

Theorem 6: We learn from each other.

The more carefully you set the foundation, the less likely it will fail. As Jane Kise in her book, *Unleashing the Positive Power of Differences: Polarity Thinking in Our Schools* (2014) asserts, we need to "listen to the reasoning of those with whom we disagree, validate their needs and fears, and vow to work together, no matter how difficult it is" (p. 4).

She appreciates two or more points of view as an opportunity to better understand others, find common ground, and discover more ways to work together. She believes this process should not only be acquired by teachers as they collaborate to find new ways to help students learn, but also by students as an important part of their education.

Time for teachers to learn together is one concern, but time within the classroom for students to learn from each other is also necessary. Ritchhart (2011) goes beyond wait time to urge teachers to allow time for students to gather and sort prior knowledge, consult with partners within direct instruction, generate questions, and reflect on observations both individually and collectively. Even such a simple routine as giving students time to jot down a few thoughts before sharing them with a partner can foster creativity.

A Saturday morning workshop in Shanghai with the school's Canadian teachers, local Chinese homeroom teachers, plus Andrew, a former Chinese principal responsible for liaison between myself as principal of BC High School SUIS (Shanghai United International Schools) and the Chinese campus administration.

We began with dyads (one Canadian and one Chinese), face-to-face in chairs, each explaining to their partner *how she or he became the teacher they were.* The partners should listen, ask questions for clarification, and then *summarize what they heard for everyone.* My rules for reporting were two: (1) Stand behind your seated partner and role-play her or him to the group: "My name is Marie, and I learned to teach by…"; and (2) If partners believed you did *not* reflect what they said accurately, they were to interrupt and help you get it right.

Purposes: 1) sharing/learning from teachers' personal history or point of view on the effectiveness of past learning opportunities; 2) extending intra-staff communications to include comparisons of professional learning in Canada and China; 3) team building for future collaboration; and 4) introducing a classroom routine for students addressing different points of view.

Collaborative learning is not confined to professional communities in schools. Chris Brown and Cindy Poortman from *Networks for*

Learning: Effective Collaboration for Teacher, School and System Improvement (2018), define professional learning networks as:

> Any group that engages in collaborative learning with others outside of their everyday community of practice in order to improve teaching and learning in their school(s) and/or the school system more widely. Our focus therefore encompasses a huge range of between-school or school-plus-other-organization network types, including research- or data-use teams, multi-site lesson study teams, teacher design teams, whole-child support teams and so on. (p. 1)

Theorem 7: We learn to be accountable

Guy Claxton (2013):

> To create the kind of culture change that is necessary, you have to read, and think, and argue, and experiment, and adjust, and try again. A Building Learning Powered School needs to be growing in its collective resilience, resourcefulness, reflection, and relationships, at the same time as it is trying to cultivate those qualities in its pupils. In short, they create a dialogue about learning, they actively encourage experimentation, and they *involve everyone in monitoring improvements that are not always measurable in the traditional ways of measuring attainment* [emphasis added]. (p. 183)

Elmore R.F. (2008), in his chapter, "When Accountability Knocks, Will Anyone Answer?" describes three related mechanisms: individual responsibility, collective expectations, and accountability:

> Our working theory posits a set of relationships among three factors: individual conceptions of *responsibility*; shared *expectations* among school participants and stakeholders; and *internal and external accountability* mechanisms. An individual school's conception of accountability, in our view, grows from the relationship among these three factors (Wagner, 1989). (p. 138)

An adjacent concern:

> To say there is a high degree of alignment between responsibility, expectations, and accountability is to say nothing specific about the purposes for which the school is aligned. Schools could, for example, have a high degree of alignment about values that stress order and discipline in the classroom and hallways but little or no agreement on academic goals. Alignment, then, refers to their consistency and strength of agreement inside the school, not the subject of that agreement. (p. 142)

Purpose, alignment, and accountability are ongoing formative processes. Listening and responding to students, parents, teachers, previous teachers, post-secondary graduates, dropouts, community service agencies, businesses employing students, local newspaper inquiries, and regional leaders/local government is critical—all having a role in providing continuous feedback.

Examples of pragmatic feedback are student engagement, efficacy of teaching methods (a la John Hattie), barriers to minority groups, levels of peer support, guidelines on best practices for teaching and learning, student government leadership, diversity in student demonstration of success in subject outcomes, and opportunities for both student and parent leadership. Teacher awareness in this regard means recognizing their need for professional learning on how to conduct accountability inquiries, not something that has historically been part of their professional lives.

We need to pursue evidence of learning. Options include former graduates and dropouts making presentations at whole school assemblies open to the public, documentation of learning experiences that were especially successful, individual advisory investigations on special interests, and subject classrooms on how their current learning relates to national issues. Another is writing articles for the school or community newspaper or local websites on how their high school education could be improved. Ongoing feedback over the years.

George Wood (2005) summarizes the situation:

> High school should be, most fundamentally, about the work of students. The quality of the papers they write, the clarity of the explanations they offer, the persuasiveness of their speeches, the precision of their drawings, the creativity of their art, the skill of their play, and the integrity of their character should be our prime concerns. Unfortunately, because

of the way we structure our high schools as well as the growing emphasis on standardized testing, our attention is too often drawn elsewhere. This shows up most clearly in what we teach and how we teach it. (p. 79)

Elmore (2008) stresses the need for collaborative decision making: "Where virtually all decisions about accountability are made by individual teachers, based on their individual conceptions of what they and their students can do, it seems unlikely that these decisions will somehow aggregate into overall improvement for the school" (p. 197).

These data are both quantitative and qualitative. Both are needed, but qualitative assessments such as students and teachers' points of view gained through interviews, questionnaires, focus groups, student presentations at assemblies, District Learning Support Committees, and community service groups, offer more in-depth evaluations of how learning is progressing.

The seven learning theorems, it should be noted, are as applicable to individuals as they are to schools, local communities, town councils, school boards, districts, counties, state departments of education, municipalities, and ministries of education, parishes, territories, and nations.

The Organization of this Book

My relevant experience is situated with practical/researched advice throughout the eight chapters: 1) Evidence for change/need for superordinate goals 2) Distributed leadership 3) Collaborative learning 4) Deeper thinking 5) Student learning ownership 6) Parents and students as partners 7) Building social capital, and 8) Foundations for change/collective accountability.

The template for the book is the template for each chapter. *Each chapter heading is an important support for change in all chapters.* For instance, collaborative skills in chapter 3 are necessary for determining both the superordinate goals of chapter 1 and democratic leadership development in classrooms, schools, districts, and communities in chapter 2, deeper thinking in chapter 4, self-regulation/student ownership in chapter 5, parents and students as partners in chapter 6, building social capital in chapter 7, and individual and collective accountability in chapter 8.

It is also international. Leading educators in the United States, United Kingdom, Canada, Australia, and New Zealand calling for generic reform reinforced by shared concerns from a broad array of countries such as Japan, Germany, Austria, Sweden, the Netherlands, Finland, and Singapore.

The online articles "Democratic Education: A Theoretical Review", (July 11, 2019) by Sant et al. carry the same message:

> There are some contextual trends within these 377 articles. The articles were mainly written by academics based at English-speaking, Western institutions. Approximately 66% of the articles were written by academics affiliated to American, British, Australian, or Canadian institutions (see tables in the supplemental information available online). The focus of the articles, nevertheless, was mostly 'generic' with almost 60% of the articles discussing democratic education in universalistic—rather than state-based—terms.

The review includes articles from authors working in academic institutions across 38 different countries. In order to maintain the focus of the study, contextual information is provided only when the context is essential to understand the nature of the authors' claims.

From a speech given at the "Seminar for the Needs for New Indonesian Civic Education Center for Indonesian Civic Education" (CICED), March 29, 2000, Bandung, Indonesia by Charles N. Quigley, Executive Director, Center for Civic Education:

> This publication looks at the importance of *the role of secondary education in the development of education around the world*, as modern economies and their labour markets need people with sophisticated knowledge, skills, and competences that cannot be developed only in primary school or in low-quality secondary schools. The publication highlights the position of the secondary education in the OECD (Organization for Economic Co-operation and Development) countries, and the need to secure access to better quality secondary education for all students in order to have a responsive and flexible upper secondary education system that simultaneously serves the needs of employers and lifelong learning [emphasis added].

Referenced research for this book: United States 64%, Canada 20%, United Kingdom 7%, New Zealand: 3%, Australia 3%, Other countries: 3%

Chapter One. Past Performance: Stuck in Neutral

Advance Organizers:

1. Understanding the culture of each school/district, with all its contrasts, is ground zero for reform. A context approach where inclusion and appreciation of students, teachers, administrators, parents, and communities' understandings, skills, and attitudes is the starting place for change ownership.
2. If we really want students to apply higher-order thinking, we must assess it. If we believe creativity, working well with others, citizenship obligations, and love of learning are vital, we need to identify observable evidence for these goals. As Claxton et al. (2013) put it, "If we do not find ways of measuring what we value, we will end up just valuing what we can measure."
3. In the same way formative assessment advises students and teachers on their learning/teaching in the classroom, schools and school districts require timely information on what is or is not working in terms of policies, attitudes, teaching methods, collaborative expertise, focus, and role formulations.
4. Moreover, if you think the challenge for high schools is confined to teaching minorities, you need only consider mounting evidence on the number of today's graduates, particularly boys, who do not read, write, or vote.
5. Hattie: Visible Learning Conference (2016) "Too many students are physically present but are neither emotionally nor intellectually involved. Part of the problem is that students spend 85% of their time listening (or pretending to listen) to a teacher talking."
6. Standardized or teacher-made tests based on memorized surface facts and procedures is a continuing problem. Unless information is used as preparation for higher level cognitive outcomes, isolated facts are useless. And contrary to the assumptions of traditionalists who oppose democratizing schools and advancing deeper thinking, their pedagogy produces students who remember less.
7. Loud labeling of students, past performance reminder, and missing range of student readiness to assist each other—all proven negatives in grouping lower-achieving students over an extended time, are bad for everyone.

8. School/district decision making is not the only concern. Within the classroom, fallacies are fixed intelligence, preaching higher-level thinking skills but confining testing to information, rewarding work over cognition, poorly integrated assistive technology, focus on reading and listening at the expense of writing and speaking, lesson planning centred on activities rather than thinking, downgrading student learning beyond a specified time, and using marks as rewards/punishment.
9. A report by the Stanford History Education Group (2016) where the authors' concern was democracy threatened by how easily disinformation about civic issues is allowed to spread, reveals students' inability to ascertain credible internet information. More specifically, they couldn't distinguish advertisements from news articles or determine sources of information, thus dispelling a common assumption that young people competent in social media are able to determine fact-based information.
10. False choices include teacher freedom to teach vs professional learning communities, district vs school decision making, inquiry vs direct instruction, phonics vs reading for understanding, academic success vs emotional and social learning, teacher support vs student self-regulation, and learning as deliberate practice vs going with the "flow."
11. Successful school improvement has one basic principle; factors/ variables that support the growth, development, and self-confidence of students are exactly those critical for attaining the same outcomes in a school's staff.
12. So, the straitjacket is that teachers, parents, and communities only know the same education system that accepts and encourages passivity, memorization as the prime vehicle for passing examinations, and student failure to learn separated from teacher responsibility.
13. Without substantial collaborative learning the probability of improving teachers' attitudes, skills, and knowledge approaches zero. The reason is that deeper thinking and transfer of ideas are best done through exchanging ideas with others. Again, what we have is a laudable goal with no credible path for realization. It is the 'what' with no 'how'.
14. Privatization along with a jam-packed schedule has a steep price: teachers do not, in any systemic way, observe each other teach, mentor colleagues, collaborate on action research, engage in joint lesson planning, devise professional learning

plans, or gather student information critical for effective teaching—all functions of an institution dedicated to learning.
15. Professional development fails because the appearance of teacher learning is conserved, but the teaching doesn't change and student learning doesn't improve.

Chapter Two. Change Leadership: Distributed Ownership

Advance Organizers:

1. Being perceived as helpful enhances trust between client and consultant; conversely, selling philosophy may inhibit trust.
2. Research deplores the 'good guy-bad guy syndrome' with the change instigators being the good guys and those who resist as backward. These observations to be appreciated, not only by external facilitators but by people within the system; their self-inflicted roadblocks just as dampening.
3. According to Hatti's Visible Learning research, based on a synthesis of more than 1,500 meta-analyses, *collective teacher efficacy* (teachers working together for the common good) is greater than three times more powerful and predictive of student achievement than socioeconomic status. It is more than double the effect of prior achievement and more than triple the effect of home environment and parental involvement.
4. Student leadership has foundations: student-chosen teacher advisors, expanded freedom of choice, daily advisories, collaborative learning expertise, school leadership credit courses, school assemblies led by students, student government as an agent for change, students leading after-school learning activities, wide participation in school/district based decision making, peer tutoring, improved language capability, teacher evaluation feedback, teacher-student-parent meetings, a learning to learn focus, and gradual release of responsibility.
5. Bad professional conduct requires a response: one being *hard conversations* that offer advice to colleagues, address ethical considerations, and critique teaching that provides little support to students.
6. Effective leadership strategies are not primarily plans or structures—they are about extending relationships: building trust, critical feeling, quality planning, resolving conflicts, learning to learn while teaching it to students, freeing students from past restrictions, building confidence through tiny victories and

large celebrations, and welcoming parents and communities as partners. Tone is important—a blend of intelligence, confidence, humility, persistence, humour, playfulness, and kindness; no better combination can be found.

7. Principal leadership requires more than sideline interest. It means facilitating professional learning community supports such as time and space, modeling conflict resolution strategies, respecting collaborative teaching and learning decisions, participating in group inquiry, instigating hard conversations with both individual teachers and groups, demonstrating trust, and helping define/negotiate collaborative leadership roles for students, parents, teachers, and community.

8. Meta-analysis of research on the effects of site-based management without the pressure and support of district found little improvement in teacher quality or student outcomes across ten British Columbia school districts.

9. From this perspective, the distinction between top-down versus bottom-up reform is an unhelpful dichotomy, and debate about their relative merit is unlikely to be productive. What is required is a truly collaborative process that builds consensus across levels, allowing *each to contribute according to its strength.*

10. District leadership is leading by learning. It affects student achievement because effective leadership provides critical support for strong professional communities and can also be a useful predictor of quality instruction and student achievement.

11. School principals change their role priorities on a daily basis. But in order to improve teaching and student learning they should spend most of their time and energy on academic and pedagogic goals. The shift is from a supervisory role based on compliance to supporting, advising, coaching, and participating in learning groups.

12. Sarason (1996): "Many teachers have two theories: *one that applies to them and one that applies to children.* Put another way, many teachers are quite aware from their own experiences of the differences in characteristics between dull and exciting conditions of intellectual activity. But their inability to see or assume some kind of identity between their pupils and themselves leads them unwittingly to create those conditions that they would personally find boring."

13. The roles and activities of leadership flow from the expertise required for learning and improvement, not from the formal dictates of the institution.
14. A warning: when educators see leaders as people they work *for*, rather than *with*, you are headed in the wrong direction. Leaders' expectations feeling more like impositions rather than collaborative/respectful efforts that empower everyone. The ensuing feelings, therefore, are more dependent on *how* expectations are delivered as opposed to the expectations themselves.
15. Recently, experts in educational change have advocated 'Leading from the Middle'—school districts learning from each other. One path is state, provincial, or territorial superintendents' associations where superintendents not only negotiate sister schools, principal pairings, and other collaborative learning opportunities but inform district leadership across the state/province/territory on school improvement successes and failures.

Chapter 3. Working Together: Alignment for Success

Advance Organizers:

1. We need evaluative criteria for both content outcomes *and* collaborative expertise while aligning resources within the district. And just as turning students loose to inquire into unknown territory takes planned support, teachers require upfront assistance as *they* learn how to work together.
2. BCTF [British Columbia Teachers Federation] (2016): "Differences of opinion are encouraged and freely expressed. Diversity is a mark of a team's strength. Team members' flexibility, objectivity, and humour promote a climate that allows for disagreement."
3. Michael Fullan and Joanne Quinn (2016): "The concept of learning communities is not wrong, but the implementation has lacked depth. If we embrace the idea that our students should be critical thinkers grounded in metacognition, then we need to *design learning experiences for adults that foster the same competencies because we cannot give to others what we do not possess ourselves.*"
4. Trust fractures, not only by people breaking their word but also by failure to clarify expectations. Organizational development role appraisal techniques work to avoid disappoint-

ment/resentment by replacing assumptions with clear expectations through out-loud, face-to-face role negotiations between superintendents and trustees, superintendents and district staff, superintendents and principals, principals and teachers, and teachers with students.
5. Opportunities for change include identifying how administrators develop, support, and sustain norms and practices that together constitute a positive ethos for the district. This includes the false dichotomy of school vs district and that having common goals does not require identical methods for achieving those goals.
6. Executing the curriculum described by Juliet Strang et al. (2007) in *Ask: How to Teach Learning to Learn in the Secondary School (2006)* will go a long way toward achieving the cultural change advocated by M. Fullan. The attitudes, dispositions, skills, and knowledge that students need to improve their ability to learn are precisely those required for teachers to change their teaching.
7. Resistance is more likely in high schools because of the strong subject department structures on which they are based. Hargreaves and Fullan (2012): "This is one of the reasons high schools are notoriously hard to change."
8. Learning to learn together is more than minor adjustments. It requires school-wide collaborative learning practices among teacher and students, students, and teachers. This includes inquiry as a subset: an interweaving of assumptions, evidence, suppositions, connections, and points of view as participants work together to plan, revise, and conclude. Hardly the past experience of teachers, and not likely to happen in any sustained way without support and considerable time.
9. Inquiry supports for students are as important for developing independence as surface information is for deeper thinking. As such, *inquiry support teams* comprised of subject teachers, PLCs, school librarians, advisories, and local organizations (public libraries, museums, municipal government, social welfare organizations, and minority leadership) to be organized as community enterprises.
10. According to Hord and Sommers (2008), collecting valuable information from classroom observations and providing constructive feedback are learned skills. Little (2002) validated this finding when she described the development of PLCs as navigation between individual autonomy and the group. How

teachers negotiate this perceived conflict will determine whether they will be guided by inquiry and reflection or strive to maintain the status quo.

Chapter 4. Cognitive Acceleration: Deeper Thinking

Advance Organizers:

1. Evidence of high schools testing accumulated knowledge at the expense of deeper thinking includes Moseley et al. (2004) who observed sixty-nine classrooms where teachers did not teach learning skills but focused on book reading, task instruction, requests for answers to questions, and providing specific information.
2. Having a growth mindset is important for improving capacity to learn anything. Being successful in science or other disciplines, then, can result in improved ability across the board. When the brain changes, neural pathways are reinforced and connectors grow.
3. Adey P. and Shayer M. from "Really Raising Standards: Cognitive intervention and academic achievement." (1997): "The Vygotskian description of the social aspect of mutual growth casts serious doubt on the notion that improving students' performance in schools is just a matter of teaching them more skills and knowledge." (P. 9)
4. A teacher needs to know how each student thinks *and* the thinking demands of each step in the lesson both by the student and the peers with whom they are working.
5. Students engaged in programming to increase social-emotional learning experience an 11-percentile gain in academic achievement. This finding highlights how interpersonal, instructional, and environmental supports produce better school performance.
6. Cognitive dissonance is making predictions based on mistaken assumptions or expectations, then confronted with a different result. An example in physics is determining average speed when a vehicle travels a distance of 60 km at 20 kilometers per hour and back again at 30 kilometers per hour. The correct answer is not 25 km/h.
7. Jo Boaler (2019): "I have observed students asking for help and teachers structuring the work for students, breaking down questions and converting them into small easy steps. In doing so,

they empty the work of challenge and opportunities for struggle. Students complete the work and feel good, but often learn little."
8. Going into classrooms, researchers determined the following: 1) The mathematics curriculum in the US is "a mile wide and an inch deep", and 2) Japan's students, regular high scorers, spend 44% of their time on "inventing, thinking, and struggling with underlying concepts" while US students are engaged in these same behaviours less than 1% of the time.
9. Advanced high school math students take calculus, performing tasks like computing closed form integrals. For problems like these, students will do categories of problems in class (e.g. integration by parts), reinforced by homework assignments. They succeed on exams if they can recognize which category the problem belongs to, recall the procedural steps required to solve it, and carry out the computation.
10. An erroneous example from an anonymous internet contributor: "Ski straight down a slope twice, once with a 25 lb weight strapped to your back and once without. Your terminal velocity will be higher with the weight because the gravitational pull will be higher but the aero drag will be the same."
11. Furthermore, the required norm at the classroom level is that taking calculated risks is essential for learning. Teachers admitting errors in thinking or in execution need to model risk-taking through "making thinking visible" routines such as, "I used to think…but now I think," where teachers stress improvement, not standards.
12. One alternative to rubrics is people—fellow learners in the same boat. Maja Wilson recommends such collaborative feedback in her writing classes. Students respond to particular sections of a classmate's writing with how they feel about an introduction, paragraph, sentence, or entire piece of writing and why. This process improves with practice. Reading and examining direct responses to either your own work or others: "I like the introduction because…" or "I don't like it because…" start with feelings and include suggestions.
13. Utilitarian characteristics of both writing *and* quality learning in general encompass *"immediate reinforcement and feedback, freedom to select, use of connections and propositions, hypotheses, and other summarizers"* (Emig, 1983).
14. Lesson planning, according to Ritchhart et al. (2011), means 1) seeing beyond memorization, work, and activity (cover the cur-

riculum and prepare for the exam) toward lessons pertinent to the discipline; what real writers, mathematicians, scientists, historians, and physicists do, and 2) recalling actions you (the teacher) remember taking when developing some new understanding of something within the discipline or subject area.

Chapter 5. Self-Regulation: Students as Independent Learners

Advance Organizers:

1. Guy Claxton from *Intelligence in the Flesh: Why your mind needs your body more than it thinks* (2015): "We must begin by seeing our emotions as contributing to our ability to act intelligently, not as impediments to such action… There are times when we wish we had gone with our head rather than our heart. But reason and emotion are lifelong partners who occasionally tread on each other's toes, not sworn enemies" (p. 103).
2. Schools expect students to learn without being taught how. The transition to self-directed inquiry with teacher guidance, the road less-travelled, can improve learning abilities of both teachers and students.
3. The 2018 summer edition of *Canada's History*, to its credit, exemplifies the above. The publication works with educators to actualize Peter Seixas' article, "Historical Thinking Concepts" (2017), of establishing historical significance (assessing relative importance, connections, predicting).
4. This has been the centrepiece of our educational history: demanding teachers getting results as *the* model of effective teaching. Also, belief in larger rewards (such as praise and recognition) as more effective than smaller ones, and that pressured students work harder and get better grades. But the overriding reason for controlling behaviour being detrimental, as Ritchhart (2015) states, is that *"fostering student independence exists as an important, worthwhile goal in its own right"* [emphasis added].
5. Ron Ritchhart and Mark Church (2020): "When we focus on students' thinking, we see them as much more. We become interested in how they come to know what they know, what questions they have, and what challenges they face. We no longer see these challenges as deficits but as interesting opportunities for exploration."

6. Hattie (2009): "When teachers seek, or at least are open to, feedback from students as to what students know, what they understand, where they are making errors, when they have misconceptions, when they are not engaged—then teaching and learning can be synchronized and powerful. Feedback to teachers helps make learning visible."
7. John Hattie (2012): "Differentiation relates more to the phases of learning—from novice, through capable, to proficient—rather than merely providing different activities to different groups of students."
8. West Vancouver teacher: "One of the surprises of this project has been how much more interactive time I have had with my students. They are so engaged with their work that I can move from student to student, coaching and providing specific feedback. I hadn't expected this. There are simply no management issues, and I have so much more time to teach."
9. The effect of competence information on students' achievement behaviours was found to be determined by whether information is perceived by students as an attempt to control behaviors versus providing information about skill level.
10. Secondary Speech and Language Pathologist: "Making thinking visible practices offer these students a path previously untraveled, giving them a voice, a purpose, and a sense of pride. I see a huge shift in attitudes regarding the learning outcomes and thinking abilities of these learners across our school."
11. We need more overt reasoning, sharing, and elaborating across many learning activities. Context is important. Connections to previous interactions, thinking routines, and learning outcomes make the most out of student discourse. The challenge of teacher and student questioning is to choose questions that are of genuine interest and *that open doors to new considerations*.
12. Tomlinson C. and Strickland C. (2005) "The goal of culture-based differentiation is not to label or pigeonhole students, but to understand and actively address the fact that a classroom that runs counter to a student's cultural norms and needs will impede that student's thinking."
13. Ritchhart (2011) holds that making thinking visible: 1) Fosters deeper learning, 2) Cultivates engaged students, 3) Realigns the roles of students and teachers to mutual support, and 4) Enhances formative assessment practice. Synonymously, it 5) Accelerates learning (even when measured by standardized tests), and 6) Escalates positive dispositions to think and learn. He

stresses that routines need to be tried, reflected upon, and then retried. All within a culture of teachers learning from each other and their students.
14. Students who are involved in their learning see themselves as assessment-capable or active learners. They know what they need to learn, where they are with that learning, and next steps. To enable students to take charge of their learning, they need to be deliberately and systematically taught how to assess their own efforts.
15. Recent observations/research from icons Michael Fullan, Ron Ritchhart, and John Hattie show that *deeper thinking benefits lower achieving students the most*. One reason, I believe, why Fullan insists on including higher thinking skills almost immediately in lesson planning.

Chapter 6. Activating Allies: Parents and Students as Partners

Advance Organizers:

1. Parents learned how to help their children attend and engage in learning by speaking with teachers and school personnel. This led to enhanced engagement by students in their schooling experiences, improvement in reading achievement, greater skills and jobs for the parents, higher expectations, higher satisfaction, and higher endorsement of the local schools and community.
2. (Dauber and Epstein 1993) found that *schools encouraging parent participation* was found to be more effective than "family characteristics such as parental education or socioeconomic level, in determining whether parents actually become involved."
3. Learning plans start with each student's concerns: Where do I need help from particular teachers, fellow classmates, or home? What kind of help is available? How do I find the time required to learn—in and out of school? Do I really understand both the content and the learning to learn outcomes in each lesson?
4. Frei (Colorado school representative): "Student-led parent/teacher conferences are incentives for the students and their parents to take ownership of their education process. We've seen the positive results as our test scores and graduation rates continue to improve, and the number of our graduating students

attending college remains higher than both the statewide and regional averages."
5. "This willingness of teachers at Thomas [School] to reach out to parents, to listen to their concerns, and to go the extra mile for their children was much appreciated by parents, and they reciprocated by extending strong support to teachers."
6. The research is unequivocal: ranking students hurts kids. A sordid fact when you consider the majority of high school tests/exams are confined to who did better than whom. Professional, formative assessments determine how students' thinking is improving and where the student needs help or enrichment. The only comparisons that make sense show how a student is progressing against learning goals.
7. As students get closer to adulthood, schools often become more isolating and impersonal. Advisory programs offer the opportunity to meet students' developmental needs because it is the one place in school where students are intimately known as 'whole people'.
8. "In the student focus groups, 98% of students responded affirmatively when asked, 'Do you think advisory helps you academically?' Students responded that their advisories helped them focus on their studies, receive critical academic support, strategize about classes and teachers, set academic goals, and belong to a group of peers striving for success."
9. Insistence on polite, respectful behaviour requires teachers modeling personal and professional commitment. Behaviour management, a synonym for rewards and punishment, has been, despite its prevalence, a colossal failure; behavioural skills don't happen through a hands-off approach waiting to see what happens, but through insistence on correct behaviour through everyday interactions between teachers and students.
10. Bryk and Schneider (2002): "In the context of power asymmetry, the burden generally falls to the most powerful party to initiate actions that reduce the sense of vulnerability experienced by others. Given the significant power imbalance between poor parents and school professionals in most urban contexts, it is incumbent on school professionals to take the lead."

Chapter 7. Building Social Capital: Team Building

Advance Organizers:

1. Producing a General Purpose Statement can assist in avoiding extremes of traditional teaching *and* progressive education, what Jane Kise (2014) calls the false dichotomy of academic achievement vs whole child education. Reconciliation, she states, starts with recognizing the other group as partners in achieving common goals, a necessary condition for whole school collaboration.
2. Online comment: "We need community cohesiveness and social responsibility. The public schools must focus on ensuring children are educated for the future of our nation, not just academically, but to ensure all children are able to see that they belong in this world as part of a greater community."
3. These goals overlap, support each other, and are almost all sub-objectives for such superordinate goals as *high academic results for all students, the ability to work with others, love of learning, learning to learn, enhanced creativity, lifelong learning, making thinking visible, deeper thinking, raising general intelligence, and democratic citizenry.*
4. The winning process for substantive change, M. Fullan (2016) insists, depends on finding "right drivers": *a clear sense of direction, coherence, interwoven policies/strategies, and an embedded culture of improvement.* The GPS, hopefully, provides the *clear sense of direction.* Attaining *coherence* through *interwoven policies and strategies* is next, all pulling and pushing toward *an embedded culture of improvement.*
5. Halbert and Kaser (2016) also provide sound advice on professional learning and improved student outcomes. Focused efforts require time—one or two years. In their experience working with BC schools, they see them finding unique ways of finding time for professional learning communities, either through staff meetings devoted to learning issues, professional book study groups, early morning sessions, or reaching out to other schools and districts.
6. Enrolling parents in courses is another possibility. One group could be young parents who enroll their pre-school children in a high school's child development/childcare course similar to one we offered in Fort Smith. Progress in achieving self-

regulated learning for students and parents would be helpful as it allows for parent time schedules/other responsibilities.
7. Schools also need to keep track of previous dropouts, and, as a school's capacity to serve a wider range of needs grows, it should invite those students back on a full or part-time basis. Knock on the doors of dropouts if you have to, as we did in Grand Rapids, MB; offer hope/improved support, and welcome them back.
8. Students as school ambassadors include school progress presentations to Lions Clubs, town councils, and other community organizations that emphasize school success in reaching agreed-upon goals as well as continuing obstacles. The tone is appreciative of teacher and parent support along the way, willingness to share mistakes as building blocks, and respect for those with opposing opinions. Conflict resolution and collaboration skills are not only learned in classes, they are an integral part of such outreach.
9. This does not imply that all student behaviour is acceptable. There is no freedom (covid or non-covid) without responsibility. And this includes <u>what you shouldn't do</u> *and* <u>what you should do</u>. Those who behave badly/disrupt others' opportunities to learn (or live) can have their freedom temporarily curtailed. Leadership from senior students can be especially helpful. We don't expect all students to be on task 100%, but behaviour that is disrespectful, intolerant, or wastes the time of others necessitates guidance, planning, teaching, and regrettably, short-term consequences.
10. Enhancing the citizenry of our students, welding schools and communities together, and using high school assemblies to collaboratively address community concerns starts with purpose. Using the current pandemic as an example, we consider the following: What do we need to learn as individuals, as a school, and as a community?
11. Whole school involvement could be difficult during the pandemic. But starting with student questions, and looking to involve the community, we might begin by asking community members such as the mayor, local physicians, other health specialists, businessmen, senior centre representatives, town council members, RCMP, Alberta-based residents, and conspiracy theorists to present their views; then respond to students' questions/concerns through school assemblies open to the public.

Chapter 8. The Distributive Property: Student Achievement/

Advance Organizers:

1. Relationships are evident in the physical nature of classrooms, student groupings, teacher accountability, teacher collaboration, observable processes for measuring results and *ways of communicating those results to students, parents, and communities*.
2. Finding the time to teach learning to learn capacities of reading, writing, and speaking is doable if it occurs in all subjects. Failing that, secondary students cannot become self-directed learners; a comprehensive literacy program is not only one of the fourteen goals it is the basis for learning anything.
3. The effectiveness of collaborative output such as dictogloss, jigsaw, and reciprocal teaching is attributed to improved language awareness as students reconstruct text and notice links between form and meaning, largely attributed to feedback from fellow students. Research again showing greater accuracy accruing from collaborative tasks as compared to individual efforts.
4. Interestingly, Giltrow (2005) showed that writers can also learn from read-alouds when the read-aloud text is not their own; teacher read-aloud/think-alouds of some students' writing benefits the rest of the class. The question then arises: *How does read-aloud-think aloud to improve reading skills differ from similar modeling designed to improve writing?*
5. Students, with their teacher's help, identify similarities and differences in terms of meaning and form between their text reconstructions and the original, which is displayed on the projection screen. Dictogloss forces students to examine grammatical structures carefully and to discuss their effects with a specific goal in mind—constructing meaning.
6. Informational texts have more difficult reading material than narrative texts. This occurs because of student inexperience with the text type and partly because students are unfamiliar with the organization and structure of informational texts. Comprehension strategies include peers accessing background knowledge, making connections, questioning, inferring, identifying main ideas and details, summarizing, and synthesizing.

7. Although the main organizational patterns were largely agreed upon, I was surprised by the number of different observations across the groups that identified patterns beyond the few I had indicated. In what I had chosen for a comparison/contrast example, they not only found other patterns, but patterns within patterns. Attacking this assignment as a puzzle to be solved, they had gone beyond my expectations. Moreover, I later learned that such patterns had become filters through which students analyzed thinking in other texts.
8. In chapter 7, I described students (with teacher support) extending school citizenship inquiry to the local community. Expanding such experience means expanding the team. Using collaborative learning, a mix of high school students, parents, teachers, school board members, business owners, local and regional government officials, politicians, and in fact, any community members, carry out investigative inquiries into community and state/provincial/national issues based on local concerns.
9. Steinberg S. R. and Kincheloe J.L. (1998): "And, while I will clarify difficult passages, I will *not* lecture on the textbook. In fact, I discourage my colleagues from such lecturing every chance I get, being sorely tempted to scream every time someone implies that the logical response to a lack of reading ability among students is to ask them to do *less* reading."
10. Enhancing communication capabilities through reading, writing, and speaking instruction in all high school courses is both a strategy for change and a goal; indispensable for achieving high academic achievement, improved creativity, and choice in a variety of learning/career opportunities, collaboration with others, upgraded engagement with their learning, participation in the governance of our democracies, and a lifetime of learning.
11. By making students, teachers, and community members equal partners in collaborative inquiries we can support active engagement with questions of common interest. Students working alongside adults mobilize student knowledge. Consequently, such partnerships develop a sense of shared responsibility for the quality and conditions of teaching and learning within particular classrooms *and* the school community.
12. To supplement classroom efforts, I asked the future teachers to research Indigenous history in Grand Rapids through the eyes of their community. They were to interview parents, grandpar-

ents, and other community members for information that could help us with the course.

13. Peer tutoring, then, along with a learning to learn curriculum and teacher advisor backing could be a life changer for disadvantaged students. These students need extensive support (intellectually, emotionally, and socially). In the suggested timetable above, there are eight hours per week available for that purpose.

14. The lessons for educators model those for local communities, counties, territories, provinces, state and national departments of education, parishes, and all democracies. Considering what is happening around the world, finding common ground is not a luxury but a necessity. The need for balancing both conservative and progressive perspectives in our democracies is paralleled by the need for compromise in our schools.

15. One function of the District Learning Support Committee is to monitor such achievement; providing information on how well goals are met, what is working, and what changes or additional incentives are required is crucial. We also need to learn *how* schools/districts support ongoing summative and formative investigations. How and *by whom*? Again, seeking to relate the parts and the whole.

16. Students, with support and encouragement from their teachers, conduct and publish research that includes gathering qualitative and quantitative data from board members, principals, teachers, students, parents, and superintendents. A teaming up that delivers needed information for improving high schools. Parents and communities have every right to better information for judging how well our schools serve their children.

Chapter 1
Past Performance: Stuck in Neutral

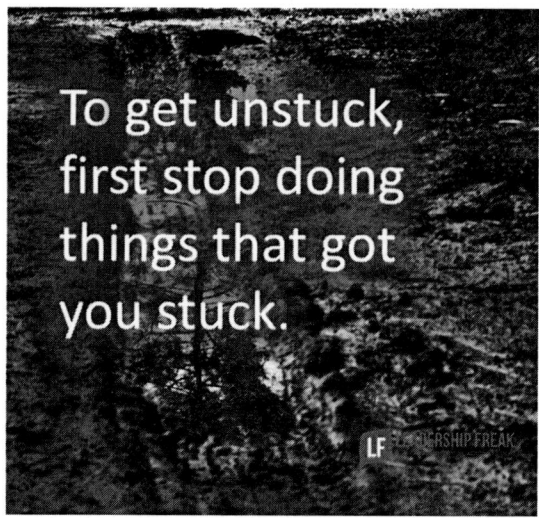

By Dan Rockwel

"Have a good day," I said, as Jack Zheng lifted himself off the stool beside me, hesitated, poked a finger at the leveled reading pieces on the counter.

"Bad day," he replied. Head down, he turned and shuffled toward the door. Jack was the last grade ten student I would test that day. Through a glass wall I watched him, head still down, as he passed through the excited chatter of Chinese BC high school students excused for the afternoon. I got it. His response underlining the frustration of students used to success—but in a different language.

He was not alone among those who scored at grade five level or less. Of the ninety-six grade ten students tested that September, only fifteen read at grade eight or nine levels. A wake-up call: the first year of the school's existence and this baseline information was important to me as principal of BC High School SUIS, Brian Butcher, Canadian consultant and teacher recruiter, and Mason Lee, Director of International Schools for XIEHE in Shanghai.

At least we knew where we stood, most secondary schools do not. As the *Canadian Journal of Education and Policy* pointed out in 1995, "schools are not themselves organized as learning institutions... They do not ordinarily collect information about their environments, or even about their students."

Karen Robson, Ontario Research Chair for "Academic Achievement and At-Risk Youth" in her online article, "Why won't Canada collect data on race and student success?" December 12, 2018, had this to say:

> Considerable research in Toronto has identified Black males as having the lowest post-secondary opportunities due to their disproportionate placement in the 'applied' stream of study. These problems are not unique to Toronto; they are only measured in Toronto.
> Lack of data does not mean lack of a problem. By not collecting data on race and other important sociodemographic factors of students, we fail to correct systemic barriers to success in our educational system.
> By conflating immigrant success with a blanket commitment to equality, we blindly assume we are doing OK as we do not have any evidence to the contrary—because we haven't taken the time to collect it.

The need to gather information relevant to the setting is reinforced by John Goodlad (2004): "It is difficult to envision a school's staff, students, and parents proceeding systematically to create new circumstances in their school without the availability of specific data on its present condition" (p. 19).

In the same way formative assessment advises students *and* teachers on their learning/teaching in the classroom, individual schools, districts, counties, provinces, territories, and federal/state departments of education require timely information on what is or is not working in terms of policies, attitudes, teaching methods, at-risk student support, parent involvement, collaborative expertise, focus, and role formulations.

Jo Chrona (2022), along with the First Nations Leadership Council of Canada, see the need to gather information on achievement levels of Indigenous students:

> In British Columbia in 2021, the First Nations Leadership Council wrote to the province's Minister of Education to challenge a campaign by the BC Teachers Federation (BCTF) to eliminate Foundation Skills Assessments (FSAs). The First Nations Leadership Council noted that eliminating this assessment and access to the results would undermine our collective ability to meet the needs of First Nations learners in the provincial school system.
>
> …this is an example of an action having an unintended adverse consequence, which was recognized by First Nations leadership. Without the data that has been provided by the assessment tools (such as FSAs), the breadth and depth of systemic inequity for Indigenous learners across the province would not be so clear, and we would lose a tool we can use to measure any potential systemic progress. Moving forward in Reconciliation means responding to the concerns and priorities of Indigenous leadership, rather than continuing to believe that non-Indigenous peoples 'know best'. (pp. 45–46)

Sighted on leaders, appointed or otherwise, this handbook suggests district/school support for interlocking learning communities facing the challenge of improved learning opportunities for minority groups, second language students, students with disabilities, of poverty, and academically advanced students. These being the square pegs failing to fit into secondary schools round holes when current opportunities for a decent life are, without a good education, quickly evaporating.

The upper tracks of almost all high schools might appear immune to these concerns as they are assigned the most experienced and qualified teachers. But academically capable students are not confined to the highest tracks and investigative interests can be stifled in status courses as easily as anywhere else. Advanced Placement courses, for instance, have the most rigid curricula because of the external examinations contributing to their status.

Moreover, if you think the challenges for high schools are confined to teaching minorities, you need only consider mounting evidence on the number of today's graduates, particularly boys, who do not read, write, or vote.

The National Youth Survey Report (2011), commissioned by Elections Canada, identified several reasons why youth do not vote. Barriers include a lack of political interest and knowledge, not knowing where or how to vote, and a lower sense that voting is a civic duty.

Reinforcing these concerns, John Hattie, an internationally recognized New Zealand researcher, had this to say: "I worry about our current factory model because for about 60–70% of the students, it's working very well, but for 30–40% it's not. And it's not always 30–40% of the struggling kids—some of our brightest kids are failing in the industrial model."

Adding to this picture, he postulated that "No manner of school reform will be successful until we first face and resolve the engagement issue—student malaise. Too many students are physically present but are neither emotionally nor intellectually involved." Part of the problem, he believes, "is that students spend 85% of their time listening (or pretending to listen) to a teacher talking." Visible Learning Conference, July 13, 2016, National Harbor, Maryland.

Jeremy Adams, a high school teacher from Bakersfield, California: "In the 1970s, teens read three times as many books as today. In 1980, sixty percent of high school seniors reported that they read a newspaper, magazine, or book on a daily basis for pleasure; by 2016 that number had dropped to sixteen percent. Teenagers are more likely to read books at thirteen than seventeen." Los Angeles Times article, August 28, 2019

Donalyn Miller, a language arts and social studies teacher from Keller, Texas, in her book, *The Book Whisperer: Awakening the Inner Reader in Every Child* (2009), describes research on "why secondary students read less and less with each passing year they are in school, and why so many students cannot comprehend the information in their textbooks or pass standardized tests" (p. 2).

In Canada, the Higher Education Quality Council of Ontario surveyed graduating students from twenty Ontario post-secondary institutions on their ability to go beyond memorization and use written or numerical information to solve problems. The results were not good. According to a Globe and Mail newspaper report, of the 7,500 students tested, almost half scored at the minimum level judged to be "adequate to succeed in today's job market." November 27, 2018

Consonant with the above, Juliet Strang, Philip Masterson & Oliver Button in (2006), report employers complaining young people lack communication, teamwork, time management, planning, and problem-solving skills—these being objectives of their learning to learn program at Villiers High School in England.

Through a mix of teaching, leadership experience, research, and reflection, I conclude that western secondary schools commonly subscribe to a disabling web of straitjackets, myths, dogmas, bureaucracies, and structures. These include misconceptions on class size effects, courses with different levels of difficulty/expectations bound to the same timeframe, university as the only viable goal, the value of all homework, inquiry as *the* answer to student motivation, learning about subjects rather than applying them, negligent evaluation of teachers and teaching, evidence of deeper learning reduced to numbers/letters, and static student groupings.

For instance, homework, according to Hattie (2009), has this caution:

> Homework in which there is no active involvement by the teacher does not contribute to student learning, and likewise the use, or not, of technologies (such as distance learning) does not show major effects on learning if there is no teacher involvement. (p. 236)

Regarding misconceptions on class size effects, Wagner T. and Dintersmith T. (2015) observe the following:

> The teacher usually drives the discussion and asks all the questions. In the 'discussions', students are playing 'guess what's on the teacher's mind' in a hub-and-spoke model, instead of forming and defending their own views. People often wonder why research on class size doesn't show learning improvements in smaller classes, and the answer is simply this: You can as easily lecture fifteen students as fifty—even if you don't call it lecturing. (p. 199)

"Mississippi Is Offering Lessons for America on Education", New York Times, May 31, 2023, a newspaper article by Nicholas Kristof, has the same message:

> Mississippi is also striking for what it didn't do. For example, it didn't reduce class sizes: Officials weighed the evidence and concluded that while smaller classes would improve outcomes, spending the money on teacher coaching and student tutoring would help even more.

As for student groupings, I inadvertently learned of a high school split between two buildings a mile or so apart. One has grades nine and ten, and the second has grades eleven and twelve. Students who fail subjects in grade ten repeat them together in the grade eleven/twelve building along with their grade eleven courses. The concern of highlighting these students as failures is offset by reducing the pupil-teacher ratio.

This is a bureaucratic solution to problems of transportation and timetabling. The research, hard as it is for teachers and the general public to accept, is that lowering the student-teacher ratio in high school classrooms has little effect. What really matters is which teacher the students get.

Perhaps I am being unfair; perhaps the most qualified (proven expertise and training) teachers were assigned to those students. But I doubt it. That's not part of the culture of secondary schools. More likely, it is the opposite—last hired/least qualified. Regardless, loud labeling of these students, past performance reminder, and missing range of student readiness to assist each other—all proven negatives in grouping lower-achieving students over an extended time, are bad for everyone.

School/district decision making is not the only concern. Within the classroom fallacies are fixed intelligence, preaching higher-level thinking skills but confining testing to information, rewarding work over cognition, poorly integrated assistive technology, focusing on reading and listening at the expense of writing and speaking, lesson planning centred on activities rather than thinking, downgrading student learning beyond a specified time, and using marks as rewards/punishment.

Balanced change starts by confirming goals beyond comparative test scores based on memory. According to educational authors Michael Fullan and Charles Ungerleider, more important student outcomes are a passion for learning, communication skills of reading, speaking, listening, and writing; self-regulation, resilience, collaborative participation, deep thinking, creativity, transfer of knowledge, respect for differences in people, willingness/skills to participate in a democracy, and concern for the less fortunate.

Quality outcomes are not being met. Consider the fact that skills needed to succeed in careers are identical to those needed to be effective citizens in a democracy. These include the ability to ask forward-thinking, stimulating questions; communicate effectively, analyze information, come to independent opinions, and collaborate well with others. Exactly where we now fail.

This relationship is emphasized by Tony Wagner, co-director of the Change Leadership Group at the Harvard Graduate School of Education, in "Change Leadership: A Practical Guide to Transforming Our Schools" et al. (2006):

> So when studies reveal that the overwhelming majority of today's public high school students leave school, 'unprepared for college', they also indicate lack of preparation to access most jobs in our economy and to assume responsible roles as informed citizens in a democracy. An eighteen-year-old who is not college ready today has effectively been sentenced to a lifetime of marginal employment and second-class citizenship. (p. 5)

Michael Fullan and Joanne Quinn from their book, "coherence: The Right Drivers in Action for Schools, Districts, and Systems" (2016):

> New learning goals require changes in how relationships between students, teachers, families, and community are structured. The shift toward active learning partnerships requires students to take greater charge of their own and each other's learning inside and outside the classroom. The new learning partnerships have the potential to create more authentic and meaningful learning locally, nationally, and globally. This more active role increases student engagement. The shift to a new balance in decision making is inevitable because students are no longer willing to be passive recipients of learning defined by someone else, are digitally connected to massive amounts of new ideas and information, and respond to traditional didactic approaches with passivity *once they have foundational skills*. (p. 93, [emphasis added])

Standardized or teacher-made tests based on memorized surface facts and procedures is a continuing problem. Unless information is used as preparation for higher level cognitive outcomes, isolated facts are useless. And contrary to the assumptions of traditionalists who oppose democratizing schools and advancing deeper thinking, their pedagogy produces students who remember less.

Ritchhart (2015) cites a study by Fred Newmann et al., "Authentic intellectual work and standardized tests: Conflict or coexistence" (2001), involving over five thousand students from Chicago Public Schools:

> He found that students who were in classrooms where they regularly encountered tasks that demanded complex thinking and elaborated communication performed better on tests of basic skills than their peers who encountered more reproductive tasks. This finding held true for students of all ability levels. However, lower-performing students are particularly

disadvantaged by a lack of opportunity. In short, students need to spend less time filling in the bubbles on tests and more time connecting the dots. (p. 166)

The impact of reduced opportunities for complex thinking and elaborated communication is supported by Robert L. Fried in his book, "The Game of School: Why We All Play It, How It Hurts Kids, and What It Will Take to Change It." (2005). He describes high schools limited to short-term memory skills accompanied by a dearth of thinking because students are not taught how to learn, make thinking visible, or appreciate mistakes. Corroborating this conclusion in their documentary film, "Race to Nowhere" (2010), Vicki Abeles and Jessica Congdon chronicle students largely working for grades—the learning being secondary or inconsequential.

If we really want students to apply higher-order thinking, we must assess it. If we believe creativity, working well with others, citizenry obligations, and love of learning are vital, we need to identify observable evidence for these goals. As Claxton et al. (2013) put it, "If we do not find ways of measuring what we value, we will end up just valuing what we can measure. And that distorts the process of schooling, and inhibits teachers from pursuing other aims that they know are more important" (p. 22).

Clear expectations are not common at the university level either; few professors model the learning required. I recall an exception where our psychology professor, in response to a multitude of mediocre efforts on my part and others, used an overhead projector to provide his own response to a test question. The detail and evidence he expected were made clear to us all. I remember his quiet message to this day: "Now do you see the difference between what you are doing and the kind of thinking and detail I am expecting?" Respectful silence from the entire class. More telling than the loudest voice.

The current undermining of higher-level goals includes teacher isolation, treating students as reluctant beneficiaries rather than partners in learning, lack of collective accountability, professional development divorced from teacher evaluations, superintendents "protecting" schools/districts from outsiders with disrupting ideas, the holy grail of control in and out of classrooms, school/district statements of intent with no plan, viewing student responses as incompetency rather than feedback to improve lessons, and exaggerating issues schools have no control over while discounting those they do.

Unrecognized false dichotomies are part of the picture. The upside of one is the downside of the other. I recall discussing a choice in teaching writing with our grade 12 English teacher, Hedy Li, in Shanghai. Having taught at R.B. Russell Collegiate in Winnipeg, Manitoba where I followed Nancy Atwell's writing workshop model as described in her book, "*In the Middle*", I wondered about the choice our teachers often made in favour of grammar instruction, seemingly at the expense of time to write. She replied, "They need both."

Other false choices are teacher freedom to teach vs professional learning communities, district vs school decision making, inquiry vs direct instruction, phonics vs reading for understanding, academic success vs emotional and social learning, teacher support vs student self-regulation, learning as deliberate practice vs going with the "flow", developing memory vs deep thinking while using osmosis as the preferred option for improving vocabulary, writing, speaking, thinking, reading, and learning to learn. We are also guilty of spavined practices such as treating parents as intruders and the tyranny of secondary teachers awarded higher-level courses/well-behaved students on the basis of longevity/divine right.

Writing is foundational for other communication abilities. Two important learning resources for students are writing and verbal presentations. The relationship between these two is rarely recognized in secondary schools. The deficit is significant. According to a survey conducted by The Chronicle of Higher Education (2006), 61% of high school teachers report their students never write a paper more than five pages. Too little practice results in poor grammar, bad organization, weak reasoning, and unproductive communication.

Matt Damon addressing a "Save Our Schools" rally, July 30, 2011:

> "I had incredible teachers. As I look at my life today, the things I value most about myself—my imagination, my love of acting, my passion for writing, my love of learning, my curiosity—all come from how I was parented and taught.
> And none of these qualities that I've just mentioned—none of these qualities that I prize so deeply, that have brought me so much joy, that have brought me so much professional success—none of these qualities that make me who I am can be tested."

They are not testable using written tests, but a passion for writing is not hard to see. Do students write on their own? Do they write about concerns/issues they deem important? Can they tell you why they enjoy writing? Can they describe what they know about their process of writing? Do they see writing improving their learning capacity? Can they define their writing strengths and weaknesses? Has writing improved their lives? How?

The use of marks is a major part of the problem. High school marks, with all their baggage (subjective judgments, grade inflation, low reliability and validity, absent benchmarks, mixing behaviour and academic progress, comparing averages using subjects with differing levels of difficulty, group marks as a convenient substitute for individual assessments, winners and losers' mentality and the resultant destruction of intrinsic motivation), do not predict success in first-year university.

As reported in Maclean's magazine, August 30, 2007, by Sarah Scott:

> High school marks don't even predict how well you will do in first-year University, says James Parker, who holds the Canada Research Chair in emotion and health at Trent University. "In our culture, high school marks are the most important thing," he says. "Yet if you look at success in first year, high school marks don't predict that very well." (p. 1)

Even China, with its eyes firmly fixed on student grades is changing its tune. Its Central Committee believes the country must emphasize sowing students' creativity and practical activities over instilling an ability to achieve certain test scores and recite rote knowledge. Suisheng Zhao (2006).

A "Learn to Think" (LTT) intervention program in China raised thinking abilities of more than 200,000 primary and secondary school students. It concluded LTT promoted the development of students' thinking ability, learning motivation, and learning strategies as well as raising academic performance. Hu (2013)

I refused to change a Mathematics 100 grade in Minitonas, Manitoba. Barry had failed the course the year before I arrived and again as my student. This occurred decades ago, but I remember his mark: 45%. He was applying to Red River Community College in Winnipeg and needed the credit to be accepted. But I had my standards. A failure is a failure. One of the most thoughtless/ignorant (amidst great competition) decisions I ever made. An oft-remembered regret that has stuck to this day. What I should have done was organize extra help from myself or his fellow students. But in that, I was the one who failed.

Seeking paths of least resistance, current change efforts are often restricted to and by (1) top-down curricular expectations, (2) the mistaken assumption that all technologies support meaningful learning, (3) the disabling attitude that sees high school culture, including school/teacher isolation, as untouchable (it is what it is), (4) bureaucratic, politically driven administrators with scant expertise in teaching or learning, and (5) failing to enlist the support, let alone leadership, of students and parents.

For example, the new British Columbia's progressive curriculum sees inquiry as *the* driving force in classrooms while acknowledging the need for additional professional learning for implementation. They call it training. But no plans for teachers to move away from isolated teaching to collaborative improvement for *any* change to occur.

This is a gaping hole in the ministry of education's plan. Without substantial collaborative learning the probability of improving teachers' attitudes, skills, and knowledge approaches zero. The reason is that deeper thinking and transfer of ideas are best done through exchanging ideas with others. Again, what we have is a laudable goal with no credible path for realization. It is the "what" with no "how".

History should teach us from our mistakes. Consider the BC Ministry of Education 1926 curriculum reform advocating student inquiry as referenced by Dr. Charles Ungerleider, former BC Deputy Minister of Education in his article, "The more things change, the more they stay the same" (2016). He decries top-down ordered change with no strategy for improving teaching other than repeating failed efforts.

Aiming for a culture of learning—socially, emotionally, physically, and intellectually in secondary schools is the preface to improvement. Missing is flexibility in the use of time, principals as fellow learners, awareness that daily exercise (at least one hour per day) improves student cognition, recognition of common learning processes for teachers, students, and parents; and facilitator (inside and outside) expertise. Assuming schools and school districts will provide such support on their own, given the dismal implementation history of secondary schools is beyond belief.

The mistaken assumption of technology standing alone (all too apparent during our recent pandemic) is the subject of an article in the New York Times by Susan Dynaski: "Online Courses Are Harming the Students Who Need the Most Help" Jan 19, 2018. She refers to evidence of online education hurting less proficient students. The technology, then, is best used as a supplement to classrooms not a replacement.

There is also evidence that students who produce large quantities of text on cellphones are unable to write well using a computer because of their addiction to the small screen. Quick communication almost demanding writers disregard rules of grammar and punctuation.

This concern is described in Nicholas Carr's book, *In the Shallows: What the Internet is Doing to Our Brains* (2020). He reveals digital media transforming cognitive processes and concentration. But not in a good way. He sees student thinking, a result of using technology/internet, as staccato-like. He evaluates his own concentration as weaker and deep reading that used to come easily has become a struggle. This echoes Jakob Nielsen's (2006) identification of the F-shaped pattern. Through eye-tracking, Neilsen observed that text read online is F-shaped—as we scroll down a page we read less and less.

Other concerns regarding the proper integration of technology in secondary schools are laid out by Andy Hargreaves et al. in "Uplifting Leadership: How Organizations, Teams, and Communities Raise Performance" (2014):

> Technology has become a mere fad in some schools and systems across the world, with dubious and sometimes disastrous results for students' learning. School districts stack up their schools with electronic tablets that become little more than fancy note-taking devices. Interactive whiteboards are used no differently than old-fashioned chalkboards. In too many cases, technology drives the teaching and merely distracts the students. At Ngee Ann (secondary school in Singapore) though, it works the other way around: technology stimulates good teachers to become even better.
>
> For instance, Ngee Ann has taken a counterintuitive approach to students' use of smartphones. In the United States and many other countries, teachers ban student smartphones in the classroom, viewing them—quite naturally—as distractions. Ngee Ann Secondary, however, sees smartphones as teaching and learning tools. They allow students to use Twitter as a feedback device. This gives shy students a way to record their responses to their learning and get involved in class discussion. It provides teachers with data about their students' learning that they can review after class and sometimes as the class is happening. Students are also "more engaged because they are using something they are very familiar with and good at," Adrian Lim explained. (p. 60)

The effects of television parallel that of smartphones. From *Thirteen Questions: Reframing Education's Conversation*, (2nd edition, 1996) by Eugene E. Provenzo Junior:

> As a university professor I have become increasingly aware of the fact that my students are often better seeing things than listening to them, of skimming information than reflecting on ideas. The image of a close friend's thirteen-year-old daughter comes to my mind. She was talking to me one Sunday morning while her father was making coffee in the kitchen. She told me about her schoolwork as she watched the television out of the corner of her eye, 'channel surfing' even after her father came back into the room to continue his conversation, she flipped from one station to another with the remote control, never staying for more than ten or fifteen seconds on a single program. (p. 220)

The affective domain is also in trouble. Jo Boaler in *Limitless mind: Learn, lead and live without barriers* (2019), introduces Shane, an American high school student determined to "help other students know what can happen when they connect with others and then match them with clubs of interest to them." He started a movement, "Count Me In". When Boaler interviewed Shane, he set out the challenges faced by young people forming meaningful connections.

Shane:

> Teenagers today have it harder than any other generation by far… Not only are they dealing with the same issues we've seen for generations, but also things like peer pressure, bullying, social isolation that can really be harmful on your upbringing and the trajectory of your life. These are now 24/7 issues for every kid because of technology and smartphones and how much they are plugged in online, yet unplugged in reality and in community. Those community connections, I think, are the key in forging something—so we can see the world just differently enough that we begin to feel a greater sense of self-acceptance and belonging. (p. 183)

Globe and Mail newspaper article by David McGinn, January 20, 2024:

> In 2019, Ontario mandated that cellphones only be used in class for educational, health and medical purposes, as well as to support special educational needs, including students with

mental health needs. Otherwise, personal devices are only to be used during lunch or recess, according to the policy.

Smartphones can support learning in some contexts, 'but not when it is overused or inappropriately used', the UNESCO report said.

That is why the report urges a nuanced approach, not bans, says Prachi Srivastava, an associate professor at Western University who specializes in education and global development.

Taking the above into consideration, the use of cell phones in classrooms suggests school wide planning. While providing a degree of safety (school shootings as an example), they can undoubtedly interrupt, distract, and diminish individual and collaborative learning.

Finding common ground on cellphone use is an opportunity for advancing democratic decision making. This suggests a school-wide investigation based on student leadership, district support, point of view awareness, conflict resolution strategies, student self-improvement plans, parent-student-teacher advisor meetings, deliberate practice, growing mindfulness, student ownership advancement, safety concerns, self-regulation, defined school citizenship responsibilities, collaborative learning, parent involvement, teacher modeling, advisory based discussions, local community input, whole school assembly presentations open to the public, hard conversations, personal accountability, and short-term consequences.

A report by the Stanford History Education Group (2016) where the authors' concern was democracy threatened by how easily disinformation about civic issues is allowed to spread, reveals students' inability to ascertain credible internet information. More specifically, they couldn't distinguish advertisements from news articles or determine sources of information, thus dispelling a common assumption that young people competent in social media are able to determine fact-based information.

Shirley R. Steinberg and Joe L. Kincheloe in their book, *Students as Researchers: Creating Classrooms that Matter* (1998), agree; they state that some academics believe students with computers are perfectly capable of gathering the information they need without the help of teachers. According to the authors, such a perspective reflects "not a unique vision for an educational future but a tired and regressive view of knowledge and learning" (p. 18).

They describe the problem:

> Epistemologically, such a position assumes that knowledge needs no interpretation, that no form of analysis or contextualization is necessary because the data speaks for itself. Anyone who surfs the net knows that information in cyberspace is produced by a wide variety of groups and individuals with an extensive range of assumptions and agendas. (p. 18)

Charles Ungerleider (2003) has the same concern:

> Students can find ample information about Canadian Confederation on the internet. But without a skillful teacher, they are unlikely to be able to construct a coherent argument about the nature of the political compromise that Confederation represents and its recurring impact on Canadian civic life. (p. 119)

As an aside, one potential antidote for disinformation is set out in "Who Owns the Learning? Preparing Students for Success in the Digital Age" (2012), where the author, Alan November, recommends teaching students how to validate online information and build custom engines for improved productive searches.

Current threats to democracy demand serious efforts to help students become life-long citizen learners with the ability to discern false premises, evaluate evidence, and expose self-indulgent conspiracy theories amid waves of social media, radio, the internet, shorthand communication, television disinformation, false dichotomies, blurbs, and corrupt websites.

Globe and Mail newspaper article (January 26, 2023):

> Vaccine hesitancy, fuelled by misinformation and conspiracy theories, led to thousands of unnecessary deaths and hospital stays and cost the health care system at least $300 million during two COVID-19 waves in 2021, according to a report that highlights the urgent risk to society of such false claims. The report, based on the work of an expert panel and published Thursday by the Council of Canadian Academies (CCA), a non-profit organization based in Ottawa, shows how misinformation is eroding trust in public institutions and exacerbating health crises.

John Hattie in, *Visible Learning for Literacy: Implementing the Practices That Work Best to Accelerate Student Learning* (2016), distinguishes "front-of-class lecturing" from "direct instruction"—one of the more effective teaching strategies in his research. His teacher education students, nonetheless, perceived direct instruction as bad, constructionism as good—constructionism interpreted as student-centred inquiry learning.

He points out that you can't think about nothing. We need to value surface information as the foundation for deeper thinking and transfer of knowledge. Selecting teaching strategies, then, is not a series of false dichotomies but linking students and student outcomes with the right choice. Hattie deplores the fact that many schools call themselves "enquiry schools", as if students can plan investigations without at least understanding some of the ideas and processes involved.

His research describes inquiry as a *standalone teaching strategy*. Many programs like enquiry-based teaching (0.31) and problem-based learning (0.16) have reduced effects as they are frequently introduced outside the context of understanding many idea*s*. This mistake is understandable. High school teachers have rarely studied either student thinking or learning to learn principles. Both professional development and university courses have, regrettably, focused on old teaching strategies (and not much variety there either) rather than how students or anyone else learn.

A caution from Michael Fullan and Mary Jean Gallagher in *The Devil is in the Details: System Solutions for Equity, Excellence, and Student Well-Being* (2020), suggests that even at the outset of acquiring surface information, usually through direct instruction, teachers should not exclude deeper thinking.

The same concern is found in Kuhlthau C. et al. *Guided Inquiry: Learning in the 21st Century* (2007), which recognizes that an extended focus on surface information, especially if the mechanics of searching skills are complex, demotivates students. Instead, they combine information location, evaluation, and how the information is to be used throughout the inquiry process—not all at the beginning.

Kuhlthau et al. (2007):

> Guided Inquiry incorporates transferable information literary concepts into the inquiry process. It does not teach isolated information skills that are difficult for students to recall and apply. Too much of the mechanics of searching and resources at the beginning of research discourages students and

distracts them from the interesting ideas and questions that motivate them to learn. Rather than attempting to teach all there is to know about *information seeking* prior to the assignment, Guided Inquiry incorporates *information location, evaluation, and use concepts throughout the research process.* Lasting information literacy is developed in practice when both information concepts and search skills in the inquiry process can be recalled and applied as needed. (p. 5, [emphasis added])

As stated, many students are ready to move past basic information to deeper thinking immediately. A child doesn't master skating before playing hockey—skating and hockey feed on each other. Just as hockey is often the motivation for learning to skate, deeper thinking is more attractive than memorizing, and furthermore, those students who can already skate have the right to play *now*.

An American history course at the University of Alberta in Edmonton early in my career was a six-week summer session. Too late to register for a mathematics course (my major), my father, a high school history teacher, suggested it. My last course in history was grade eleven Canadian history. In high school we learned surface information: who, what, and sometimes why—all that would be needed on the provincial exam. But this was a different story. The professor told us we were responsible for all the surface information—he expected us to learn that on our own.

He told us the assignments and final examination would be answering a choice of questions with an argumentative essay. I remember one: "Were the founding fathers of the American Constitution selfish reactionaries?" The response was to be 'Yes' or 'No' with evidence. There were fifteen questions on the final exam and we had to choose three. A world away from high school and many other undergraduate courses as well. We needed deeper thinking and a good memory. Challenging and elevating, it remains one of my most valuable educational experiences.

Instead of endorsing panacean teaching strategies, ministries of education should support collective accountability where successful methods *rise from within*. A voice in the wilderness: back in 1964 John Holt, in his book, *How Children Fail,* while recognizing the value of insiders driving change, wrote, "This is the only kind of educational research that will ever actually improve education—research done *by teachers*, in their own classrooms, to solve what *they* see as their problems." (p. 212)

He suggested teachers examine carefully what kinds of teaching work best. We need to recognize particular teaching practices as helpful, useless, or harmful. Again, he stresses that only teachers can ask such questions based on their experience.

Wiliam and Leahy, authors of *Embedding Formative Assessment: Practical Techniques for K-12 Classrooms* (2015), quote Sir Richard Livingstone, the president of Corpus Christi College at the University of Oxford three centuries ago:

> The test of a successful education is not the amount of knowledge a pupil takes away from school, but his appetite to know and his capacity to learn. If the school sends out children with a desire for knowledge and some idea of how to acquire and use it, it will have done its work. Too many leave school with the appetite killed and the mind loaded with undigested lumps of information. (pp. 169–170)

The attributes teachers need for improving their teaching are the same skills, knowledge, and attitudes that increase students' ability to learn. There are other similarities: Brownlie and Schnellert (2009), maintain that student motivation is linked to personal relationships with teachers as well as "students' sense of voice and choice in the classroom" (p. 5). Likewise, teacher motivation is also a function of personal relations along with their own sense of voice and choice.

Individual classrooms are not the only settings for change. Secondary schools exist where students, individually or as tasked groups, are recognized as full associates. See Chapter 6: "Activating Allies: Parents and Students as Partners."

I recall student Jackson Yang's suggestion for scheduling Science 10 at our British Columbia high school in Shanghai. He reasoned that since Chinese students had already mastered the learning outcomes for Mathematics 10 in previous grades and only needed the associated English vocabulary, and that Science 10 contained biology/earth science topics for which they had little background, we needed more time for Science 10.

Jackson suggested four months for Math 10 and six months for Science 10. The change contributing to a 100% pass rate from ninety-six students in the subsequent BC provincial examinations in both courses.

My time as a ministry of education consultant using approaches such as *survey-data-feedback* for determining prior knowledge/concerns, building trust through *role clarification/negotiation, mistakes as building blocks, point of view awareness,* and *promoting intellectual conflict* taught me that context is just about everything. Creative responses to learning obstacles requiring active collaboration and contribution from those directly involved.

A creative response to a learning problem: while superintendent of the South Slave Divisional Board of Education in the NWT, moving toward a district goal of an equivalent graduation rate for both Indigenous and non-Indigenous students was achieved, in part, by establishing a full day child-development course at PWK High School in Fort Smith. Under the leadership of the principal, Coralie Bryant, it allowed single parents to attend high school regularly while their children became the subjects of the course.
Guy Claxton et al. (2013):

> Taken together, we (along with many others) believe the arguments for a radical rethink of the priorities and practices of education are overwhelming. And so is the direction in which all these arguments are pointing. If you want that world-class flexible workforce, coach young people in the *pleasures and skills of learning.* If you want to help young people prepare for the stresses and uncertainties of twenty-first century life, help them to be *more resilient.* If you want them to be able to join the world of self-organizing, resourceful learners…give them the *confidence to experiment and collaborate.* (p. 27, [emphasis added])

Organizational development methods can model democratic, professional ethics by respecting individuals, wide perspectives, open-ended thinking, and decision-making inclusiveness at every level. But it is not the only game in town. The challenge for change also embraces confluent learning where feelings/awareness conjoin with thinking, a well-defined learning to learn curriculum aimed at student independence, and collaboration abilities in everyone, in particular teachers learning from each other. The current learning culture best described as isolated workshops for isolated teachers.

In the United States, researchers determined that while 90 percent of teachers reported participating in professional development, most teachers also reported it was totally useless (Darling-Hammond et al. 2009). Thus, they concluded, the real issue isn't teachers being provided professional development, but that typical efforts do not impact teachers' practice or student learning.

The chasm between what we want changed and how to make those changes has been rarely addressed or even noticed. According to M. Fullan (1982), (as true today as it was yesterday) teacher training institutions, although recognizing the need, have failed to prepare teachers with the necessary perceptions/skills to implement change in schools. Their emphasis, he asserted, is on teachers knowing their subjects and fitting in with current school systems.

Hank Levin: "If you can't make a school a great professional place for its staff, it's never going to be a great place for kids." Interview with Ron Brandt (December 1, 1992). Successful school improvement has one basic principle: variables that support the growth, development, and self-confidence of students are exactly those critical for attaining the same outcomes for a school's staff. Sarason (1990).

Sarason (1996) also suggested that many faculties of education have little contact with schools and are poorly organized to effect change. He contended there is no evidence today's teachers with five years of university are more capable than those like my father, who, with no preparation time, taught seventy students from grade one to grade ten in a one-room rural school.

Barth (1990):

> Few professors ever work in public schools and few school people ever work in higher education. Curiously, the education profession has made membership in its two major wings all but mutually exclusive. A citizen in one is suspect in the other. (p. 106)

Current teacher training still results in lesson plans with student activities disconnected from previous knowledge, teaching answers to questions on tests, ignoring formative assessments needed to power subsequent lessons, and failing to clarify or model expectations.

My experience over the years is that teachers, when asked to reflect on how they learned to teach, consistently ranked (high to low frequency) the following: trial and error, a teacher who taught them in school, a colleague, and practice teaching. Rarely mentioned—reading and research. Never mentioned—university methods courses.

Hardly surprising really, considering that universities, especially at the undergraduate level, mirror high school passivity/regurgitation of information—not the stuff of active, personal engagement needed to challenge bad educational assumptions. Education faculties have, disappointingly, become increasingly irrelevant to high school reform.

Thirteen Questions: Reframing Education's Conversation 2nd edition (1996) edited by Joe L. Kincheloe & Shirley R. Steinberg:

> In most instances, schools of education represent the most conservative sector of university life bent on reproducing values designed to maintain the status quo while de-skilling teachers through a labyrinth of how-to methods courses devoid of any substantive content (p. 53)
> Schools of education cannot succeed in preparing future teachers for leadership positions and to be agents of change if they continue to advocate the consumption of neatly packaged instructional programs that are presented as the panacea to difficulties students face in the acquisition of pre-packaged knowledge. (p. 54)

So, the straitjacket is that teachers, parents, and communities have experienced the same education system that accepts and encourages passivity, memorization as the prime vehicle for passing examinations, and student failure to learn separated from teacher responsibility. To this are added absent collaborative learning skills, scarce professional reading when evaluating teaching/learning evidence, sorting students rather than teaching them, and subjective student marks as *the* measurement of their own success.

School boards are also under increasing fire. Board accountability being confined to fiscal issues, legislative task requirements, personnel problems, and pet projects while failing to articulate local community interests or connect them to governing. They avoid penetrating parental/community input. It appears that there is neither time nor inclination for trustees to pursue educational purposes or engage in discussions pertaining to improved learning or teaching.

Understanding the culture of each school/district, with all its contrasts, is ground zero for effective change. Everything affects everything. Determining students, teachers, administrators, and parents' understandings, skills, and attitudes within a particular setting is the starting point. Thus, the first step for needed *change* is *"What do we know? Where are we at?"*

Going forward we remind ourselves of two facts: the first is that the dominant support for student learning is teaching quality. The second is that the current system of professional development—a sad mix of teacher privatization, absent support, and zero accountability—is a proven failure.

Hattie (2012) observes passionate and inspired teachers as focused on what to teach, difficulty levels, rate of progress, and how their teaching affects students' success. Such target setting, however, is not seen by many high school teachers as their concern; their focus on students doing homework and completing assignments. Their job restricted to 1) covering the curriculum, 2) providing resources and activities, and 3) maintaining order in the classroom.

The most prevalent method of professional development, isolated workshops, doesn't work. There are two contrasting situations to avoid: the first is administrators taking little interest in teachers' learning/new experiences with no encouragement/support for sharing, accountability, or follow-up. The second mistake is to swing hard the other way and over-supervise. Armed with a fistful of checklists, narrow expectations, and a specific number of classroom visitations; principals, inspectors, and supervisors strangle the very creativity they seek to enhance.

Observing how other teachers teach/learn is germane, but seldom happens. And, as stated, teachers rarely read learning studies in depth. This may be the result of the unfortunate message of teacher unions, traditional school culture, and ministries of education: (1) teachers have mastered their subjects and they understand how students learn, and (2) lesson planning is personal taste.

With little or no leadership from ministries of education, the job is left to school districts, teacher unions, and "professional development." This means individually attended workshops, outside conferences, and ministry of education lectures—all supporting stopped-up, isolated teacher learning.

Privatization along with a jam-packed schedule has a steep price: teachers do not, in any systemic way, observe each other teach, mentor colleagues, collaborate on action research, engage in joint lesson planning, devise professional learning plans, or gather student information critical to effective teaching—all functions of an institution dedicated to learning.

Although substantial numbers of school districts are aware of the potential impact of professional learning communities, they are not common in high schools. And when they exist, are rarely provided direction or resources. Strategies for realizing distributive leadership are noticeably absent; little attention is paid to supportive conditions and processes.

Effectively mixing research/expertise and teacher problem-solving requires more than 'practical' decisions based on previous understanding of what works, much of it concerned with control, or the studies of university researchers. Growth in decision making is rather the result of systemic reflection: collaborative thinking/inquiry as part of a *learning to learn* literacy curriculum modeled for students *by* teachers.

Roland Barth (1990) concluded the following in *Improving Schools from Within: Teachers, parents, and principals can make the difference*:

> Probably nothing within a school has more impact on students in terms of skills development, self-confidence, or classroom behavior than the personal and professional growth of their teachers… When teachers observe, examine, question, and reflect on their ideas, and develop new practices that lead toward their ideals, students are alive. When teachers stop growing, so do their students. (p. 49–50)

Correspondingly, Faye Brownlie and Leyton Schnellert (2009) urge teachers to incorporate "approaches that build student engagement and lead to active, strategic, and self-regulated learning… One-time workshops are out. Working together over time to understand and support students and their learning is in!" (p. 16)

The need to understand and support students and their learning is underlined by Judy Halbert and Linda Kaser in their book, *Spirals of Inquiry For equity and quality* (2016). They rightfully point out that citizens would be concerned if "a medical team was funded by the public to attend conferences, seminars, workshops and meet with coaching partners in order to learn more about everything except the health issues that their patients were currently confronting" (p.66).

They report:

> It is still too common to hear people planning a school or district professional day by asking some version of: What would we enjoy learning—or doing? Who is available? Anybody have a good idea for a topic? How much would it cost to bring in a well-known speaker? What will we do for lunch?" instead of, "What is it that our students really need us to learn? Who is best positioned to help us? On what resources can we draw?" (p. 66)

Halbert and Kaser also have concerns about trust and challenge. They underscore these issues through Helen Timperley's book, *Realizing the*

Power of Professional Learning (2011):

> Opportunities for adult learning need to occur in environments characterized by both trust and challenge, because *change is as much about emotions as it is about knowledge and skills*. Expectations for change can touch raw nerves *if teachers see these expectations as a reflection on their competence*. If emotional issues are ignored or glossed over, teachers may develop defensive postures as a way to protect themselves from exposing vulnerabilities. If, on the other hand, we allow educator vulnerabilities to dictate the professional learning agenda exclusively, we are unlikely to make the changes that our learners require. (p. 70, [emphasis added])

A no-nonsense consultant from Australia, Peter Cole, encapsulates the situation in his paper, "Professional Development: A Great Way to Avoid Change" (2004). Professional development fails because the appearance of teacher learning is conserved, but the teaching doesn't change and student learning doesn't improve.

Real change embraces individual and group learning ranging from defined targets, clarifying prior knowledge, acquiring surface information, modeling, deliberate practice, intensive thinking, and metacognition to guided/independent inquiry. Quality learning emphasizes student ownership, formative assessment, emotional intelligence, collaborative learning, and gradual release of responsibility. "You in your dark corner and me in mine" hasn't worked. It's time to move on.

Chapter 2
Change Leadership:
Distributed Ownership

Simon Sinek: *"Leadership is a way of thinking, a way of acting, and most importantly, a way of communicating."*

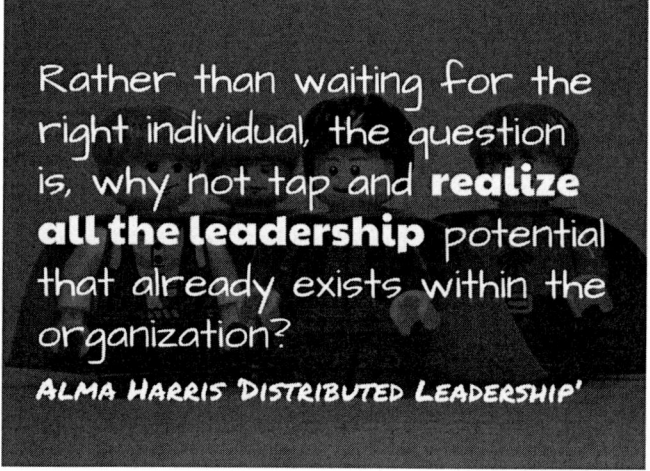

Rather than waiting for the right individual, the question is, why not tap and **realize all the leadership** potential that already exists within the organization?
ALMA HARRIS 'DISTRIBUTED LEADERSHIP'

Tony Wagner et al. in their book, *Change Leadership: A Practical Guide to Transforming our Schools* (2006), report the work of Tony Alverado who received national U.S. acclaim for his leadership while serving as superintendent of Community School District 2 in New York City. He created a model for raising student achievement scores built on a program of focused and intensive professional development of teachers.

Recruited to San Diego, he failed as badly as he succeeded in New York. By replacing his experience in New York with a singularly top-down approach, the result, especially in high schools, was a disaster. Different context, workshops imposed on teachers, lectures to teachers by consultants, ignored parent and teacher input, restrictions on achievement information, supervisors looking over the shoulders of teachers, and fear mongering those who resisted; all contributed to a vast disappointment.

Michael Fullan [online article] "The Role of the District in Tri Level Reform" (2010):

> The San Diego strategy failed because the pace of change was too fast, the strategy was too unidirectional from the top, relationships were not built with teachers and principals, and, above all, the strategies did not really build capacity—which is the development of the collective knowledge and understandings required for ongoing instructional improvement that meets the needs of each child. (p.296)

The lesson (again) is that force feeding doesn't work and people are not sheep. Here we draw on the experience of Wendell L. French and Cecil H. Bell Jr. of the University of Washington in "Organization Development: behavioral science interventions for organization improvement" (1973):

> A common mistake is for external or internal consultants, in their enthusiasm, to be "selling" a kind of utopia instead of helping clients with their problems. For example, they may be perceived as selling trust, openness, cooperation, and the like.
> While we believe these are good things, they are probably best worked on in the context of helping the client system *solve those problems perceived as interfering with organizational effectiveness*. In other words, being perceived as helpful enhances trust between client and consultant; conversely, selling philosophy may inhibit trust. (p. 173, [emphasis added])

They go on to deplore the "good guy-bad guy syndrome" with the change instigators being the good guys and those who resist as backward. These observations are to be appreciated not only by external facilitators, but by people within the system: principals, district personnel, teacher-leaders, superintendents, and school boards. Their self-inflicted roadblocks just as dampening.

This is where organizational development and current educational change efforts come together; analyzing concerns, strengths, suggestions, and prior knowledge of individuals and groups as the point of departure. As M. Fullan set out in Change Leader: Learning to Do What Matters Most (2011):

> The more my colleagues and I grappled with change challenges, the more I realized that the most effective leaders use practice as their fertile learning ground. They never go from theory to practice or research evidence to application. They do it the other way around: they try to figure out what's working, what could be working better, and then look into how research and theory might help. (p.xii)

Agreeing with G. Colvin's book, "Talent is Overrated" (2008) and his characteristics of deliberate practice: repetition, feedback on performance and results, and intellectually challenging work, Fullan sees change as self-motivating through a confluence of success (student and teacher achievement), ethical purpose, freedom and capacity to choose, and social interaction with co-learners.

He reinforces this conclusion by citing John Hattie's mega studies evidence that "high expectations for each student", the previous leading influence on student learning, has been, after more study, surpassed by "collective efficacy", an upshot of "collaborative expertise"—becoming effective with others.

"The Power of Collective Efficacy" (2018), an article by Jenni Donohoo et al., defines the term: A team of individuals sharing the belief "that through their unified efforts they can overcome challenges and produce intended results" (p. 41).

Their summary:

> John Hattie (2016) positioned collective efficacy at the top of the list of factors that influence student achievement. According to his Visible Learning research, based on a synthesis of more than 1,500 meta-analyses, collective teacher efficacy is greater than three times more powerful and predictive of student achievement than socioeconomic status. It is more than double the effect of prior achievement and more than triple the effect of home environment and parental involvement. It is also greater than three times more predictive of student achievement than student motivation and concentration, persistence, and engagement. (pp. 41–42)

Productive citizenship as a superordinate goal for students remains important. Others are improved engagement levels/success of Indigenous learners, other minorities, second language students, students with disabilities, of poverty, academically advanced students, and indeed, all students. Such goals motivating not only teachers, but administrators, parents, and local communities.

Distributed leadership depends on both individuals *and* groups. Participation through district committees, principals' professional communities, and school-based learning communities improve learning capabilities of both. Often we think of individuals, especially those with titles, as the only leaders. But interlocking communities of all types, each with their own collaborative style, accomplishments, and divergent thinking also have leadership responsibilities.

This includes students. Student leadership, including school research (both their own school and others) not only benefits the school, but prepares high school students for freedom, responsibilities, and opportunities as democratic citizens.

This leadership has foundations/supports: student-selected teacher advisors, advisory planning time per day, collaborative learning expertise, school leadership credit courses, virtual/personal connections with student leadership in other schools/districts, student government with expanded opportunities, students leading after-school learning activities, teacher modeling and encouragement, participation in school/district decision making, room for playfulness, language capability across the disciplines, a learning to learn focus, and gradual release of responsibility.

Harris (2014) on facilitating distributed leadership, credits working with "educators in Wales, England, Russia, Australia, Malaysia, and many other countries" (p. xv) for influencing her thinking and writing:

> In very practical terms, to be most effective, distributed leadership has to be carefully planned and deliberately orchestrated. It won't just happen. Therefore, those in formal leadership roles have a key role to play in creating the conditions for distributed leadership to occur. They are responsible for making it happen. Formal leaders have to model distributed leadership by actively encouraging others to take the lead, at appropriate times. They need to invite others to lead and to reinforce the idea that leadership is about expertise as well as responsibility. They have to facilitate the professional collaboration of others. (p. 41)

Roland Barth (1990) makes the case for developing a community of leaders:

> The kind of school I would like my children to attend is one where *everyone* gets a chance to be a leader. Various studies suggest that about 80 percent of first-grade students feel good about who they are. By sixth grade only 20 percent feel good about themselves. And, by the end of high school, perhaps 5 percent. Clearly, schools are not very good at helping students to feel self-confident, instrumental, and worthy. But a school can be far more than a place that allows only some students to serve on the student council or a place that encourages only a few teachers to be departmental chairs. School can be a place whose very mission is to ensure that everyone becomes a school leader in some ways and at some times in concert with some others. (p. 171)

Relationships are central in Anthony S. Bryk and Barbara Schneider's book, *Trust in Schools: A Core Resource for Improvement* (2002). They contend that *school improvement* and *social resource development* feed on each other over time; success at school improvement expanding and deepening the trust/social capital necessary for other successes.

A warning: when educators start to see leaders as people they work *for*, rather than *with*, you are headed in the wrong direction. Leaders' expectations feeling more like impositions rather than collaborative/respectful efforts that empower everyone. Such ensuing feelings often being the result of *how* expectations are delivered vs the expectations themselves.

Trust is important in any relationship; sometimes taking years to grow, much less to lose. And since conflict is often based on perceived violation of expectations, it is important those expectations be clear. Again, this applies to both individuals and groups. Groups finding common ground, improving relationships, maintaining trust, and eliminating misunderstandings requires attention. One resource is the Role Appraisal Technique described in Chapter 3—a two-way process of clarification and renegotiation.

Beyond misunderstandings, bad professional conduct demands a response. As defined by Jennifer Abrams in her book, *Hard Conversations Unpacked: the Whos, the Whens, and the What-Ifs* (2016), hard conversations address ethical considerations, offer advice to colleagues, and critique teaching that provides little support to students.

The canon of not criticizing colleagues regardless of bad behaviour/ unprofessional teaching decisions has been around a long time. Teachers aware of poor ethical conduct/teaching hurtful to students, but remaining silent, have long disabled our profession. As far back as 1968, Daniel N. Fader and Elton B. McNeil in *Hooked on Books*, attempted to increase awareness of this deficiency:

> Is it professional courtesy that causes so even a reception of such uneven work? Does our charity overcome our critical instinct and confuse our search for truth… In short, public criticism of one teacher by another is as little encountered in the so-called profession at conventions as it is in the so-called profession in schools. It is exactly this remarkable absence of interior criticism that causes the profession to remain so-called. (p. 14)

Barnett Berry, a contributor to the book, *Democratic School Accountability: A Model for School Improvement* (2006), has the same concern. He sees teachers "discouraged by 'the lack of professionalism among (their) colleagues' and the 'blue collar' responses of teacher unions. They are anxious for new forms of accountability." He quotes a teacher (Deidre) within a peer review process who "believes teachers must enforce teaching standards because administrators do not or cannot do it themselves." (p. 101)

> I have been working with this one teacher and if he can't or won't adapt and learn then he should be out of the classroom. I don't have the final say, but as someone who will have worked with this person over a period of time, I believe that my observations are more valid than a 20-minute interview by the administration. If we want to be viewed as professionals then we must hold ourselves and everyone else to a high standard. (p. 101)

Abrams (2016) concurs:

> We need to speak up for the field, advocate for the democratic ideals on which our profession was based, speak for students who don't have a voice, for the best teaching possible for all students, for the professional cultures we deserve to work in and for the next generation of educators. (p. xii)

She sees hard conversations in a number of forms:

> They range from a formal evaluation conference in which you tell someone they need to improve, to the briefest com-

ment on behavior at a team meeting; from a colleague-to-colleague discussion in a parking lot, to the rollout of a district initiative that prompts resistance. Hard conversations occur between colleagues, with administrators, at team meetings, and with any adult connected to the school. The content can be teacher or administrative behavior, lack of follow-through, not meeting performance expectations, responding to a challenging communication, or about other 'goings on' that happen in schools. Whenever you feel uncomfortable or fearful, have second thoughts, or avoid saying something, you are circling a hard conversation. (p. ix)

Abrams differentiates hard conversations from clarification efforts, coaching sessions, cease and desist warnings, mental issues, false dichotomies, or "thank you, you are done here." Instead, they are directed at "generative, collegial communication for the sake of our profession." Hard conversations "facilitate professional growth as well as results in classrooms" (p. ix).

Support for hard conversations: 1) defining the problem 2) determining the point of view of the person you are advising, and 3) seeing mistakes as helpful if we learn from them. The most encouraging element, Abrams notes, is when the recipient asks for help.

Other considerations: How solid is my information? What background information on this person is pertinent? How does this person's role influence my concerns? Does the behaviour violate well-known professional/public expectations? What ethics are involved? What positive information about this person can I share so he understands this is not personal? How do I focus on behaviour, not personalities? How do I convey both empathy *and* need for growth? Does this person have the necessary skills/experience to adjust? How can I support this person carrying out needed changes? How can the school?

Hard conversations are not restricted to adults: scenarios are teacher to teacher, teacher to professional learning community, principal to teacher, local community to teachers, teaching staff to principal, teacher to principal, student to student, student to teacher, and student to principal: all contributing specific, honest feedback bent on improved behaviour/ethical standards. Again, we learn what we teach. By helping students learn how to initiate and receive hard conversations we improve our own capabilities.

True story: A teacher heard an unethical rumour about his principal, took some time before confronting her, and found the rumour to be baseless. He then apologized for taking so long to get clarification. As he got up from his chair to leave, she motioned him to stay. "Have you spoken to anyone else about this?"

A long hesitation. "Yes," he replied, and named two teachers on staff, his wife, and a few friends. The principal nodded slowly. "I would appreciate you speaking with each of these people and setting them straight."

"Of course." And started to get up from his chair.

"And another thing. Those people you misinformed also need to clarify this with whomever *they* spoke to." The teacher hung his head.

"Now you see how false rumours hurt us all. This could have just as easily happened to you. You lost control the minute you shared a rumour before getting the facts."

Elevating relationships is the issue. The goal is not simply to grow one type of PLC; culture change is dependent on interlaced collaborative learning groups large and small: subject departments, school management committees, advisories, principals' groups, parent advisory committees, sister schools, virtual learning groups, resource teachers, educational assistants, ad hoc study groups, regular classes, District/School Learning Support Committees, student government, whole school assemblies, after-school activities, subject assemblies, and staff meetings.

As Harris emphasized, this will take work, resilience, and patience. According to Richard F. Elmore, a leading expert on how change might happen, the future is bleak. Speaking at a forum on education reform sponsored by the Aspen Institute, the American Enterprise Institute, and the Harvard Graduate School of Education on October 21, 2012, he concluded that schooling *as we know it* will inevitably fail.

"I do not believe in the institutional structure of public schooling anymore," Elmore said, noting that his long-standing work at helping teachers and principals professionalize their practice is "palliative care for a dying institution." He then predicted "a progressive dissociation between learning and schooling."

Deadening teacher boredom, emotionally flat teaching, rambling professional development divorced from the classroom, failure to make thinking central in lessons, principals glued to administration/personnel issues, separation of teaching and learning, non-existent student input on what is taught and how it is taught, few parent inclusion mechanisms—all feed into Elmore's assertion that learning and schooling are two different animals. Unlike wine, secondary schools have not improved with age.

The direction has changed. Not so long ago, under the banner of school-based decision making, isolating schools from the district seemed right. The results were disappointing. A meta-analysis of research on the effects of site-based management without the pressure and support of districts found little improvement in teacher quality or student outcomes across ten British Columbia school districts: Peter Cole & Linda Laroque in *Struggling to be 'Good Enough', Administrative Practices & School District Ethos* (1990).

They observed the need for balance. In one successful district:

> District administrators were peripatetic, demanding, and supportive; schools were autonomous but accountable. Principals were important figures not only at the school level, but also in the operation of the district. Such a high level of principal involvement in, and influence over, district decisions distinguished this district from all others. The district motto might have been 'growing together'; we labelled it Jointure District. (p. 7)

The research is controversial. Goodlad and colleagues in "Ecology of School Renewal" (1987) believed that the school must become autonomous: "it is educationally counterproductive for the rest of the schooling hierarchy to interfere with the teacher's educative activities." (p. 36)

On the other hand, Sedlak et al. in *Selling Students Short: Classroom Bargains and Academic Reform in the American High School* (1986), saw isolation, on its own, as insidious to teacher growth:

> The fact is, autonomy contributes to *irresponsible and disastrous teaching,* as much as it is essential to imaginative and effective teaching... There are many decisions about what to teach, whom to teach, or what standards and expectations individual teachers *should not make alone* in their classrooms without a strong sense of professional responsibility and the guidance of professional standards. (pp. 121–122, [emphasis added])

The balanced approach is described by J. Douglas Willms in his book, *Vulnerable Children* (2002):

> Many community-builders, especially those working at the grassroots, have *correctly argued* that top-down reforms,

with standards and processes rigidly prescribed by experts and policymakers, do not usually work. Many reformers would also argue that governments have been slow to learn this lesson. But the reverse is also true: communities that try to achieve renewal without seeking outside resources are less successful in achieving their aims.

From this perspective, the distinction between top-down versus bottom-up reforms is an unhelpful dichotomy, and debate about their relative merit is unlikely to be productive. What is required is a truly collaborative process that builds consensus across levels, allowing *each to contribute according to its strength*. This process must seek to strike the right balance between pressure and support from outside the community, and the capacity and will of those working within. (p. 367, [emphasis added])

Top-down intervention has its place. Ken Jones (2006), acknowledges different levels of accountability in the United States:

One might envision at least three cases where the state would take on a more assertive role: (1) to investigate claims or appeals from students, parents, or the local community that the local accountability system is not meeting the standards set for such systems (2) to require local schools and districts to respond to findings in the data that show significant student learning deficiencies, inequity in the opportunities to learn for all students, or lack of responsiveness to students, parents, or communities, or (3) to provide additional resources and guidance to improve the organizational capacity of the local school or district. (p. 25)

In the 90s, school-based management was implemented in Edmonton, Alberta. Michael Strembitsky, superintendent of public schools at the time, was interviewed by John O' Neil on December 1, 1995. Mr. Strembitsky:

You might think that once schools began making more decisions, the need for the central services would diminish. *With us, it turned out to be the opposite.* People who had all the answers when they couldn't make decisions found that they could benefit from a second opinion, especially if it was free. *In fact, the demand for district services went up, but it was a different kind of service.* The schools didn't want people who told them what they had to do. Schools were looking for advice that they could sift through to see whether it made sense for them.

By law, in Edmonton the principal was held accountable. But principals could not be a one-person show. *We did attitude surveys of staff, parents, and students every year in every school, examining issues of confidence, support, communication, goals, working conditions, and recognition.* We had indicators to tell us *where that involvement at the schools was successful, and where it was not.*

It comes down to your belief in people. If you believe that people want to succeed—want to make decisions, want to serve—then you must free them to do their work. That's when you get commitment from people and support for what they're trying to achieve. This applies to all people, whether they are in the central office, the principal's office, or the classroom.
[emphasis added]

I recall isolated high schools in northern Manitoba. At times, when class sizes are small, the range of interests/abilities needed to support learning is low. Students learn from each other as well as from the teacher. Even the absence of one key student can shrink class motivation/momentum. Learners are learners. A small number of teachers, isolated from external influence, have the same problem. Change is always difficult, expertise is sometimes missing, and collaborating on solving learning problems is new. At times, the result is retreat to the classroom. Small is not always beautiful; it can be stifling.

Stephen E. Anderson, in his paper, "The School District Role in Educational Change: A Review of the Literature" (2006), has the following advice:

1. Evince the belief that teachers working collaboratively with a strong sense of collective accountability can work with students and parents to achieve a high standard of learning for all.
2. Designate specific district targets for at-risk student groups and measure evidence of progress.
3. Such ongoing investigative research, as noted earlier, is an opportunity for student government to go beyond school dances, graduation celebrations, and supporting charities to *gathering information that directly supports social, emotional, and academic growth for both students and teachers.*

4. Provide support for a range of interlocking (vertical and horizontal) professional learning communities *setting progress criteria* for goals such as quality academic achievement, citizenship characteristics, ensuring opportunities and fairness for minority groups/underserved students, local community mindfulness, love of learning, reading, writing; and belief in one's ability to improve thinking.

District leadership is leading by learning. It affects student achievement because effective leadership provides critical supports for strong professional communities and can also be a useful predictor of quality instruction and student achievement. Shifting gears from judging individuals to collective expectations and mutual support is critical for improved teacher morale.

Within this framework, M. Fullan's (2001) summary of leadership styles are still pertinent: *coercive* for enforcing defined behaviours, *affiliative* as valuing personal relations, *democratic* as inviting participation with the goal of consensus, *authoritative* vision based on leaders' knowledge/moral values, *pacesetting* as modeling commitment, and *coaching* through observation. All existing to one degree or another in every school and school district; each founded on different motivational assumptions, *and all just as appropriate for groups as they are for individuals.*

These overlap Leithwood's (1986) principal categories of *administration, human relations, pet projects,* and *problem solving.* No category being exclusive, Leithwood estimated the percentage of principals' intent on problem solving as no more than 10%.

Principal leadership requires more than sideline interest. It means facilitating professional learning community supports such as time and space, modeling conflict resolution strategies, identifying false dichotomies, respecting collaborative decisions, participating in group inquiry, having hard conversations with individual teachers and groups, demonstrating ethical behaviours, and supporting leadership roles for students, parents, teachers, and community. Overall, clear personal investment by the principal in the teaching-learning improvement process.

Sharing leadership has its limits. Wright L. (2008) reminds us that distributed leadership does not imply reduced responsibility for formal leaders. She believes that too often:

> It gives minimal attention to the roles, responsibilities or circumstances under which the formal leader (i.e. the principal or

superintendent) must exercise leadership. To simply ignore the legislation and policies that define the role of the principal and hold principals accountable for their actions and school-based results, would pose significant ethical, professional and organizational concerns. (p. 3)

Leadership at all levels requires positive personal relations, but not at the expense of results. Our job to model democratic values/personal respect while maintaining Leithwood's problem solving resolve. This, along with sharing doubts, mistakes, and contradictions; such honesty necessary so others know it is safe to do the same

Barth (1990):

> Suggestions for teacher and principal to move a school toward a community of leaders imply a level of personal security on the part of the principal as well as teacher. To publicly articulate a personal vision, relinquish control, empower and entrust teachers, involve teachers early, accord responsibility to untried teacher-leaders, share responsibility for teacher failure, accord responsibility to teachers for success, and have confidence that all teachers can lead, principals have to be psychologically secure individuals who are willing to take risks. The principals' personal security is a precondition on which communities of leaders rest. With some measure of security on the part of principals these ideas have plausibility; without security they may have little. (p. 140)

More evidence for principal role reform as reported in Wagner T. et al. (2006):

> *Education Week* research polled ten thousand principals who reported 27 % of the day in any kind of instructional development, with 86% spending part of each day managing school facilities and maintaining security. Additionally, 55% of their teachers "strongly disagree or somewhat disagree that their principals talk with them frequently about their instructional practices. (p. 199)

Anthony James Aylsworth (2012) describes changed roles for administrators. He states that administrators, as well as teachers, must be learners: questioning, examining, and working with others to find opportunities for school improvement and enhanced student learning. The outdated pattern that students learn, teachers teach, and administrators manage is no longer valid.

Visiting classrooms will take practice. Richard Elmore, interviewed in 2010, from "Leading the Instructional Core" Volume II, Issue 3, had this advice for principals observing classes for the first time:

> I want you to take ten deep breaths, and I want you to walk into the room and sit down. Look at your watch, shut up, and don't say anything for 15 minutes. Then, as soon as the fifteen minutes are up, you are authorized to speak. But the thing I want you to think about is that the first thing coming out of your mouth should be a question to which you don't know the answer…the point is, learn to think of yourself as a *leader of learning*, and try to model the practice you expect other people to engage in. (p. 12)

Principals closely involved in the learning does not mean they have the luxury of being non-political. Tony Wagner et al. (2006) addresses this consideration by quoting Boston Superintendent Tom Pryzant:

> The kind of leader you want, someone who is closely tied to the improvement of instruction, is exactly what we need. But if a school or district head is not also a good politician, it doesn't matter how much they know about instruction. They might not last ninety days. (p. 207)

Two examples: In 1967, as principal of Frontier Collegiate Institute, a residential school in Cranberry Portage, MB, we were challenged with the responsibility of improving literary skills of students from across northern Manitoba. One idea that surfaced was to dramatically increase the number of visuals connected to ideas and words in all subjects. At the time, this meant teacher-prepared transparencies using overhead projectors, filmstrip projectors, 16 mm movies, and single concept loops.

An explanatory note from Jerry Storie's book, *Becoming Family: Living and Learning at Frontier Collegiate* (2015):

> The very mention of the word 'residential' has connotations that would colour many people's views of FCI. As I write this, the Truth and Reconciliation Commission has just completed its sessions across the country, focusing on a particu-

larly distressing and destructive chapter in the history of Aboriginal peoples. The federally-sponsored, and primarily religious, residential schools that are the focus of so much anguish across the country were based on a government policy of forced assimilation. There is another history of residential schools, sometimes called boarding schools, which crosses cultures and generations and has had a much more positive influence on its students and society. The residential component of the high school operated by Frontier School Division (FSD) since 1965 is categorically and demonstrably different from the type of institution being examined by the Truth and Reconciliation Commission. (p. 12)

He offers evidence:

The level of commitment to the students by individual teachers was exceptional, as former FCI students recognized. David Yeo, who began teaching at FCI in 1968, and would go on to become one of the longest-serving area superintendents in FSD history, fondly recalls the connection teachers made with students. Describing the early days he says, "Every teacher on the staff had a group of students that were assigned to you. Actually, the kids chose which teacher they wanted. So that was kind of a mentoring program and each teacher had so many kids, 25 or 30, whatever it was and you were kind of responsible for, you were their connection. So, we had things at our house you know, on a Saturday afternoon if the weather was nice, we'd barbecue or often we would take the kids to The Pas or Flin Flon and shopping at night. You were involved with the kids at night." Pondering the question of why FCI had succeeded, even with many students who had failed previous attempts at their home school or at other high schools in the province, Yeo said it boiled down to "simply people caring about how these kids did, period." Yeo went on to say that the principal at that time, Mr. Jack Orchard, adhered to this principle: "There was no question, kids came first" (pp. 175–176).

To complete the leadership example—increasing the visuals meant increasing the budget; we invited the Official Trustee, Mr. Ken Jasper, to a one-day workshop setting out the value of visual connections for our students. All of the leadership came from the teaching staff—no outside facilitator (or costs) required. We had a clear objective (increased funding for visual aids) and staff consensus. Building cohesion and glue within a team is not that difficult when the goal is clear and the means to that goal is within reach.

We set up stations for each audio/visual piece of equipment in separate classrooms with teachers who felt confident in their ability to demonstrate their use in helping students learn, all based on their experience. The rest of the staff, including the facilitators, were rotated through the stations. Mr. Jasper and other central office staff scattered among the rotating groups.

We were successful. The budget was increased to $10,000, a considerable sum at the time. The best outcome, however, was the increased application of visuals across the curriculum over the years. So much so that IQ scores of that beginning group of G10 students (yes, they were all tested back then) increased by one standard deviation after one year. This was totally unexpected. Especially when we had all been taught through our education classes that IQs were fixed at birth.

More recently, connecting visuals with ideas and words is backed by research: Oakley B. et al. in their book, *Uncommon Sense Teaching: Practical Insights in Brain Science to Help Students Learn* (2021), report:

> The basic idea is straightforward. A picture with an accompanying verbal explanation can help students grasp a concept much more quickly than either a picture or a verbal explanation alone. This is because working memory typically has both a hearing and a seeing component (these are the multi parts of a multimedia theory). Simultaneously using both visual and verbal explanations allows students to make better use of their limited working memory. (p. 199)

The second example is not so positive. Grade nine classes at MBCI in The Pas, Manitoba, were ability grouped when I arrived as the new principal. Writing an article in the local education newsletter, I outlined my arguments against such streaming. Many of the teachers read the article—some discussed it with me privately.

The reasons included the message of low expectations for those in the lower classes, that students learn from each other, and that a larger range of abilities is helpful; confident students helped others build confidence; that often the top grade nine classes went to those teachers with the most experience, and that grade nine students are too young to be slotted for life.

There was resistance, but not directly from the staff (42 teachers). My mistake was not discussing/confronting their dissatisfaction. Instead, I advised Management Team (so much for team) with representatives from each subject department that I couldn't live with grade nine streaming and that the following year we would have mixed-ability classes.

The only people, to my knowledge, who supported me were the two guidance counsellors. I did it anyway. By disrespecting some teachers' views I won the battle but lost the war. From that time forward my relations with many of the teachers went sideways.

There could have been compromises. One would have been to start with a few grades nine mixed-ability classes with teachers who volunteered to work on providing enrichment opportunities for the more advanced students, and also build peer tutoring into those classes so teachers could see learning benefits for all students. But unfortunately, since I thought it was so obviously the right thing to do, I didn't see these alternatives.

Marzano et al. (2005) refer to redistribution of power where the school leader involves teachers in the design and execution of important decisions. According to his study, school principals know the benefits of professional learning communities. They just don't think they have the time to provide the leadership required due to their administrative roles.

Principals involved believed that time for discussions with parents, teachers, and students wasn't there. They also claimed they didn't have the power and authority for teachers' professional development. They saw their main job as providing a peaceful atmosphere for teachers and students. The conclusion was that they appreciated PLCs and found them beneficial but didn't believe they could make them work effectively.

The results also revealed that although principals are aware of professional learning communities benefiting schools, they spend limited time, authority, power, or interest in putting them into practice. Most of their time was spent on managerial/office work such as paperwork, meetings, minor concerns, and official reports.

Charles Ungerleider in *Failing Our Kids: How We Are Ruining Our Public Schools* (2003) had similar concerns:

> The majority of school principals simply do not see regular classroom-based instructional supervision as part of their role unless it is for the purpose of evaluating the teacher. This is unfortunate for at least two reasons. First, it does not

help support good teaching and improve the overall quality of teaching. Second, it does not diminish the distance between principals and teachers.

He criticizes opportunities for peer observation: "Almost all teaching occurs simultaneously. The few teachers who are not engaged in teaching are usually involved in preparation for teaching. That preparation almost never involves peer observation." (p. 174)

Brownlie and Schnellert (2009) summarize Sir Ken Robinson's (2007) research:

> The practice of principals' promoting and participating in teacher learning and development activities has a more profound impact on students than any other practice. To develop collaborative, community-minded classes that are focused on learning, school leaders need to participate in staff learning communities. Both formal and informal leaders play a key role in modeling learning. (p. 20)

Such efforts demand time. One bad policy is rotating principals from school to school after only a few years in each school. In general, shorter terms for principals and superintendents reduce the following: knowing people well, supporting collaborative learning teams, finding consensus for long range plans, becoming politically astute, reaching out beyond your school/district, gathering allies, and using long term evidence for ongoing school/district formative assessments.

"How the world's most Improved educational systems keep getting better, 2010", the report by Mourshed, Chigiuke, and Barlow shows a record of improvement from leadership that sticks around:

> Once installed, they have staying power; the new median tenure of the new strategic leaders is six years and that of the new political leaders is seven years, thereby enabling continuity in the reform process and development of the system pedagogy. This is in stark contrast to the norm. For example, the average tenure of superintendents of urban school districts in the US is nearly three years. (p. 107)

In an online article, "10 Traits of Successful School Leaders" (2021), Joseph Lathan provides further evidence of the need for extended tenure of principals:

> Change, while good, can also be disruptive when it occurs too frequently. In the case of school leadership, it has been documented those frequent turnover results in a negative school climate, which in turn has a negative effect on student performance. Principal turnover has a more significant negative effect in high-poverty, low-achieving schools—the very schools in which students most rely on their education for future success. The negative effect of principal turnover suggests that principals need time to make meaningful improvements in their schools. One study found that it takes, on average, five years of a new principal leading a school for the school's performance to rebound to the pre-turnover level. (p. 11)

The evidence from the US is that principals spend less than 25% of their time on issues pertaining to teaching and learning, the rest in their offices, outside meetings, or other administration duties. In order to address these concerns, SAM (School Administrator Management) schools delegate these duties to a school administrator who works with the principal to gradually increase the principal's time on student learning-related work.

Management aspects require attention. Ways need to be found to ensure these tasks are taken care of or eliminated. Some went so far as to hire a recently retired principal to act as the principal's advisor in accelerating the process. According to M. Fullan (2012), in the first two years of SAM, "principals increased their instructional leadership time to 75% while the level of student achievement doubled." (p. 166, [emphasis added])

Lee and Smith (1996) found that achievement gains for eighth and tenth grade students were significantly higher in schools where teachers took collective responsibility for students' academic success or failure. In a similar study, Cuttance (2001) determined that when pedagogic leadership works in parallel with strategic leadership, teacher-leaders and administrative leaders develop new roles and responsibilities.

One top-down and bottom-up initiative supporting change leadership is laid out in Chapter 6 of Networks for Learning: Effective Collaboration for Teacher, School and System Improvement, edited by Chris Brown and Cindy L. Poortman (2018) entitled "Austria's Lerndesigner Network: The dynamics of Virtual Professional Learning in interschool networks", by Livia Roessier and Tanja Westfall-Greiter. "The goal to improve excellence and equity across the Austrian school system by installing a change agent role (Lerndesigner) in each school.

"The role quickly took on a life of its own and gained the support of system stakeholders, a key success factor in a country with a federalist structure. The role has since become a defined teacher leadership function...for which teachers acquire certification in a university accredited program." A key feature is cohorts of Lerndesigners networked virtually. Their focus to "explore how top-down strategies responsively supported eyelevel network development in the interest of system development and how these efforts led to a network with a life of its own" (p. 92).

This reform was aimed at researched evidence on a lack of educational mobility and equity in a public school system founded on ability grouped tracking. "In other words, teachers—often under the pressure of their pupils' parents—tend to determine marks based on their perceptions of the appropriate educational path the pupil should pursue rather than on their actual abilities" (p. 93).

The Lerndesigner role is different in that, although mandated, it allowed appointees to define responsibilities within their own school. This while simultaneously carrying out other roles: classroom teachers, facilitators, coordinators, members of school development teams, and subject team leaders. Their appointments often based on their innovation record, ongoing professional learning, and "willingness to take on responsibility for school development" (P. 97).

This nationwide initiative had its bumps: "Lerndesigners had to first learn to network and participate in a network in order to gain from networking. Back at their schools, role-taking and role-making was a struggle for some, as they indicated in a survey in 2010" (p. 98).

Similarly, we have criteria identified by Westfall-Greiter and Hofbauer (2013) for identifying colleagues acting as teacher-leaders:

* Sees what needs doing beyond their work as teachers;
* Takes on a task beyond their classroom responsibilities;
* Takes on responsibility for the school's success;
* Breaks ranks and becomes noticeable for colleagues (from actively contributing to directly intervening) (p. 100)

Their program was comprised of six development areas deemed essential for fostering change in the learning culture: 1) mindfulness of learning 2) difference and diversity 3) competence orientation 4) 'backwards design' curriculum development 5) differentiated instruction, and 6) assessment.

As researchers have recognized, student motivation/engagement needs work. The reason schools use marks/praise/rewards is that we, as teachers, don't believe successful learning is enough on its own to motivate students. We see our product as so poor we think we need external incentives. And because we grew up in this situation when we were in high school, we can't see any other way of doing things.

Tony Wagner and Ted Dintersmith, authors of "Most Likely to Succeed: Preparing Our Kids for the Innovation Era" (2015), relate an experiment on the value of marks carried out by Lawrenceville School, reputed to be one of the best U.S. private schools in the country:

> It ran a fascinating experiment with students taking core science courses. When students returned after summer vacation, they were asked to retake the final exam they had completed three months earlier. Actually, it was a simplified version of the final, as the faculty eliminated any detailed questions that students shouldn't be expected to remember a few months later. The results were stunning. When students took the final in June, the average grade was (87%); when the simplified test was taken in September, the average grade was (58%). Not one student retained mastery of all important concepts covered by the course. Following this experiment, Lawrenceville completely rethought the way courses were taught, eliminating almost half the content to emphasize deeper learning. When it repeated the experiment in subsequent years, the results were far more satisfactory.
>
> This Lawrenceville experiment is something more schools should do. If most students who get A's in June have retained almost nothing by September, what did they really learn? And if the carry-over from year to year is minimal—meaning the content covered in one year *never* gets revisited, what exactly has a year of study done for the student? (pp. 41–42)

Ken O'Connor, in his book *How to Grade for Learning: Linking Grades to Standards* (2002), seeks to make grades less punitive while contributing to student learning. He chooses neither eliminating marks as Alfie Kohn recommends, nor retaining their current reward and punishment emphasis. Instead, he wants grading that encourages and supports learning over adjudication and sorting.

His recommendations/guidelines:

1. Include students in evaluation practices—individually and as a class.
2. Use the median rather than the mean while considering quantity or quality along with only some of the evidence, keeping zeros out of calculations. This allows for diminishing the impact of a few stumbles.
3. Disdain punishment through grades for attendance, tardiness, misconduct, or lack of effort. Grades to communicate student achievement and nothing else. Decisions to be exclusively based on weighted content outcomes/priorities for a particular course.
4. Recognize that grading is subjective and emotional—equity means treating students differently.
5. Provide more chances for success. This means eliminating marks from failed past performance once success occurs.
6. Grades can contribute toward feedback, encouragement, and re-instruction.
7. Grades required for university entrance require consistent marking with schools and across districts.
8. Fairness, including no group marks for individuals when assessing collaborative learning.
9. Seeing past stifling rubrics to fairly evaluate creativity, depth of thinking, and promote encouragement/motivation.
10. Alternative forms of assessing achievement—writing, interviews, and performances.

Alfie Kohn, in his foreword to Maja Wilson's book, *Rethinking Rubrics in Writing Assessment* (2006) asks a rare question, "What's our reason for trying to evaluate the quality of students' efforts?" Possible objectives: 1) ranking students against each other, 2) rewarding them so they work harder, or 3) providing feedback that will not only help them become more adept but become excited about their learning.

Kohn:

> But I worry more about the success of rubrics than their failure. Just as it's possible to raise standardized test scores, providing that you're willing to gut the curriculum and turn the school into a test-preparation factory, it's possible to get a bunch of people to agree on what rating to give an assign-

ment, providing that they're willing to accept and apply someone else's narrow criteria for what merits that rating. (pp. xii-xiii)

Too often, when marking writing, elements such as spelling/grammar are the focus rather than sense of purpose, reader enlightenment, or new ideas. Holt, as discussed, generally advises teachers/peer tutors (Hattie effect size 0.55) to determine *what and how* students are thinking as opposed to brushing aside wrong thinking and handing over the right answer. Rubrics are often too simplistic to be useful. Student thinking far exceeding short descriptions on a four-level scale.

Sarason (1996) had a similar concern. How do teachers' views of teaching and motivation differ from the views of their students? Do students think about these issues? Can they talk about them? In Sarason's words, "How do teachers explain and discuss their theories of learning and thinking with their students? In short, to what extent were the why's and how's of learning an explicit focus and subject of discussion in the classroom?" (p. 220).

To answer the above, observers were assigned to classrooms with the following questions:

1) When a child did not know or could not do something, did the teacher's response in any way attempt to find out how the child had been thinking or how the child might think—in contrast, for example, to telling and showing a correct procedure?
2) How frequently did a teacher say, "I don't know", and go on to discuss how he or she would think about going and *knowing*?
3) How frequently and in what ways does a teacher take up and discuss the role of asking questions in intellectual inquiry or problem-solving? (pp. 220–221)

These discussions did not happen. The ground rules took precedent: *First*, in the view of both students and teachers, getting the right answer was far more important than how you got it. *Second,* there is only one way to think about and get the right answer, and *third*, thinking is not complicated.

Sarason then took these observations to the teachers. He confronted them after a discussion in which they had "critically examined their experiences as students in their college courses." *He then explained the similarity of their complaints with what their students might have.*

Some teachers saw the similarities, some could not. They had two reservations: 1) "there was little or nothing in their training that would enable them to handle the issues in the classrooms", and 2) "even if they wanted to or could handle them, the demands of curriculum coverage leave little time for such matters." (p. 222)

His analysis:

> Many teachers have two theories: one that applies to them and one that applies to children. Put in another way, many teachers are quite aware from their own experiences of the differences in characteristics between dull and exciting conditions of intellectual activity. But their inability to see or assume some kind of identity between their pupils and themselves leads them unwittingly to create those conditions that they would personally find boring. Classroom learning is primarily determined by teachers' perceived differences between children and adults, a fact that makes recognition of communalities almost impossible. (p. 222)

O'Connor's suggestions hit directly at the reward and punish mentality of high schools. Usually, only attaining learning outcomes within a certain timeframe earns a pass. Instead of making students repeat an entire course, one alternative is to identify which outcomes in the failed course still need to be learned, then provide the support required to achieve them. This could be integrated into the succeeding course or through extra help outside the regular timetable.

Other recommendations are those of Christensen L. (2004–2005). She doesn't put any grades on individual papers, nor use tests or extra credits. Her expectations/criteria include the ability to write an essay that demonstrates understanding of historical or literary material or the use of historical facts to critique documents. Other criteria are skills such as active listening, sticking to topics, and taking notes.

Homework is viewed as an extension of work in class—readings that provide background for the kinds of writing expected. But Linda also allows extra time for those having difficulty and provides personal support through phone calls, lunch time conferences, or after school. This support is in contrast, she contends, with classes where all papers are graded and students who get high grades receive little feedback or encouragement.

Maja Wilson from "Rethinking Rubrics in Writing Assessment" (2006): "Grading policies should not only help students to engage in the hard work of writing but should also encourage us to become better teachers." (p. 85)

Years ago, some Ontario high schools, with the ministry of education's blessing, instituted a program called "Credit Recovery." Students mastered key learning outcomes from failed courses while taking the succeeding course or were placed in a low-enrollment course where they were helped to gain credits for courses they failed. (*As previously stated, there are concerns here—this is best done within a wider range of student capabilities*)

Reward and punishment for students has been around for a long time. As in most high schools across North America and China the prevailing teacher culture embraces it heartily—speaking Chinese in classes teaching English as one example. Others are our response to cheating or handing assignments in late, or students rewarded by teachers with improved marks for working hard, paying attention in class, and helping others.

One further observation: While we, as teachers, generally favour various reward/punishment classroom scenarios, we deplore them if they are enacted on us. In my last high school, the Chinese administrators punished Chinese teachers for not flashing their ID over the machine at the school entrance. One teacher was threatened with a 20% reduction of her monthly salary if she continued to ignore this order.

Professionalism is not a matter of fulfilling/enforcing the terms of the contract, job description, or required policies. These are technical requirements. Professionalism is embracing and embodying the values of a supportive, caring, and committed learning community in everyday actions big and small.

Motivating students is no different from motivating teachers. Egregious effects of the carrot (marks) and the stick (identified student failure) are rarely, if ever, discussed in staffrooms or staff meetings. PLCs at every level need to take a hard look at the limits of praise, rewards, and punishment.

Alfie Kohn (1999):

> Even if it were just as easy to be a successful learner without intrinsic motivation, I believe that the desire to wrestle with ideas, sample literature, and think like a scientist is also valuable. I think we should want children who want to learn, who not only have reading skills but actually read. As Richard Ryan and a colleague argue, it is not enough 'to conceive of the central goal of 12 years of mandatory schooling as

merely a cognitive outcome'. Instead, we should aim for children who are 'willing and even enthusiastic about achieving something in school, curious and excited by learning to the point of seeking out opportunities to follow their interests beyond the boundaries of school'. (p. 147)

The assumption that school marks positively influence student effort is often wrong. Research by Butler R. (1988), comparing the effects of feedback vs marks, concluded that students *who only received comments* showed greater improvement over those receiving either a *combination of marks and comments* or simply *grades*.

The motivational 3C's from Alfie Kohn deserve a place at the table; all hallmarks of self-regulated learning: (1) collaboration amongst students—reciprocal learning as part of the LTL curriculum (2) content that has learning nested in real-life concerns of the community, and (3) student choice—investigating issues pertinent to individuals. Real-life community concerns are emphasized by Maja Wilson (2006). She quotes Andrea Lunsford on nineteenth-century college learning:

> Students regularly gave public speeches on matters of importance to society, in forums open to the entire college and the surrounding community...writing was part of the student's effort to understand and impact his society, as he often wrote out his ideas in preparation for his oral presentations. Assessment of these ideas was woven throughout each presentation as professors, fellow students, and community members questioned and argued with the student, forcing him to refine his ideas and arguments—a process that inevitably strengthened future performance. (p. 13)

In the past, educational icons such as Madeline Hunter and Carol Cummings clarified the difference between feedback and praise. Knowledge of results coupling a learning behaviour with a particular learning outcome as opposed to a bribe designed to elicit a certain action. The first is an effort to clarify cause and effect; the second is a blatant attempt to control.

Elmore R. (2008) sees large scale improvement as improbable without supports: "*strong, stable, and consistent incentives*" for both individual teachers and for PLCs seeking more uniform internal accountability (p. 117).

His recommended incentives: 1) encouragement and support 2) access to special knowledge 3) time to focus on the requirements of the new task, and 4) time to observe others doing it—all critical for supporting change.

He refers to a study by Newmann, Rutter et al. (1989):

> The responsiveness of administrators to problems of practice—with help, support, and recognition—was most strongly related to teachers' perceptions of community within a school. Interestingly, they found no independent effect of teachers' perceptions of principals' leadership, teachers' participation in professional development, or teachers' participation in organizational decisions on either teachers' sense of efficacy or community. This latter finding is interesting not so much because of what it says about principal leadership and professional development per se, because the schools in the sample represented a full array of practice in this regard. It is interesting because it suggests that principal leadership, professional development, and participation in decision making by teachers *have no effect on teachers' sense of efficacy and community unless they are deliberately connected to tangible and immediate problems of practice.* (p. 61, [emphasis added])

Elmore's five principles for establishing distributed leadership:

1. *"The purpose of leadership is the improvement of instructional practice and performance, regardless of role"* (p. 66).
   He stresses that the only *theory of management that counts* puts improvement of practice and performance at the centre—"the creation of *settings for learning* focused on clear expectations for instruction." (p. 67) All other skills being instrumental to that challenge. Those who have a higher degree of knowledge, skill, and competence should be expected to spend some portion of their work engaged in the improvement of practice across schools and classrooms.
2. *"Instructional improvement requires continuous learning"*—learning as social *and* individual. Teachers, along with students, differ greatly in their need for support and encouragement. Examples are quality mentoring, timely interactions, honest appreciations, metacognition, making thinking visible, specific feedback, hard conversations, cognitive acceleration, deliberate practice, external resources, and focus. Leadership

attending to the feelings, thoughts, and actions of particular teachers over the long haul
3. *"Learning requires modeling."*
"If learning, individual and collective, is the central responsibility of leaders, then they must be able to model the learning they expect of others. Leaders should be doing, and should be seen as doing, that which they expect or require others to do. Likewise, leaders should expect to have their own practice subjected to the same scrutiny as they exercise toward others." (p. 67)
4. *"The roles and activities of leadership flow from the expertise required for learning and improvement, not from the formal dictates of the institution."*
"Large-scale Improvement requires a relatively complex kind of cooperation among people in diverse roles performing diverse functions. This kind of cooperation requires understanding that learning grows out of differences in expertise rather than differences in formal authority." (p. 68)
5. *"The exercise of authority requires reciprocity of accountability and capacity."*
"If the formal authority of my role requires that I hold you accountable for some action or outcome, then I have an equal and complementary responsibility to assure that you have the capacity to do what I am asking you to do. All accountability relationships are necessarily reciprocal." (p. 68)

This last principle comports with his incentives/supports for helping others change. It also fits with freedom/choice and ways of holding ourselves and others accountable. The challenge is moving away from a culture of compliance where top-down directives disable intellectual discourse needed for sustained improvement. Our improved culture sees *new norms of questioning, dialogue, and debate. Everyone aboard invariably means diminishing status differences and supporting untitled leaders at every opportunity.*

Rea Taylor Gill, in her book, *A School as a Living Entity* (2011), also addresses such concerns. Referring to an article in the *Ivy Business Journal* by Edgar Schein et al., Rea describes the problem:

> Hierarchical top-down leadership/social structure that relies on the ability of the leader to compensate for a structure that does not recognize the inherent living nature of an organization. In reality, it is *neither* the leader *nor* the subordinate

that needs to learn to change the way they relate to one another in order to compensate for the mechanical top-down hierarchical structure, but rather it is the *structure* that needs to change in order to enable collaborative, cooperative, associative relationships. (p. 24)

She emphasizes the point: "In other words, what is needed is a structure with a hierarchy that shifts the authority depending on the specific expertise and particular function needed in a given context" (p. 24).

Other voices advocating in the same direction includes circumventing chain of command, with Hargreaves and Fullan (2012) proposing that resources for change "sometimes go direct to the teacher and not always via the superintendent and then the principal" (p. 67).

A disheartening example of constricted leadership is Kylene Beers, in *Adolescent Literacy: Turning Promise into Practice* (2007) witnessing the following:

> An urban high school, facing growing pressure about not reaching AYP (adequate yearly progress) for two years in a row, put "low-achieving" ninth graders (i.e. students who did not reach the minimum pass score on the eighth grade Texas Assessment of Knowledge and Skills test) into a "remedial reading class" that proved to be nothing more than a TAKS test-preparation class.
>
> It didn't matter that the teacher wanted to teach students reading strategies that she knew would help them in their content area classes (which in my mind include English class); it didn't matter that the teacher knew she needed to teach students with texts at each student's instructional reading level.
>
> The principal had purchased a test-prep program that promised to help students reach AYP, and he decided that was the curriculum. When I asked him if he thought that particular pre-packaged program was really going to help close the reading achievement gap, especially for the groups of students in his school that were not making AYP (African-American students, Hispanic students, and the economically disadvantaged students), he explained. "It's got to. NCLB demands it." "NCLB demands what?" I asked. "That we close the achievement gap," he said. *How do you know that happened?* I asked. "Kids pass the damn test," he said, walking off. (p. 3)

Andy Hargreaves et al. in *Uplifting Leadership: How Organizations, Teams, and Communities Raise Performance* (2014), see pressure vs support, passion vs performance, the insatiable desire to learn vs the uncompromising demand for success as false choices.

Collaboration and competition can be complementary. Both contributing to the motivation of students, teachers, principals, superintendents, and schools. I am reminded of principal meetings in China where we gathered under the leadership of Mark Butcher, principal of BC High School Sino-Canada, to meet in pursuance of better ideas/sharing of successes and failures and improved learning opportunities for our students while still competing as private enterprises. Friendly rivalry having its place at the table.

Senge P. (2012) concurs:

> I do not agree that competition is inherently bad. I am the type of person who enjoys competition and have always loved competitive sports. I believe that under the right circumstances, competition can enhance learning. But I also believe that many of our modern societies, such as the United States, have lost appreciation for the healthy balance between competition and collaboration. The two can coexist. Indeed, they do so in most healthy living systems. (p. 54)
> Note – *shades of Rea Taylor Gill above*

Supportive teacher commitment, I believe, is key to student motivation. Are lessons bad copies of old ones, or are they well prepared, honest efforts to develop deep thinking? Jaime Escalante comes to mind—the AP calculus teacher at James A. Garfield High School in East Los Angeles, where high expectations combined with quality support resulted in extraordinary success for underprivileged students.

There are obstacles: I recall a principal's response when discussing how his school could improve the low graduation rate of Indigenous students, "Well, we won't reduce our expectations." He was implying, I believe, that the only way to accelerate the graduation rate would be to lower standards.

Educators do not respond well to fiscal rewards or threats of punishment for much past getting to work on time. Motivation results from a sense of purpose, the desire to solve tough problems, the kinds of incentives/supports set out by Elmore, and ultimately, success. Collegiality, mutual respect, and improving learning opportunities are both a process and a result. Michael Fullan and Joanne Quinn, in their book,

Coherence (2016), believe people have a built-in wish to belong to organizations contributing to something more important than themselves.

An abject lesson: student-marked tests of fellow students in a teacher-directed process, with the teacher losing information needed to inform subsequent teaching. But even worse, receiving students concentrating on the score—not areas for improvement. An example of traditional school culture obscuring teacher awareness only a few feet away.

Professional teachers who love their subjects, learn to model/share different stages of their own writing/thinking with students and colleagues, demonstrate how writing improves thinking, courageously do read aloud/think-alouds, and how they learned to think for themselves in high school or university are to be appreciated out loud. Far from seeing school as an opportunity for growth, young teachers often experience a grind; their teaching in a rut, while more experienced teachers suffer from the same pressures as students.

The necessary shift from students memorizing information to reading/analyzing high-level text, fitting it with prior knowledge, asking oneself important questions, and working with each other in creating/communicating new learning, all within the students' chosen time frame, is more than a small leap.

Students depend on personal, formative feedback for achieving subject outcomes *and* becoming their own teachers. Considering the teacher step-by-step control in the past, no one expects students to immediately learn on their own. It is in the collaborative learning of students and teachers that both succeed.

Change is needed. The hard news is that student motivation is on a downward slide from primary to secondary school with a small upswing in their last years while teacher morale, intrinsically entwined with student motivation (the chicken and the egg), tracks this trend along with districts and schools continuing to embrace decrepitude over reform.

Recently, experts in educational change have advocated "Leading from the Middle"; school districts learning from each other. One potential path is superintendents' associations where they could not only negotiate sister schools, principal pairings, and other collaborative learning opportunities but also inform leadership everywhere on school improvement successes/failures.

Another potential driver could be ministries of education. Assuming ministries understand the need for change and how change occurs, they are uniquely positioned to strengthen, advance, and support serious improvement strategies across state departments of education, national departments of education, counties, provinces, shires, and territories; Elmore's five principles for harnessing/enhancing teacher initiatives as examples.

Things are not improving. A statement by Stanley Kutcher, a psychiatry professor at Dalhousie University in Halifax and the Sun Life Financial Chair in Adolescent Mental Health, as reported in the Globe and Mail newspaper on January 23, 2013: "The level of expectations, both from the students themselves and their families, has become a greater issue adding to stress in the past 15 years. The expectation is that everybody gets an A. It's a real issue. We've had grade inflation [in high school] for two decades."

Michael Fullan and Mary Jean Gallagher in *The Devil is in the Details: System Solutions for Equity, Excellence, and Student Well-Being* (2020) came to the same conclusion: "Stress is high and increasing at a rapid pace for students from all SES levels. For students these days, the modal response to schooling is either alienation (if you live in destitute circumstances) or stress/anxiety (if you are swept up into the academic rat race)." (p. 15)

Senge et al. from *Schools That Learn* (2012):

> "There are many ways to measure a successful school," wrote New York Times education reporter Michael Winerip in 1999. But the only measure that matters to commentators and politicians, he added, "is performance on standardized tests. As long as that is true, those backpacks are likely to be full each night starting in grade nine and maybe earlier.
> This situation leaves over-pressured students with two basic alternatives: cope or disengage. More and more of them disengage. The system then tracks them into classes for underachievers where they no longer will be challenged. Others try to cope, trapped in the conflict between competing against their peers (and pleasing their parents and teachers) versus being true to their own well-being. The end result is a lack of motivation and engagement, waste of their potential, and a diminishing of the contribution that they could make to society. (p. 33)

It gets personal. Barth (1990):

> Our daughter tends to work slowly and carefully and thoughtfully, and gregariously, savoring and wondering

about and getting lost in things along the way. Unfortunately, more courses, more homework, more after-school activities, higher expectations, constant time on task, more accountability, and more demands to produce do not represent a very good prescription for her. I believe the word *curriculum* comes from the Latin for 'a little race track'. Running this race track seven days a week is taking a toll... Where is 'time on the margins...for reflection, pleasure, and interaction with colleagues'? These are not frills. Humans *learn* through reflection, pleasure, and interaction with colleagues. I do, you do, and high school students do. In short, why do those who move reflectively and precisely and happily either have to abandon reflection, precision, and interaction in order to finish so much so fast—or burn out on the race track? At best, I think we end up with more production and less learning. (p. 174)

A British Columbian high school student's online message:

This is why I refer to school as the stress factory.
Whenever I get a bad grade on a certain subject, they call my parents and say that I am doing terrible in this subject. At least my parents know I'm trying hard, because lots of the teachers seem to look at the negative and try to harass us so they can get us in trouble OUT of school! They say good grades get you into good schools, which is true, but the stress won't help! I hate this!
I just kinda had an epiphany. So, you see, grades were invented as an incentive to learn, but it shouldn't be taken so far. Everyone I know freaks out about getting the grades to get into the top 10%, most of them try to take all AP and pre-AP and stay up all night so they can get that one grade up. I just think that really it's all unfair because some minds naturally hold more information than others and the purpose of school should just be to give you some information to help you in the future, not to stress you out so much you have to start taking anti-depressants and caffeine pills to stay awake all night. I think there's a fine line between school giving you a healthy amount of challenge to encourage learning in a safe and friendly environment, and being so stressed about school that you break down and cry.

Chapter 3
Working Together: Alignment for Success

"For the things we have to learn before we can do them, we learn by doing them."
–Aristotle

Concept Map 2

District School Support

Professional Learning Communities

Classroom Teacher *(In Pic; Alan Levine)*

Jo Boaler, in her book *Limitless mind: Learn, lead, and live without barriers* (2019), provides strong evidence that neural pathways are strengthened by people learning from each other. She reports a study at the University of California where 60 percent of African Americans were failing a calculus course while no Chinese Americans were failing the same course. Uri Treisman, a mathematics professor at the university, after considering traditional explanations, observed that while the Chinese Americans worked collaboratively, the African Americans studied alone.

He then organized workshops for vulnerable African American students as part of establishing an emotionally supportive academic environment for everyone. During the workshops, the students worked on solving mathematics problems together. In the space of two years the African Americans and Latino students outperformed both white and Asian counterparts.

Boaler also exposes a false assumption amongst high school teachers—that their students actually know how to work together:

> The fact that it took work to teach students how to collaborate with each other after they had spent thirteen years in school speaks to the problems in our school system, where the common pattern is that teachers lecture and students work through problems alone. (p. 168)

An online comment from a teacher: "There's a myth that, if you place people into a group, they will automatically function well as a group. But you've been in a classroom that doesn't have rules and structure. So don't assume that a group will become high performing simply because it consists of multiple people sharing a space."

Teachers often observe that students sitting beside each other does not mean group learning. They saw students not challenging each other in a serious way, perhaps afraid of being perceived as rude/hurting friendships or not having enough practice giving and receiving honest feedback.

Similarly, Diane Wood's study (2007) found that too often, professional learning communities spend more time building camaraderie than focusing on professional development that would improve classroom practices.

More qualitative data was obtained by researchers. Instructional teams failed because: (1) they spent little time discussing teaching practices or planning lessons, (2) their discussion of instructional matters was usually transmission of information, and (3) they failed to move to higher levels of group practice by analyzing teaching practices in relation to student work or thinking.

It is important to get beyond the usual school discussions. Too frequently teacher talk consists of casual comments on student behaviour/motivation, test marks, student diversity, or time to finish the course. Lack of a common vocabulary consistent with the complexity of teaching and learning is also a problem. Distinguishing between teaching and learning methods demands precise talk, quality description, and a common vocabulary. *Activating prior knowledge* has precision; *introduction* does not.

According to Wood, protocols became problematic. Due to their rigorous structure, they tended to lead teachers to a quick consensus rather than fostering collegial inquiry and questioning of ideological stances. Protocols also failed to help participants search for external expertise that might be needed to improve teacher and student learning. In many schools, rules of engagement became the content of the meeting instead of the tools to navigate it. As a result, many schools in the study failed to see changes in student performance.

The goal is for PLCs to become effective teams of learners. Practical advice: start where you are, use what you have, and do what you can. Starting where you are is assessing prior knowledge, current beliefs, concerns, and interactions (Theorem 1). Using what you have is building on that knowledge through a learning approach in the service of important educational goals, and doing what you can means applying the other six theorems.

Exchanging ideas on student learning along with teachers' changing role has important ramifications for the entire school. From the Canadian Journal of Educational Administration and Policy's article,

"Change Forces: Implementing Change in a Secondary School for the Common Good" (2012), by Wayne Melville et al.:

> Successful implementation was based solidly on *professional, cultural, and democratic change forces*. For administrators who seek to implement reforms, this is an important understanding for two reasons. The first is that reforms cannot be rushed, or forced, into narrow bureaucratic timelines. The development of the level of community that can effectively utilise the power of these change forces is a time consuming, and labour intensive, process. The second reason is that *the process of developing a community that is capable of taking implementation risks is also the process by which teachers learn how to change and are given the capacity to change.* (p. 23, [emphasis added])

Michael Fullan and Joanne Quinn from *Coherence: The Right Drivers in Action for Schools, Districts, and Systems* (2016):

> The concept of learning communities is not wrong, but the implementation has lacked depth. If we embrace the idea that our students should be critical thinkers grounded in metacognition, then we need to *design learning experiences for adults that foster the same competencies because we cannot give to others what we do not possess ourselves.* (p. 63, [emphasis added])

Zeichner and Liston in their book, *Traditions of Reform in U.S. Teacher Education* (1990), long before PLCs existed, criticized reflection that assumed positive results regardless of quality: in some instances, the reader is left with the impression that as long as teachers reflect about something, whatever they do must be worthwhile.

Furthermore, Mel Ainseow, David Bares, and Jill Martin in their article, "Taking school improvement into the classroom" (1998) concluded that current school collegiality doesn't, in itself, result in changes in classroom practice. Their research suggests teachers need to observe other teaching models in order to distinguish between what they are presently doing and their aspirations. Otherwise, professional learning communities reinforce existing practices instead of addressing learning issues. Perhaps their most important conclusion is that gaining new insights is more likely to come from observational studies in specific contexts.

Despite such concerns, professional learning communities are still described as the answer. Consider the words of Milbrey W. McLaughlin and Joan E. Talbert's *Building School-Based Teacher Learning Communities: Professional Strategies to Improve Student Achievement* (2006) on the cover of their book: "Building on extensive evidence that school-based teacher learning communities improve student outcomes, this book lays out an agenda to develop and sustain collaborative professional cultures."

A different story, however, within the book: "Available evidence about the relationship between school-based teacher learning communities and positive student outcomes is promising and consistent—but thin" (p. 129).

The apparent contradiction is understandable. There are problems with interpreting the effectiveness of professional learning communities. Different contexts with an interacting diversity of teaching expertise, principal support, time constraints, teacher-leaders, facilitator availability, and changes in principals, superintendents, and boards muddy the waters.

And unless learning goals have accompanying criteria, valid comparisons are difficult. When schools have goals such as improved creativity, democratic responsibilities, and love of learning along with specific subject outcomes, comparing student achievement across schools is more than a challenge.

Hargreaves and Fullan, in *Professional Capital: Transforming Teaching in Every School* (2012), use principals or district personnel demanding results from PLCs as an example of push while creating pushback. Its opposite, pull, is described as attraction to the team through its comradery of positive energy, ambitious goals, and success in improving student achievement. Not mentioned are legs, a third set of exercises found in fitness gyms. Your legs get you to places where you can pull and push. Within culture change, legs can be seen as building relationships/creating mutual strength and trust.

Concept Map 2 depicts support as a two-way street—the upward arrows each with two components. One is emotional/cognitive support from teachers for both PLCs and school/district leadership in *their* quest for an improved culture. The second is success: professional teaching that results in upgraded student motivation/love of learning, improved exam results, and boosted school/district morale.

District and school support (up and down) benefit from sequences found in organizational development/visible thinking routines such as RAT (Role Appraisal Technique), Alter-Ego, and Ladder of Feedback:

clarifying expectations, bridging perceptions, and ongoing formative assessment.

Role: A set of connected behaviors, rights, obligations, beliefs, and norms as conceptualized by people in a social situation. Trust fractures, not only by people breaking commitments but by failure to clarify expectations. Role Appraisal Technique avoids disappointments and resentments by setting and updating those anticipations. This is done through negotiations between inter-connected roles.

Role clarification *is* how we work together. The traditional RAT begins with the focal person or group presenting an analysis of their role to those with whom they interact—its purpose, related duties, and history. The second step is setting out expectations (skills, behaviours and attitudes) for the interacting group—what is needed from them in support.

This is another two-way street. Those individuals or groups not only respond, but they also have requests/demands of the focal person or group so they can carry out *their* jobs. Areas of confusion/doubt are worked out while arriving at agreed-upon commitments from both parties. In my experience (often principal and teaching staff), this process is highly appreciated. Centred on mutual respect, democratic values, and hard conversations, RAT can impact clarity of purpose, school-wide effectiveness, formative assessment, distributed leadership, morale, confidence, conflict resolutions, and trust.

Conflict resolution is the focus of an article by Tony Keller in the Globe and Mail newspaper (October 13, 2023). He references a book by R. Fisher et al., *Getting to Yes: Negotiating Agreement without Giving In 3rd edition* (2011), where "non-adversarial bargaining only works when both parties want a deal." Their four basic principles: "*separate people from the problem,*" "*focus on interests, not positions,*" "*invent options for mutual gain,*" and "*insist on using objective criteria.*" These being resolution strategies across individuals, small groups, and nations. ([emphasis added])

The Alter-Ego routine, as described in the introduction, where a teacher interviews another on a topic, then role-plays the interviewee to the rest of the group (along with ongoing corrections from their partner), also supports conflict resolution. Taking even a short walk in someone else's shoes, especially a fellow teacher with opposing views, opens room for common ground. It also, as previously stated, introduces a workable classroom process for students addressing different points of view.

Ongoing formative assessment of both individuals and collaborative groups incorporates "Ladder of Feedback." The recommended sequence for providing feedback: (1) ask for any needed clarifications, (2) appreciate specific thoughts/awareness, (3) raise questions/concerns, and 4) offer suggestions. And finally (not the least important), the person or persons receiving feedback to thank those providing it.

Effective professional learning communities learn by doing: teachers examining data/information, visiting each other's classrooms, supporting each other, sharing research in pursuit of student learning solutions, instigating hard conversations, developing common formative assessments, setting a limited number of SMART (Specific, Measurable, Ambitious, Relevant, and Time-Bound) goals, and, when appropriate, requesting the district for additional expertise.

Guided inquiry is not only a subsection of a learning to learn curriculum for students, but also how professional learning communities approach their job. This includes locating information, collaborative learning, deep thinking through shunning distractions, resilience when the going gets rough, writing as a thinking tool, and self-analysis through reflection. Response-ability, another important attribute, *is* the "learning by doing" theorem described earlier.

The result of such efforts, when done well, is improved resilience in meeting setbacks/new demands such as changes in administrators. Collaboration is common in other professions; we need to be part of the growing movement of physicians, social workers, scientists, engineers, architects, and lawyers learning/working together. Therein lies the growth, development, and self-esteem teachers seek.

One example of modeling rather than telling: students invited to witness (fishbowl fashion) a professional learning community meeting, then, using the Ladder of Feedback, provide observations to the PLC before reporting back to their classmates.

Unfortunately, current high school culture avoids such off-road suggestions. For instance, it is sometimes recommended, as Janet Giltrow suggests in *Academic Writing: Writing & Reading in the Disciplines 3rd edition* (2002), that teachers demonstrate their own writing while explaining choices, false starts, failures, relationships within sentence structure, meaning, and purpose, or highlight grammatical structures with which students have been struggling.

Such teaching allows students an in-depth look at a creative process that is observed, not described. Another is for department heads or teachers with proven expertise to volunteer to teach (with observers) at least one class with a history of learning problems.

There are other impediments. As Peter Coleman and Linda La Roque (1990) reported, we suffer from, "the narrowness of the current emphasis on the classroom and the school as the only important units of analysis with respect to quality" (p. 10).

Opportunities for change, they contend, means identifying how administrators develop, support, and sustain norms and practices that together constitute a positive ethos for the district. As discussed in Chapter 2, this includes the false dichotomy of school vs district and that having common goals does not require identical methods for achieving those goals.

Their six centres of administrative and instructional effort: "paying attention to instructional issues; requiring school accountability; managing change and improvement; eliciting commitment; treating members and clients with consideration; and gaining community support" (p. 4).

Guidelines for group effectiveness include avoiding personal attacks in favour of an honest discussion of learning and teaching. Others are listening skills, providing quality feedback, examining evidence, recognizing differing points of view as an asset, not a hindrance; identifying false dichotomies, summarizing interactions, hard conversations, sticking to topics, reaching consensus, and gatekeeping that recognizes that just because people are quiet doesn't mean they lack ideas.

Skepticism on teacher preparedness for learning communities is found in Sam Kaner's book, *Facilitator's Guide to Participatory Decision Making* (2014):

> Most individuals working in groups do not know how to solve tough problems on their own. They do not know how to build a shared framework of understanding—they seldom recognize its significance. They dread conflict and discomfort, and they try hard to avoid it. Yet by avoiding the struggle to integrate one another's perspectives, the members of such groups greatly diminish their own potential to be effective. They need a facilitator. (p. 32)

Seeking outside help from those with more experience or training is nothing to be disdained—instead, it may indicate maturity. These supports may be interschool, district personnel, provincial/state departments of education, or professional learning networks around the country or the world; examples being described in *"Networks For Learning: Effective Collaboration for Teacher, School and System Improvement"* (2018), edited by Chris Brown and Cindy L. Poortman.

More evidence for collaborative expertise. Carrie Leana of the University of Pittsburgh did a study titled "Social capital: An untapped resource for educational improvement" (2017) where she measured teachers' paper qualifications and competencies as well as collaborative expertise against student learning. Teacher qualifications turned out to be important; nevertheless, students with highly qualified teachers *and* collaborative expertise did better.

DuFour et al. in "Learning by Doing: A Handbook for Professional Learning Communities at Work" (2006), state that schools need to regard time as a tool, not a limitation:

> Many teachers have come to the conclusion that their job is not just difficult—it is *impossible*. If schools continue to operate according to traditional assumptions and practices…individual teachers working in isolation as they attempt to help all of their students achieve at high levels will eventually be overwhelmed by the tension between covering the content and responding to the diverse needs of their students in a fixed time with virtually no external support. (p. 77)

Balkanized teacher culture is a feature of many high schools. As Hargreaves and Fullan (2012) report:

> Balkanized cultures attach their loyalties and identities to particular groups of their colleagues with whom they work most closely, share most time, and socialize most often in the staffroom or department workroom. The existence of tightly insulated subgroups in a school often reflects and reinforces very different outlooks on learning, teaching strategies, discipline, and curriculum. In balkanized cultures, teachers may not be *isolated*, but they are quite *insulated*.
> These are more likely in high schools because of "strong subject department structures on which high schools are based. This is one of the reasons high schools are so notoriously hard to change." (pp. 115–116)

I was never part of such a closed group, but I know them: department heads fixed on external exams, early re-streaming of students to raise scores, and forced decision making; in some cases, flexibility/choice (regardless of student progress) reduced to teachers being on the same page every day. In one case, a first-year teacher was told by her department head to submit one hundred lesson plans prior to school opening.

A summary of differences between effective PLCs and less substantive efforts:

- Trust and confidence in relationships with fellow teachers.
- Acceptance of the need for systemic change.
- A sense of agency. Collaboratively designed lesson plans.
- Choice and voice still available for individual teachers on how to learn/teach.
- Open-ended learning opportunities.
- Interlocking roles negotiated from the inside. Teacher to teacher classroom observations/videos for PLC use.
- Tight loops (planning-action-impact data sequence).
- Extended time to learn by doing.
- Activating prior knowledge.
- Decisions by consensus.
- Collective accountability for results
- Flexibility in temporarily assigning students to teachers based on need.
- Teacher leaders/distributed leadership.
- Employing LTL principles of resourcefulness, reciprocity, responsiveness, resilience, and reflection within professional learning individually and as a team.
- Focus on deep thinking, making thinking visible, naming thinking, and cultivation of routines for specific thinking processes.
- Hard conversations.
- Acceptance of criticism.
- Modeling learning *within* Direct Instruction and Guided Inquiry.
- Scheduled time to meet.

All more easily said than done.

Comparable expectations for Professional Learning Community members are those set out by the BCTF (British Columbia Teachers Federation) as described in the BCTF Summer Conference 2016 for their committees:

1. The team needs to share clear objectives, values, and common goals, and know how to focus on the task at hand.
2. Team members need to know who does what and willingly accept the influence and leadership of members who have skills pertinent to the immediate task.
3. Team members need to feel that their specific concerns are appreciated.

4. The team needs to find a way to make decisions that are trust enhancing. Not being open and frank with colleagues is just as corruptive as stating untruths or leaving obligations unfulfilled. Leaving your thinking to the imagination of others is a bad road to a bad place. At times, it's not what you say that kills trust, but what you avoid.
5. The team must act with integrity and honor its commitments.
6. The team must be good at listening, clarifying what is being said, showing an interest in what is being said, feedback, and learning.
7. The team must look at the way it operates and assess its own effectiveness. Team members take the time to stop and learn and ask themselves, 'what do we do well as a group?'
8. Differences of opinion are encouraged and freely expressed. Diversity is a mark of a team's strength. Team members' flexibility, objectivity, and humour promote a climate that allows for disagreement.
9. The team is willing to identify what works to create the ideal circumstances and try to recreate those circumstances to bring change.
10. The team exerts energy toward creating a vision of what can be.
11. Roles are balanced and shared to facilitate both the accomplishment of tasks and feeling of team cohesion and morale.

Any team, regardless of purpose, depends more on inside behaviour than outside supports. Internal accountability is only possible with a certain level of trust. As such, Bailey and Jakicic in *Common Formative Assessments: A Toolkit for Professional Learning Communities at Work* (2010), also set out norms for working together:

1) Focus on student learning.
2) Task conflict over interpersonal conflict.
3) Decisions based on quantitative and qualitative data.
4) Commitment not to blame students.
5) Putting aside personal preferences for the good of the team.

Commitment to the PLC is critical: They suggest consensus-building strategies where consensus is defined as the clear "will of the group" rather than unanimous support:

1) Build shared knowledge of the student learning problem. 2) Define the problem, determine the criteria needed for an acceptable solution. 3) Participate in solution input. 4) Refine potential solutions. 5) Pick one fitting the criteria. 6) Set out the final consensus.

One process for initiating Professional Learning Communities is Theorem 1—gathering prior knowledge: concerns, strengths, and expectations from individual teachers and students as preparation for functioning as a group. This inside information critical for deciding whether to go forward or not.

Interview Guide

1. What are the learning goals for students in your school?
2. How do teachers and students in this school work together to achieve those goals? What is the current level of trust? What strengths are available? How have you improved the teaching in your school in the past? How do you know?
3. Can you identify previous teacher-leaders/student-led initiatives? How did this happen?
4. What is the history of collaboration in your school?
5. Have you participated in working committees? Under what circumstances? For what purpose? What did you learn?
6. What concerns do you have about forming a PLC? What suggestions do you have to deal with those concerns?
7. How can individual teachers contribute to a successful PLC?
8. How do you see a PLC spending its time? What activities would help you become a better teacher? A better PLC? A better learner?
9. What support do you feel is necessary for success? From whom?
10. Is teacher autonomy consistent with PLC decision making? How much autonomy/support from administrators/other teachers does a PLC require?
11. How would the group assess how well it works together? What would success look like?

My main conclusion from leading such investigations/change support is that teacher analysis of context is vital for ownership. After taping individual interviews, I sorted teacher responses into themes. Each theme, along with a set of relevant interview quotes were hung on walls. At the first meeting, participants are seated, then asked to circulate and read all the material *without speaking*. Reading these collections silently, participants recognize their own contributions while other contributors can only be surmised. Groups of four or five then discuss the data, then summarize each theme into one or two sentences. Their summaries are then added below each theme.

Teachers will recognize their own comments and can guess which comments belong to others, but they don't know for sure. One surprise for most teachers and myself as facilitator, was the high level of agreement displayed under each theme. Even for issues that, I would learn later, were rarely discussed.

In small groups, they discuss connections among the themes. In addition to cause and effect, comparison and contrast, relative importance, and other deeper thinking, they work to identify key concerns/issues/logjams blocking progress. Examples are disruptive relationships among the teaching staff (progressive vs traditional), lack of support *from*, or missing communication *with* parents/community, student engagement levels, streaming students, administration focus, teacher leadership, role clarifications, teacher privatization, student leadership opportunities, meeting time, or lack of collaborative expertise.

The overarching objective here is not only widespread analysis, what Peter Senge in *Schools That Learn* (2012) calls "systems thinking", but hometown ownership—a growing understanding that their problems are the direct result of *what was, or was not done, in large part by themselves*.

The resulting cognitive map is the starting point for investigating push and pull issues, growing strengths, collaborative time, documenting reflection, student citizenship/leadership development, whole-school accountability, inter-school and inter-district connections, cognitive acceleration, teacher-leader responsibilities, hard conversations, making thinking visible, motivational issues, expanded parent involvement, democratic values, finding consensus, local community learning integration, principal's role, collective learning in and out of the classroom, aligned planning, recognizing false dichotomies, self-differentiated learning, conflict resolution skills, role negotiation and clarification, making thinking visible/formative assessment, data analysis, or effective decision-making.

Jeffrey Gantz in his two and one-half year 2016 research paper, "Action Research by Practitioners: A Case Study of a High School's Attempt to Create Transformational Change" is the direct opposite of the above. Initiated by top management where involvement by teachers was required, if not coerced, the abbreviated success of the intervention, clearly recognized by Gantz, was due to lack of teacher ownership.

His post-mortem concluded that instructional improvement cannot be isolated from wider, long-term concerns affecting the school. Gathering overall concerns, strengths, and interests using the above OD (Organizational Development) interview-data collection group feedback/analysis model, then, offers a better chance of success, not just initially, but for ongoing formative assessment.

We need to correct the misconception that organizational development interventions are restricted to outside facilitators. French W. and Bell C. (1973):

> One use of the term that is common with practitioners and laymen alike is that an intervention is something the outside consultant does to the client system. The major shortcomings of this definition are, first, that it does not provide for the client system doing something to itself without the assistance of an external, or even internal, consultant; and, second, it denies the joint collaboration that takes place between the consultant and client. In OD programs, individuals and units within the organization often initiate activities designed to improve their functioning and do so on their own. These activities can clearly constitute OD interventions. (p. 98)

Careful, objective, and open teaching observations are beginnings of teacher awareness. For instance, Shayer and Adey, in "Really Raising Standards: Cognitive intervention and academic achievement." (1997), describe two classes in an Australian high school where the teachers professed to be enhancing high level thinking within an individualized, self-paced process. Driven by workbooks with low level recall demands, its exposure by outside observers included lack of cognitive conflict and its effect—student boredom.

Finding ways for students to visibly demonstrate learning outcomes is important. A mathematics lesson taught by a Chinese secondary teacher in a Chinese high school in Shanghai comes to mind. At the end of the lesson, the teacher asked each student to stand and explain what they had learned.

Some stood by their desks as they reflected on their learning; others used the chalkboard for more detailed explanations. This was not a summary of what the teacher had taught during the lesson. Their reflections showed extended thinking to applications in other subjects, usually sciences—how their learning connected with other areas of mathematics, and how they came to those conclusions.

Learning to learn together is more than minor adjustments. It requires school-wide democratic practices among teachers and students, students, and teachers. This includes team inquiries as a subset: an interweaving of tentative assumptions, playfulness, humour, evidence, suppositions, connections, and points of view as teachers/students work together to plan, revise, and conclude. Hardly the past experience of teachers, and not likely to happen in any sustained way without support and considerable time.

Kuhlthau et al. in *Guided Inquiry: Learning in the 21st Century* (2007) describe inquiry supports for students as just as crucial for developing independence as Hattie's surface information is for deeper thinking. As such, they believe *inquiry support teams* comprised of subject teachers, PLC's, school librarians, and local organizations (public libraries, museums, minority leadership, and immigrant support groups) should be organized as a community enterprise.

They see the library as the students' inquiry laboratory where information access is taught and learned. They report that in the absence of such support, "too often the result is blatant copying, narrow fact finding, and unimaginative repetition of an author's work, with little real learning on the part of the student" (p. 22).

The particulars of inquiry learning may vary from school to school, but the underlying principle is the same: students choose a topic of interest to them, study it in depth, and share what they have learned. This process does not begin in high school; Kuhlthau et al. see elementary and middle schools as essential for future efforts.

Secondary school students' learning centres on the inquiry process, building on the knowledge and strategies they have acquired throughout elementary and middle school. Through these years, as students' capacity for abstraction and independence increases, the Guided Inquiry team gradually releases responsibility to them.

Students learn the difference between *gathering a few facts in response to a question and dealing with more complex inquiries that require serious thinking and learning*. Kuhlthau et al., then, describe an information search process (ISP) composed of seven stages: the *first* stage is the teacher *initiating* the process by setting out a unit of study.

The *second* stage has students *selecting a topic* within the unit of study. Choices here depend on availability of information, student personal interest, assignment requirements, and time. The *third* stage is *exploration* where the student works on *deciding a focus*. As students gather information, they explore inconsistencies, false choices, points of view, and other elements of deeper thinking and investigation. They *build on what they know, work with other students, and receive teacher guidance along the way.*

Formulating a focus is *fourth* and has the same considerations as selecting a topic—preference based on past experience, assignment, and time. The *collection* stage is *fifth*: gathering information that *defines, extends, and supports* their focus. As confidence and interest grows, a sense of ownership and expertise ensues.

The foregoing is preparation for the *sixth* phase: sharing their work with others. The *seventh* stage is *assessment:* self-reflection and feedback from peers. *These considerations/stages are also applicable to teacher and school inquiry processes. What is good for students is good for us.* Theorem 2—we learn what we teach.

Daniels H. et al. (2001):

> As much as we may achieve by making our science, history, English, math, and other content classrooms challenging, authentic, and collaborative, teaching them as disconnected subjects still limits student learning. In the wider adult world inquiring, problem solving, and gaining new skills is rarely as compartmentalized as this. And so pathfinding high schools must find ways to bring subjects together. And this means not just plugging a little statistics or geography into a literature lesson where appropriate. Rather, it involves guiding students to conduct in-depth inquiry that starts with an important question and then to pursue that question by using all the subject-area skills and knowledge needed for that particular investigation. This is the kind of higher-order thinking and problem solving that colleges, the business world, and our communities are asking that public school graduates be able to do. (p. 141)

Guided inquiry is also the prewriting stage of the writing process while exploring and formulating ideas. The result, at times, is a document to be presented to fellow students, advisories, or school assemblies. Guided inquiry is the domain of all writers—their precursor to success. Specific skills to include chaining (where references in the research provide further opportunities to learn) along with summaries, paraphrasing, and questioning.

Learning how to improve lessons benefits from collaborative routines such as LAST (Looking at Student Thinking). Ritchhart (2020) begins with a caveat: "As with most protocols, the artificialness of structuring a conversation is weighed against the benefits of making sure the discussion is complete" (p. 235).

The steps:
1. A teacher presents students' work to the PLC. The teacher then asks, "What do you see?" The purpose is to become aware (objective, open observation) of all features of the work. (5–7minutes)
2. PLC speculates about the students' thinking. "Where do you see thinking?" What parts of the work provide evidence? PLC to make connections to different kinds of thinking such as deductions, cause and effect, and prediction. A concept map of the suggested thinking might be helpful here. (5–7 minutes)
3. PLC gathers questions about the thinking and understanding of the students—not the lesson itself. Frame questions to get at broad issues along with specifics. Questions should be important to the questioner *and* open doors to expanded thinking. (5–7 minutes).
4. Discuss the implications for teaching and learning. What is needed to further extend and build on students' thinking? Suggestions should be practical as well as having general implications.

Executing the curriculum described by Juliet Strang et al. (2007) in *Attitudes Skills Knowledge: How to Teach Learning to Learn in the Secondary School* (2006) could go a long way toward achieving the *cultural change* advocated by M. Fullan. The attitudes, dispositions, skills, and knowledge that students need to improve their ability to learn are precisely those required for teachers to change their teaching. Growing such a curriculum with students through teacher modeling, collaborative learning, and multiple teaching strategies is how that change happens.

Learning to learn can be summarized as follows: students and teachers do best when they stand back from information or ideas and think about them objectively. Reflective learners assimilate new learnings, relate it to prior knowledge, and adapt it for their own purposes. Over time, they develop creativity, ability to think critically, and heighten consideration of their own thinking. Teachers encourage such thinking when they design opportunities for students to critically evaluate and create their own discourse.

Rosemary Hipkins, a New Zealand authority on teaching metacognition, identifies research where learning-to-learn practices improved results for lower-achieving students. She stresses *the importance of keeping expectations open for those who have not done well in the past.*

She refers to a study by Zohar, A. & Ben D. (2008) titled "Explicit teaching of meta-strategic knowledge in authentic classroom situations" where eighth grade science students were assigned to treatment and comparison groups with equal numbers of high and low achieving students. The result: low and high-achieving students in the treatment group *outscored even high-achieving students in the comparison group.*

Teacher attitudes/belief systems are critical. In an attempt to explain teaching behaviour, Ritchhart (2015) describes the work of Alan Schoenfeld and his colleagues at the Teacher Model Group in Berkeley who developed a "goal-oriented decision-making model of teaching" in which knowledge of a teacher's goals and beliefs "provides the basis for understanding much, if not all, of a teacher's behavior" (p. 41).

It suggests teachers are *not guided by teaching methods so much as by belief sets*—orientations about "teaching, learning, and the meaning and purpose of school." Their explanation:

> Changing teaching is much more than giving teachers a new set of practices to deploy. In fact, teachers may employ a new method of instruction only to find that it falls flat and doesn't achieve the kind of lift its proponents had promised. They then discount the method, ignoring completely how their expectational beliefs have undermined the new instructional practices. (p. 41)

Acting as action theories, Ritchhart lists five belief sets that "lay a foundation *for* our expectations in learning groups":

> 1) Focusing students on learning vs the work. 2) Teaching for understanding vs knowledge. 3) Encouraging deep vs surface learning strategies. 4) Promoting independence vs dependence. 5) Developing a growth vs a fixed mindset. (p. 42)

Ritchhart:

> As we worked our way through different types of modeling in this chapter, our progression has been from the informal, ongoing, and embedded to the increasingly explicit, focused, and directed. All these types of modeling have their place in

> the classroom. However, as a force shaping the culture of a classroom, school, or organization, it is the informal modeling that has the most power. It is this kind of model that tells students who we really are and what we really value. As the Sizers said, "The students are watching." They see us in our glory and our ignobility. However, rather than seeking to hide our weaknesses, struggles, and shortcomings—which students will inevitably see and notice anyway—we can open ourselves up authentically to our students and show them what it means to be an ongoing learner. (p. 137)

It's all about authenticity. There is no way that any teacher, through her words or actions, can convincingly exhibit high expectations for students if she doesn't believe it. You also cannot model risk-taking, reflection on thinking, and learning from your mistakes in the abstract. It is in the sharing of personal experience that improved relationships and trust happen. Effective behaviours, a la John Holt, rise from within.

Expectations also include curricular outcomes. Each content objective is an opportunity to improve learning skills. As Juliet Strang et al. (2006) recommends, implementing a learning to learn curriculum effectively means using a split-screen approach where content outcomes are achieved while teaching related learning to learn attitudes, skills, and knowledge.

An important point they make is that learning to learn doesn't happen in a vacuum. Strang et al. emphasize the importance of learning attitudes, skills, and knowledge taught in conjunction with subject outcomes; for evidence they reference failed study skills programs isolated from academic learning in the past.

Next is language where teachers through their interactions with students, clarify thinking routines that have become the norm. Noticing, naming, and underlining thinking is developed day by day by drawing attention to specific instances. Two examples are 'Compass Points'—considering an idea or proposition from different angles: excitements (the upside), worries (downside), determining additional information, current opinion, and next steps. Also 'Chalktalk', a group process for activating prior knowledge *or* summarizing group learning. Not confined to classrooms, these routines also work for PLCs.

Time for teachers to learn together is a concern. But time within the classroom for students to learn is also necessary. Ritchhart goes beyond wait time to urge teachers to allow time for students to gather and sort prior knowledge, consult with partners within direct instruction, generate questions, and reflect on observations both individually and collectively. Even such a simple tactic as giving students time to jot down a few thoughts before sharing them with a partner can foster creativity.

With autonomous lifelong learning as the goal, a parallel learning to learn curriculum will take considerable time/effort to cultivate a different perspective in students used to being told what to do, when to do it, and receiving marks (rewards) every step of the way. Alfie Kohn maintains in *Feel-Bad Education* (2011) that students may resist a "more active, probing form of learning." He quotes a grade ten student's comment to a teacher, "We see what all this is about now. You are trying to get us to think and learn for ourselves." "Exactly right!" said the teacher. The student replied, "Well, we don't want to do that." (PP. 39–40) Agreeing with this concern is Sizer (1984) who found that secondary school students, as a trade-off for not having to do too much, are willing to be submissive.

To illustrate a range of views, we have a sample of online teacher comments regarding PLCs:

"PLCs are a complete waste of time, but they have made Rich DuFour and the Bride of DuFour rich."

"Teachers can be great alone, but are exceptional when working together. Imagine taking all of the great minds in the school together and coming up with the best resources, lessons, assessments, and ideas on how to be successful with all children—that's what PLCs are about."

"Schools have been, for a long time, collaborative and cooperative communities. The offerings from DuFour, are nothing new. Unfortunately, school boards are paying these people a ton of money to tell them things that are hardly profound. What a waste of already limited resources."

"As I see it, schools are one of the last environments that do not use collaboration. When professionals in other disciplines look from the outside in, our structure is bizarre—a bunch of professionals with the same goals and the same clients…isolating themselves in different rooms, not comparing notes, not benefiting from each other's input, not problem solving together, not brainstorming, not idea sharing. We are each other's greatest resource. PLCs finally allow us to take advantage of the resource we have in each other for the benefit of students."

Learning to work well together is a priority. As noted previously, it is the legs that support both the pull of motivating others through modeling, quality goals, respect, and local evidence and push in the form of active reading, peer feedback, writing to learn, critical feeling, and hard conversations. Improving the capabilities of critical analysis, creative confidence, passion for teaching and learning, respect for differences in people, and concern for the less fortunate depends on its success.

This is how change happens: teachers using learning processes that increase their capacity to teach students those same processes. The concept map at the beginning of this chapter displays the centrality of PLCs as both catalyst and product: small groups of collaborating teachers sorting themselves out within an LTL agenda that puts learning at the forefront for themselves and their students.

Making the case for learning to learn as a strategy for change, Rosemary Hipkins, Chief Researcher at the New Zealand Council for Educational Research, concluded that professional growth, student voice, metacognition, self-regulation, community support for learning, and lifelong/life-wide learning all have strong connections with learning to learn, while expressing the concern that teachers don't always connect involving students in assessment/learning decisions with a learning to learn approach.

Learning well starts with noticing. Star hockey player Patrick Kane, while being interviewed on-ice, explained why the Chicago Blackhawks were in a slump. He said his team was focused on their losing streak—they needed a win. Too much. With some insight, he believed these distracted players from paying attention to the here and now (like seeing the puck). In keeping with Kane's observation, recent research concludes that students receiving only informational feedback do better than those given marks or feedback with marks. Keeping your eyes on the prize can be bad advice.

According to Hord and Sommers (2008), collecting valuable information from classroom observations and provision of constructive feedback are learned skills. Little (2002) validated this finding when she described the development of PLCs as navigation between individual autonomy and the group. How teachers negotiate this perceived conflict will determine whether they will be guided by inquiry and reflection or strive to maintain the status quo.

Research suggests five guidelines for all professional learning communities:

1) Diagnosing concerns using prior knowledge/analysis/planning routines.
2) Applying the district's General-Purpose Statement (more about this in Chapter 7).
3) Focusing on group *and* individual learning skills.
4) Adapting/adopting thinking routines that address team relationships, intra-group conflict, finding common ground, role clarification, visible thinking, and decision making, and
5) Ongoing assessment of PLC impact on student achievement.

PLC's own learning/teaching experience, as stated, is the right place to start. But when stuck, new input is often required. Consequently, PLCs cannot effect change by ignoring the abundance of information, evidence, and analysis of those who have gone before. Reading research is another form of collaboration. Unless professional reading, individually and collectively, is highly regarded and utilized, real change is handicapped; awareness of both teaching/learning experience and research is critical for quality decision making.

Improving teachers' vocabulary that describes teaching and learning is important for internalization. Making vocabulary such as *"thinking routines"*, *"making thinking visible"*, *"reflection"*, *"formative assessment"*, *"constructive conflict"*, *"model"*, *"independent learners"* a part of professional meetings and student interactions pulls thinking to new levels.

Reading and writing in the subject areas are important supports for learning to learn. Vacca and Vacca's book *Content Area Reading: Literacy and Learning across the Curriculum* (2011), is a learning to learn book. Making thinking visible, modeling expectations, inductive approaches, exemplary teaching methods, ownership of change, and student partnerships—all supports for effective change.

How do we renegotiate mutually supportive roles over time? How do we analyze PLC progress in improved thinking/effectiveness regarding a) lessons b) thinking about thinking c) group dynamics d) awareness of cognitive resources related to tasks, and e) planning and monitoring plans? One answer, as in the LAST example, is building concept maps over extended periods—as helpful for teachers as it is for students.

Lesson study, a mainstay for improving instruction in Japan, is a well-studied and highly successful form of professional learning—but only if teachers are provided the time, support, and resources needed to make it a success. Lesson study has been used as a dominant form of professional development in Japan for years. Its curriculum focused on fewer curriculum topics in depth within a Japanese educational culture that has a long tradition of outside observers in classrooms.

In lesson study, teachers collaboratively plan, develop, or improve a lesson, field test the lesson in a classroom—observe it, make changes, and collect data to determine the impact of the lesson on student learning. This usually occurs over a period of months.

According to research by Siebrich de Veries and Rilana Prenger in *Networks for Learning: Effective Collaboration for Teacher, School and System Improvement* (2018), lesson study is:

> Characterized by active collaboration and research; it is practice-based, student oriented and teacher directed… Although its impact is mainly based on small-scale qualitative research, it also appears to be a powerful tool for teachers to improve their teaching practice. (p. 135)

They describe the backdrop to the Netherlands professional development as:

> "traditionally top-down, imposed *quick fix and one-shot* workshops, conferences and seminars, and, to a lesser degree, long-term, teacher-directed, practice-based collaboration and research. Moreover, a student-based orientation is not a common practice for Dutch teachers. Just as in other Western European countries, work pressure in schools is high." (p. 135)

A caution from Senge et al. (2012) on creating schools that learn:

> People in schools and other organizations often create teams that hold deep conversations about their purpose, the nature of their organizations, their shared values, and their goals. Yet they appear to be unaware of the political and social forces that have shaped the system around them and that their silence on many issues contributes to the conditions with which they struggle. This makes it more difficult to see the interconnections in their actions and inaction, where to apply leverage, or even that they are part of creating the system. (p. 254)

Toby Greany and Jill Rodd, in *Creating a Learning to Learn School* (2003) see learning to learn as a unifying force for disparate initiatives through a coherent philosophy. *Teachers' learning capacity/leadership* as indispensable for advancing student ownership, love of learning, making thinking visible, distributed leadership, high expectations, and democratizing schools. The school growing along with the teachers, students, and the local community.

In summary, professional learning communities accelerate learning capacity through considered action, deep thinking, and emotional connections; assessing current knowledge on a particular learning issue, gathering pertinent research, working together, identifying alternate strategies when stuck, learning from mistakes, developing a common vocabulary, awareness of forces supporting or restricting change, and reflecting on their actions through active listening, critical reading, writing to learn, and rich conversations.

Chapter 4
Cognitive Acceleration: Deeper Thinking

"What we want to see is the child in pursuit of knowledge, and not knowledge in pursuit of the child." George Bernard Shaw

In the past, the ability of high school students to think abstractly was assumed by chronological age, but we now know that capability to form hypotheses/ expand reasoning varies considerably from student to student. Information uncovered by Shayer, *Learning Intelligence: Cognitive Acceleration across the curriculum* (2003), shows that less than half of grade eleven and grade twelve students are operational thinkers, a considerable drop in performance compared to previous decades.

The reason, Shayer suggests, is high schools testing accumulated knowledge at the expense of deeper thinking. In addition, he was aware that teachers, as described previously, do not teach students how to learn, citing Moseley et al. (2004), who observed sixty-nine classrooms where teachers did not teach learning skills but focused on book reading, task instruction, requests for answers to questions, and providing specific information.

He then developed two-year programmes using outside facilitators for those children identified as unable to think beyond the concrete.

Aimed at fast forwarding students' abilities, he called it "cognitive acceleration." These programmes substantially improved mathematics and science entry level testing grades. More importantly, the children also showed improvement on predicted grades in other subjects such as English and history. This last evidence fits with his goal, not improved grades but improvement in students' general thinking abilities; essentially an increase in intelligence.

Having a growth mindset is important for improving capacity to learn anything. Being successful in science or other disciplines, then, can result in improved ability across the board. The brain changes, neural pathways are reinforced, connectors grow—layers of myelin allow information to travel efficiently through our brains.

Shayer worked with Piagetian groups of concrete and formal. The concrete stage in mathematics meant testing a child's ability to put things in order, establish logical relationships, and plot simple graphs. The formal stage involved testing more abstract thinking, including the ability to predict. He did not advocate cognitive acceleration for every lesson. Instead, he only replaced 25% of the usual science curriculum.

Outside input should not overshadow the central role of Vygotsky's Zone of Proximal Development (the range of abilities that a person can perform with assistance but cannot yet perform independently) within cognitive acceleration. Its success directly dependent on teacher expertise in drawing out students and promoting collaborative thinking.

Adey and Shayer:

> CA interventions in any subject area and at any age encourage students to describe and explain their ideas, to feel unafraid of getting things wrong, and to engage in constructive polylogue with colleagues while teasing out a group understanding." (p. 6)

This reinforces, as stated in "Really Raising Standards: Cognitive Intervention and Academic Achievement" (1997), "the extra-intellectual power that is available to a child when her thinking is mediated through social interaction with adults or peers… The extra half-skill the child may need to knit to his own to create a completed skill may just as well come from what another child says and does as from her own behaviour. (p. 119)

They offer colleague Carolyn Yates' 'jig-saw puzzle' analogy:

> Sitting around a table collaboratively completing a jigsaw, one person fitting in a piece often stimulates another: 'Ah! Now I see where this piece goes.' If one of these players is a teacher who actually knows pretty well how the puzzle goes together, she can ask framing and focusing questions to aid the process and occasionally add a piece herself, but unless the students construct much of the puzzle themselves it will not be their own and (to come out of the analogy) they will not have gone beyond their present level of reasoning. (P. 66)

Cognitive acceleration was founded, in part, by the work of Reuven Feuerstein back in the 1950s in working with children traumatized by the holocaust. He had applied content-free learning of basic cognitive processes across all subject areas to children of Middle Eastern immigrants in Israel who were doing more poorly than average Israeli children. He called it Instrumental Enrichment. According to Shayer, it was a "metalearning intervention programme in the sense that it teaches students how to learn" (p. 10).

Hattie (2009), in his research on effective teaching strategies, rated Shayer's cognitive acceleration at 0.60, placing it in the upper tier. The approach consists of three drivers: (1) cognitive dissonance as recognizing a conflict between past knowledge and new awareness/information (2) reflection on learning to learn choices/strategies/variables, and (3) high quality dialogue among peers with teacher support.

His measurement of teaching impact deserves consideration. Extensive meta-analysis of the relative impact of each strategy is based on the results of pre and post-lesson testing. The impact on each student's learning is calculated as the ratio of the student's score change to the average standard deviation of both tests. Looking at all the strategies, Hattie determined the average impact at 0.4. This means about half of the strategies are below this score and half above.

As an aside, Douglas Fisher et al., in *Visible Learning for Literacy: Implementing the Practices That Work Best to Accelerate Student Learning* (2016), recommend the same formula for classroom use: teachers determining the impact of a unit of instruction using the ratio of the difference in class averages of post-test and pre-test to the average standard deviation of both tests.

There is criticism of this process. Some researchers are concerned that Hattie took no cognizance of individual studies with wide ranges of teaching expertise. One online researcher had this to say: "They are full of tiny, brief lab studies, studies with no control groups, studies that fail to control for initial achievement, and studies that use measures made up by the researchers."

Hattie's supporters, nonetheless, see his impact calculations more simply as guidance for teachers in choosing teaching strategies/approaches. The purpose is to make relative comparisons of different influences on student achievement while inviting teachers to collect their own proof of what does or does not work. They suggest his formula is only one piece of evidence for deciding lesson planning along with student reflections, teacher observations, and other pertinent information.

High quality dialogue with teacher support cannot be overstressed. It is the interaction from student to student as well as teacher guidance on moving thinking forward that makes the difference. All dependent on collaborative/reciprocal learning skills among students and teachers.

Consider a statement from Adey and Shayer's book: "The Vygotskian description of the social aspect of mutual growth casts serious doubt on the notion that improving students' performance in schools is just a matter of teaching them more skills and knowledge" (p. 9). Higher level thinking/making thinking visible, then, as part of a learning to learn program in conjunction with content knowledge paves the way.

With this in mind, Hattie (2012) recommends lesson planning that takes into account:(1) where students are at in their cognitive abilities (understanding patterns and relationships, seeing different points of view, discerning evidence, making use of analogies, or still at the concrete stage of learning), (2) clear thinking outcomes, and (3) working with students to monitor a suitable improvement rate. Importantly, cognitive acceleration, he believes, carries with it other positive effects such as motivation, improved strategies to learn, and student confidence.

Hattie:

> A major message that Shayer draws from this research is the important role played by teachers in structuring learning to ensure that students create their learning for themselves and with their peers, particularly when the lessons have two or three steps of the important concepts at or just above the level of thinking used by the student. This means that a teacher needs to know how each student thinks, and the thinking

demands of each step in the lesson both by the student and the peers with whom they are working. This, he claims, stops peer learning or collaborative learning from degenerating into the 'blind leading the blind'. It requires teachers to intervene to keep the learning moving upwards all of the time in relation to the demands of subject knowledge being taught. This notion of teaching 'at or +1 above' where the students are thinking is a major theme. (p. 106, [emphasis added])

As stated, Hattie links other student learning variables/dispositions to new learning. This includes *motivation to learn, past learning strategies, and confidence levels*. Information processes at work: working memory, acquisition capacities of recording, organization, retrieval—all leading to improved understanding. Students' prior knowledge still the beginning point, but also encapsulating self-efficacy, anxiety levels, performance, and goal orientations. Social and emotional learning again supporting intellectual growth.

We need to know our students well. Driving home the inclusion of social-emotional learning with academic excellence, the man believes teachers "can develop and enhance students' confidence in tackling challenging tasks, resilience in the face of error and failure, openness and willingness to share when interacting with peers, and pride in investing energy in actions that will lead to successful outcomes" (p. 45).

He also sees students as 'choosers' aimed at imposing:

> Some sense of order, coherence, and predictability in their world. We make choices about how to interpret events, about alternative courses of action, and about the value of making these decisions. These choices aim to *protect, preserve, and promote* our sense of self such that we can 'back ourselves'—that is, maintain a sense of self-esteem. A major purpose of schooling is to enable students to 'back themselves' as learners of what we consider worth knowing. (p. 45)

The significance of the social-emotional component for academic achievement is also illustrated by Halbert J & Kaser L. (2016). They offer the example of Birgit, a suburban high school English teacher—her student participation and success rate the highest in a diverse community. Based on these results, Louise, a school counsellor, offered to work with Birgit to identify the reasons for her success.

Halbert and Kaser:

> For years, Birgit had made it her practice to speak with each of her learners every day about some aspect of their personal lives, unconnected to their study of English. Being in her class was a personalized experience, not because she dramatically shifted her learning and teaching strategies on an individualized basis, but because she took the few moments available to her as learners came to her class to connect with them. They came to her class to learn because they knew she cared. Birgit didn't have access to the evidence of John Hattie that the effect size for positive teacher-student relationships is 0.72. She just knew that connection was important. (p. 24)

They summarize research on the impact of social-emotional learning (SEL):

> Students who are engaged in programming to increase SEL experience an 11 percentile gain in academic achievement. This finding matters. Researchers have highlighted how interpersonal, instructional, and environmental supports produce better school performance. (p. 24)

Further evidence for success in teaching deeper thinking: Philip Abrami and colleagues analyzed 117 studies on teaching critical thinking. The teaching approach with the strongest empirical support was explicit instruction: *teaching specific ways to reason and solve problems*. This in contrast with studies where teachers asked students to solve problems without explicit instruction where students experienced little improvement (Abrami et al. 2008).

Lesson planning, according to Ritchhart et al. (2011), means 1) seeing beyond memorization, work, and activity (covering the curriculum and preparing for the exam) toward lessons pertinent to the discipline; what real writers, mathematicians, scientists, historians, and physicists do, and 2) recalling actions you (the teacher) remember taking when developing some new understanding of something within the discipline or subject area. All based on your previous learning/prior knowledge.

The goal is to move from learning about the subject to doing it: solving problems, making decisions, and developing new understandings using the methods and tools of the discipline. Examples: Mathematicians—patterns, hypotheses, deductive and inductive thinking, direct and indirect proof, assumptions, congruity of a particular mathematics with the real world. Readers—interpretations, predictions, connections, visualization. Historians—perspectives, evidence, explanations, comparison/contrast, sequence/timelines. Writers—coherence and cohesiveness, vocabulary choice, summaries, connections, analogies.

Types of thinking across all subjects is also important: Ritchhart and colleagues identified eight "high-leverage thinking moves" essential for increased understanding:

> 1) Observing and describing what's there 2) building explanations and interpretations 3) reasoning with evidence 4) making connections 5) considering different viewpoints/perspectives 6) capturing the heart and forming conclusions 7) wondering and asking questions, and 8) uncovering complexity/going beyond the surface (p. 11)

Cognitive dissonance needs more explanation. The gap between what students initially know about a learning outcome and the outcome itself is not always cognitive dissonance. New learning targets don't necessarily contradict students' prior knowledge. Cognitive acceleration, then, is more than bridging gaps between prior knowledge and new information/thinking processes.

Rather, cognitive dissonance is students making predictions based on mistaken assumptions/expectations, then confronted with a different result. An example in physics is determining average speed when a vehicle travels 120 km at 40 kilometers per hour and back again at 60 kilometers per hour. The correct answer is not 50 km/hr. Another is the belief by most teachers, parents, and school boards that lowering the pupil-teacher ratio in high schools, in itself, improves student achievement. Or private schools as inherently more effective than our public education system. Also, that schools with an abundance of homework automatically have high standards.

Because of the specialized outside support, many schools cannot implement Shayer's cognitive acceleration—its fundamental principles, still, *are* pertinent in advancing student *and* teacher thinking. We start by making learning visible. You can't work with what you can't see. Other requirements are student collaboration proficiency and teacher coaching skills.

Teaching students how to collaborate in their learning, as previously stated, needs work. Sam Levin and Susan Engel, co-authors of "*A*

School of Our Own: The Story of the First Student-Run High School and a New Vision for American Education (2016) had this observation:

> Once again, it seemed wild to me that we never got to practice true collaboration in school. Time and again, it seemed, there was a skill with which we were expected to leave high school that we never really practiced while we were there. On top of that, I knew from the baseball diamond and the basketball court and the farm and the garden that collaboration felt incredible. If it was something we needed to learn, and something that was rewarding to do, why the hell was it missing entirely from the school day? (p. 38)

They are just as critical of current high schools on deeper thinking:

> Given the fact that using evidence to back up a belief or opinion is one of the prime components of higher-order thinking, Shtulman's data suggest that kids are graduating from high school no more sophisticated in their ability to reason than they were when they began. In my own lab we have data supporting this. Asked to convince others of their position on a controversial topic, students at the best colleges in the country have difficulty backing up their arguments with evidence. (p. 35)

Note: Andrew Shtulman is a cognitive developmental psychologist at Occidental College who studies conceptual development and conceptual change, particularly as they relate to science education.

The learning process, a series of approximations for *both students and teachers*, starts with concerns: What do I already know about the targeted learning? What related experience do I have? What abilities do I have that will support me? How much effort is required? Who do I get to learn with? What are my chances of failing? How do I protect my sense of well-being? What help is available? What kinds of thinking are needed? Will I improve my capabilities and at what cost?

A needed part of the teacher's role, then, is creating safety in the workplace. This starts by expanding time for success. An example is the process of writing, drafting, and re-drafting—at times, weeks, months, even years. As every writer knows, the initial effort can be daunting, but it's a start.

In Shanghai we worked with students preparing for international mathematics contests. Students struggled with problems for weeks before coming up with a solution or asking for help. The point is that grading/marking first efforts makes no sense. As an aside, contrary to the perception of many westerners, Chinese students are not simply memory banks; they love having time to think deep and succeed.

Jo Boaler (2019) reports research by TIMSS (Trends in International Mathematics and Science Study) in fifty-seven countries. Going into classrooms, researchers determined the following: 1) The mathematics curriculum in the US is "a mile wide and an inch deep," and that 2) Japan, a regular high scorer spent 44% of their time on "inventing, thinking, and struggling with underlying concepts" while US students were engaged in these same behaviours less than 1% of the time.

Her summary of American classrooms:

> Many times, I have observed students asking for help and teachers structuring the work for students, breaking down questions and converting them into small easy steps. In doing so, they empty the work of challenge and opportunities for struggle. Students complete the work and feel good, but often learn little. (p. 53)

Keeping this in mind, Boaler, while in China, also observed math lessons in classrooms. She reports:

> In a number of high-school math classrooms, lessons were approximately one hour long, but at no time did I see students working on more than three questions in one hour. This contrasts strongly with a typical US high-school math classroom, where students chug through about thirty questions in an hour—about ten times more. The questions worked on in Chinese classrooms were deeper and more involved than the ones in US classrooms. (p. 54)

High schools, as compared to elementary schools, do not display student thinking with assignments (including unfinished work) on classroom walls/school hallways. 'To be continued' is important because it leads to considering next steps/choices and other problem-solving efforts over simply grading the work. It is thinking in progress.

There is safety in numbers. Peer partners or even small groups—carefully chosen by both the students and the teacher, reduce the risk to individual learners. Schools with programs such as RTI (response to intervention) where diagnosing individual students' learning challenges early is followed by immediate attention also reduces students' feelings of risk. Peer tutoring, resource teachers, educational assistants, and auxiliary parent programs including extra reading support in primary grades or Later Literacy for upper grades, offer such supports.

Furthermore, the required norm at the classroom level is that taking risks is essential for learning. Teachers admitting errors in thinking or in execution need to model risk-taking by demonstrating visible thinking routines such as: "I used to think…but now I think," where teachers stress improvement, not standards.

Rubrics, constructed with the participation of the class, also come into play. Instead of being confined to scorekeeping, they are better used as guidelines for improved performance. Formative assessments without marks/grades send the same message. It takes time and error to succeed. Resiliency, along with feelings of confidence, are the product of taking public risks. Feeling safe reduces the risk of trying.

While clarifying expectations for district goals as well as those within each subject is important, the thought arises that Maja Wilson's criticisms in *Rethinking Rubrics in Writing Assessments* (2006) apply not only to writing but to most high school courses.

She asserts that while success criteria for writing outcomes help clarify expectations for both processes and products, rubrics should not drive instruction. They should not be, as some teachers and students believe, a guide to getting good marks. It's not that they are totally bad; they just don't tell the whole story. As she puts it, "quality is more than the sum of its rubricized parts" (p. xv).

Another critic, Linda Maybry, a department of teaching and learning professor at the Vancouver Campus in Washington State, maintains that rubrics tend to produce vacuous writing—no depth of thinking. That is the difference, she claims, between good ideas presented in a standard communicative format, and great ideas set out in a more penetrating, creative way that inspires more complete understanding, relationships, insights, and higher levels of knowing.

There are others. Within "Thinking through Assessment," a chapter in *Adolescent Literacy: Turning Promise into Practice* (2007), Linda Rief, in a discussion with other language consultants, had this to say:

> I worry, Devon, about all the resources for rubrics and checklists that you mentioned. I, too, often see these printed as posters, with kids having little understanding of what these lists mean and how they could use them. *Too often*

teachers use them to assess students with little understanding themselves of how to teach or how to succeed at accomplishing these characteristics or traits. And if they don't know, how can the students figure them out? (p. 267, [emphasis added])

The importance of clarifying expectations remains. To that end, Susan Brookhart, in her book, *How to Create and Use Rubrics for Formative Assessment and Grading* (2013), recommends the following:

1. Start with a dozen or more copies of student work. These should be different tasks so that the rubrics reflect performance descriptions for general learning outcomes, not specific assignments.
2. Have students sort their work into three piles: high, medium, and low quality based on the concepts and skills involved.
3. Students/teachers write specific descriptions for each pile. Focus on what was done and why each piece is categorized as it is. Be as specific as possible.
4. Compare and contrast the descriptions and determine criteria for each.
5. For each criterion, write descriptions of quality at as many levels as you need depending on how many distinctions you see as useful.

She also described positive evidence for the use of rubrics: Hafner and Hafner (2003) investigated college biology students' use of rubrics for *peer assessment and teacher assessment* of a collaborative oral presentation. There were five criteria: organization and research, persuasiveness and logic of argument, collaboration, delivery and grammar, and creativity and originality. Originally the rubric was developed and then modified with discussion and involvement of the students.

The same rubric was used for a required course assignment three years in a row. The instructors determined that peer evaluation was accurate, matched teacher input, and was consistent across classes. Students were able to accurately give feedback to their peers, and their information matched that of their instructor.

Her advice includes the following points:

1. The best rubrics are those built with students. They help define the criteria.
2. Students contribute their prior knowledge, thus inspiring ownership.
3. Common curriculum outcomes are supported by deciding on criteria for success.
4. Focus on general knowledge/skills.
5. Only use for complex learning outcomes. Help students apply the criteria to examples.
6. Students need to look at their own work, decide which criteria are appropriate and which are not, then develop an action plan for improvement. This process moves students forward in providing their own feedback—an important ingredient in becoming self-sufficient.

One alternative to rubrics is people—fellow learners in the same boat. Maja Wilson recommends such collaborative feedback in her writing classes. Students respond to sections of a classmate's writing with how they feel about an introduction, paragraph, sentence, or entire piece of writing and why. This process improves with practice. Reading and examining direct responses to either your own work or others: "I like the introduction because…" or "I don't like it because…" start with feelings and include suggestions.

Such feedback includes what might be there instead of simply correcting for mistakes in grammar, spelling, and sentence construction. This process allows a student to see their writing and alternatives through the eyes of others. This applies to my own efforts; I look at sections of this book and imagine how a teacher, a principal, a superintendent, a parent, or a high school student might respond. I also know authors who tape their writing, then listen to their words being played back as if they were hearing them for the first time.

Maja sees collaborative support from teachers and fellow students as vital in the teaching/learning needed for speaking and writing. The reader/listener is invited to pay attention to the following: How do these words affect me? What does the paper make me think? "How do the writer/speaker's choices contribute to or take away from *the way these words interact with my thinking?*" (p. 38).

What is apparent is that you can't teach writing the same way I used to teach mathematics—piece by piece, step by step, drill and skill. Quality feedback depends on finding insight through disagreement. Ladder of Feedback has its place here—fellow students seeking clarification, expressing appreciation or concern about a portion of the writing along with comments/suggestions.

Maja Wilson: "If we start with the assumption that we should read our students' writing in the same way we read literature, we can borrow many of the methods we use to teach reading and response" (p. 95).

Reading Response: agreement/disagreement with the ideas in the text. Reaction to how the ideas in the text relate to your own experience. Reaction to how ideas in the text relate to other things you've read. Your analysis of the author and audience. Your evaluation of how this text tries to convince the reader and whether it is effective.

These strategies can be modeled for students—write aloud/think aloud is one way of engaging in such feedback in a fluid manner, a direct contrast to checklists and static rubrics in its public thinking and immediate feedback.

They also apply to other subjects; problem solving aloud in mathematics and the sciences, modeled by teachers, then practiced in dyads or other small groups by our students. Thinking is analyzed together with feedback close to the action.

I recall Dr. Riffel and faculty education colleagues at a meeting responding to my master's thesis—an action research intervention at Brooke School in Rivers, Manitoba. At one point, I was asked to clarify what I had written. I did, and the immediate response was, "Write that." Personal and immediate feedback at its best.

Maja recommends graphic organizers. A matrix to keep track of suggestions: who says what, why they say it, and what the writer decides to do as a result. Her point is that assessment is not always done after the student is finished. Writers assess on the fly, choices based on some assessment already made. This is equally accurate for learning of any kind. Assessment woven throughout all secondary school subjects.

She and her students don't use such words as organization, word choice, or voice. Their common language is about making subjective responses public, transparent, and useful. They rearranged the writing, decided on what words worked best, compared how their words were perceived by others, and became, in her view, "more and more expressive in their writing."

She points out that Duke University in 2002 recognized the role of receiving meaningful feedback on applicant's admission essays. Applicants were told that since sharing, feedback, and revision were important to composing, they should list those who provided help and how they were helped.

Read aloud-think aloud, or thinking aloud in problem solving during mathematics and science classes are opportunities for teachers and students to acknowledge dead ends, and errors in thinking. Perhaps the school should pass out T-shirts with the slogan. "I tried, I failed, I conquered," or "No risk-no win." This reminds me of a classmate at the University of Alberta (Edmonton) who bragged that he was taking Ed Psych 952 while the rest of us were only taking Ed Psych 476 because he was repeating the course.

The above applies to teachers. We too are afraid of making mistakes, often fearing the same level of criticism as we did when we were students. Again, the strategies for reducing risk are the same as the suggestions for managing students' risks.

This observation is backed by a comment in "Spirals of Inquiry For equity and quality," Judy Halbert & Linda Kaser (2016):

> Years ago, after a few days in a first teaching position, one of us was approached by a couple of experienced colleagues who cautioned that being too open in asking questions, seeking help or exposing vulnerabilities were not professionally smart behaviors. This could have been the end of a promising career had not a wise principal refuted their advice. Nevertheless, the message was loud and clear. (p. 68)

Jo Boaler (2009) exemplifies the difference between fixed praise and growth praise as "You have a degree in science? You are a genius!" as compared to, "You have a degree in science? You must have worked really hard."

Guy Claxton et al. in *The Learning Powered School* (2013), also recommend "using comments that focus on effort, habit, and disposition…not on carving the world into things they are 'good at' or 'not good at'." Their advice comes with a warning:

> However, there can be a problem with praising people too much for effort, as there is with praising them for ability. If a pupil has already picked up on the fixed-mindset bug, they can easily hear praise for effort as a confirmation of their lack of ability… The safest thing is for teachers to develop the habit of interesting their students in the learnable skills and strategies that underpinned their performance, and to be continually looking for ways to expand and strengthen those learning muscles. (p. 80)

Amy L. Eva, writer of an article entitled "Why We Should Embrace Mistakes in School" also focuses on learnable skills and strategies. Her cited research compared a "direct instruction" group, where students learned step by step how to solve mathematical problems with a second group called "productive failures".

"Productive failures" struggled alone until the teacher intervened, helped analyze mistakes with the students, and then, together, they determined the correct solution. In the final test, common for both, productive failures came out on top for both simple and complex problems. The difference is palpable: ownership is critical for building confidence *and* success. Productive failures were taking charge of their learning, albeit with some help, whereas the direct instruction group was copying ideas.

Eva also described new research suggesting overconfidence as an asset. It seems the more confident you are in your incorrect response, the more likely you are to embrace the new learning. This is consistent with cognitive dissonance. Being confident and then learning you misunderstood by a wide margin reinforces corrective feedback. The greater the margin of error on your first response, the more interest/focus you have in getting it right.

The first years of my career included teaching Euclidean geometry to grade 10/grade 11 students in Minitonas, Manitoba. Deductive reasoning. Each problem required students to prove a required outcome using past deductions (theorems) and assumptions (postulates) along with some given relationships. It was a compulsory university entrance course. No other levels were available. And no other high school course employed, in its consistency, such deductive reasoning.

Each problem included a labeled geometric diagram or a description for the student to construct:

Diagram:

Given: _____
Required to prove: _____

Statements Reasons

_____ _____
_____ _____

Therefore, _____ (Reason)

This was half of Mathematics 10; the other half was algebra. For algebra I chose at random 8–10 students to work at chalkboards (two chalkboards per room, the rest seated at their desks in traditional rows) while I dictated improvised questions from the back of the room.

This was all about immediate feedback/guided practice, but even when I detected errors (easily observed at the boards) or those at their desks (I moved up and down the aisles like an osprey flying over Shuswap Lake—eyes sighted on fish/key errors), I simply put my finger next to them. That was often enough. In short order they would hear a step-by-step explanation of the correct process from a student. Day after alternate day—boring for those who learned more quickly, for others essential for success.

That took care of the routines. But the real challenge, as mathematics teachers know, is students applying algebra to problem solving. This is where modeling the thinking can help, along with productive failing/individual support from the teacher and other students. Such thinking requires visualization, sequence, recognizing relationships, working backward, seeing the situation from different points of view, and then representing the variables with symbols.

Geometry is not so different. Learning to apply comparison and contrast, visualization—especially useful with rotations, translations, and reflections; and transferring past reasoning to new geometrical configurations takes deeper thinking and time.

Beyond the fundamentals, students worked alone at their desks. Only when they had completed the problems in the text could they move to a table at the back of the room and individually or collaboratively, solve the extra-tough problems I dreamed up or copied from past provincial exams.

I didn't ask them to hand in their work and I never marked it. They were responsible for finding their own mistakes—with help. I sat at my desk with a pencil and blank sheets of paper, and the textbook opened. When they struggled enough and felt lost, they left their seats and stood behind my desk. My job was to provide as *little* help as possible. Sometimes asking where they felt stuck and responding with either one clue, or, as I recall, simply pointing to one or another feature of the geometric diagram, a related theorem, or what was given, or to a particular reason for a statement.

This is an example of immediate, useful feedback—not the same effect if received a day or three later. Students need minimal support at the time of their struggles. Too much is just as bad as too little. These were my 'productive failures', admittedly at a smaller scale than the previous researched example, but still effective.

At times there were three or four students looking over my shoulder. Often, as I recall, when pointing out one feature of the diagram/problem based on student comments, one or more of the students left without a word—they had seen the light. They never handed in their "work," and the tougher the problems, the more they seemed to enjoy the class.

I never gave tests beyond compulsory school Christmas and Easter exams in any of the grades (9–12) nor homework where they could practice mistakes, ineffective thinking, or confusion. This is not to say these are always bad. But my experience at the time led me to believe that too much struggle on your own without support doesn't end well. Enrichment for homework—yes. Learning the fundamentals—no. This experience similar to the positive qualities of the productive failures in the research discussed earlier.

I didn't waste any of the thirty-seven minutes per class by looking to see if they had completed homework or what consequences I could dream up as punishment. I have never regretted not trying to distinguish between students who could have done it, but didn't, and those who needed help. I taught my last grade twelve class in Minitonas from grade nine to graduation. Their average mark on the grade twelve final provincial examination was close to 90% with no failures. The average failure rate over the province in those years ranged from 25% to 40%.

This success was heavily supported by context missing today. Semesters didn't exist; there were no five month *or longer* interruptions to learning mathematics. Second, I taught these students for the previous three years (grades nine to eleven). I knew them well, both as mathematics students and as people. Today, in most high schools, math teachers teach one or two grades—with little experience in what their students have already learned or what they need for later learning. Compared to my four years with the same students, they have five months.

I contemplate the usefulness of secondary school mathematics; such a small fraction of students goes on to further study/use in occupations. One thought is that past success instills confidence when encountering any new learning—positive reflection bolstering assurance in other situations—all embracing struggle. Another is Shayer's evidence that deeper thinking in one subject improves learning capability overall.

What was considered success in the past, though, won't cut it now. Recognized goals for students then—achieving high grades, getting along with teachers, and working hard. At times, such goals as learning to learn or productive citizenship were espoused at graduation ceremonies, but that was about it.

John Holt (1964) had some things right. He pointed out that when a student makes an error, teachers rarely attempt to find out why. The thinking that led the student astray is never determined. Instead, the student is simply told the right answer. Unless erroneous thinking is addressed, the same error will be repeated.

Presently, high schools ignore mistakes and reward right answers. Exactly the wrong approach; discussion of wrong answers leads to exploring paths to both correct and incorrect solutions, all leading to resilience for future hard slugging.

Boaler J. (2019):

> For students to experience growth, they need to be working on questions that challenge them, questions that are on the edge of their understanding. And they need to be working on them in an environment that encourages mistakes and makes students aware of the benefits of mistakes. This point is critical. Not only should the work be challenging to foster mistakes; the environment must also be encouraging, so that the students do not experience challenge or struggle as a deterrent. Both components need to work together to create an ideal learning experience. (p. 49)

We need more professional learning in this area. I recall Dr. Tony Riffel, as head of Administrative Studies in Education at the University of Manitoba, describing an 'Error Analysis' course for teachers in the early seventies. This coincides with Holt's comments—error analysis as a stepping stone for determining how a particular student thinks.

Knowing students well is critical for teachers' ability to accelerate students learning from each other. As an example, Jane Kise (2014) points out that extroverts gather energy from interaction with others, while introverts prefer solitude and reflection. These predilections suppress each student to a degree, but she maintains everyone is capable, over time, of improving collaborative learning *and* reflective dispositions.

One example of making thinking visible is a Physics 11 lesson in Shanghai. Because my students were well on their way to being prepared for the final examination in June (going beyond memorization, use of formulas, and problems from previous final examinations) there was room for more.

Taking a page out of Vacca and Vacca's book, *Content Area Reading: Literacy and Learning Across the Curriculum, Tenth Edition* (2011), an old friend from my days as a high school consultant, we spent time improving reading and language skills using the physics text from day one—almost mandatory for second language students.

Early on, we worked on key words identifying cause and effect, comparison and contrast, sequence, problem-solution, different ways of identifying the meaning of a word through context, close reading, checking for understanding, especially of graphs and tables, and semantic webs to assist connections with prior knowledge. They used classmates as an important resource, and good memories developed over time. One of my students told me, as a six-year-old, he had memorized over three thousand language symbols. They all did.

Instead of the usual physics labs back home where students follow step by step instructions leading to a known result and are then graded on how well they describe their efforts, I wanted them to at least taste what physicists do—predict. Too often students learn *about* writing, physics, and history but are offered pathetically few experiences *as* writers, historians, mathematicians, or physicists. Writing (the only way anyone learns to write), across all high schools, is granted little time, almost always confined to a few pages.

Directions: Set up an inclined plane consisting of a length of aluminum approximately 3 feet long and 8 inches wide. Use books to raise one end on a table where the lower end is a distance from the table's edge. Each of the five groups of 4–5 students to select a steel ball. The task appears simple enough: to *predict the horizontal distance traveled by the ball beyond the lip of the table before it strikes the floor*. Same size ramps, students choose height, distance from the ramp bottom to the edge of the table, and ball weight. Tape measures and weight scales available.

Each group prepares a presentation to the class with calculations along with their prediction and result. This requires group planning, communication skills, clear assumptions, and collaborative learning. Needed understanding: ratio and proportion, similar triangles, force resolutions, sequencing, and analyzing disparities between prediction and the actual result. Knowledge of how mass, distance, force, acceleration, and velocity are related is essential. No trial runs before the prediction. It would have spoiled the fun.

Visualization, like all abilities, improves with use. This prediction reminds me of Einstein riding a ray of light when developing his theory of relativity. Different points of view can be helpful. Relevant experiences could be roller coasters (available in Shanghai), a toboggan full of people going down a snow-covered hill (not so much), wheelchair ramps, playground slides, or skateboards on slopes.

There are three stages to be considered: (1) the ball rolling down the incline, (2) the ball rolling horizontally to the edge of the table, and (3) the ball falling through the air until it strikes the floor. Except for rolling friction and air resistance, the horizontal velocity after reaching the bottom of the incline remains constant until the ball strikes the floor.

The emphasis is on thinking awareness, followed by reflection as part of their presentations. Teacher role: to observe students' thinking and not do it for them. The process then involved group planning, predictions, execution, and student presentations to the entire class. This took close to a week. I observed group meetings and answered some questions without taking over the thinking. Presentations, including questions and comments from the rest of the class, took two, seventy-minute periods.

Each group chose their own slope, steel ball, and distance from the table edge. There would be no right answer for all. Being close to their prediction was the goal, but the analytics on why they were off the measured result were just as important. Rolling friction vs sliding friction, choice of slopes, and distances from the bottom of the plane to the edge of the table were all part of the extended questions and answers during the presentations.

Was there cognitive dissonance? When a group calculated their prediction, the horizontal distance traveled by the steel ball through the air after being released, did this surprise any students based on any similar real-life experience? Did the calculation seem unrealistic? What other expectations based on past knowledge/experience could be part of the learning here?

The concept of gravity bears scrutiny. At times, I believe, students find right answers without a clear understanding of the concepts involved. I was especially tuned into students' conversations that indicated such misunderstandings.

Wagner T. & Dintersmith T. (2015) had the same concern:

> Advanced high school math students take calculus, performing tasks like computing closed form integrals. For problems like these, students will do categories of problems in class (e.g. integration by parts), reinforced by homework assign-

ments. They succeed on exams if they can recognize which category the problem belongs to, recall the procedural steps required to solve it, and carry out the computation. (p. 89)

An erroneous example from an anonymous internet contributor: "Ski straight down a slope twice, once with a 25 lb weight strapped to your back and once without. Your terminal velocity will be higher with the weight because the gravitational pull will be higher, but the aero drag will be the same."

This miss understanding that acceleration from the greater pull of the earth on the larger mass is exactly offset by the increase in pull needed to accelerate that same mass. Galileo at the Leaning Tower of Pisa observing heavy and light balls hitting the ground simultaneously with the same acceleration/final velocity. Cognitive dissonance for bystanders sometime between 1589 and 1592.

Appreciation for physics in solving real situations, the value of group work in advancing individual learning expertise, and pride in presenting their thinking went beyond memorization/standard problem solving in the past. Reflecting on the physics lesson and similar prediction opportunities over the following month, I summarize our learning together as paying particular attention to the kinds of thinking needed to be successful predictors: visualizing the ball accelerating down the plane, along with force changes in each of the three stages, as an example.

What I did observe from my student desk within the class, was an improvement in the quality/enthusiasm of questions asked each group from the rest of the class during/after their presentation. Others were social-emotional outcomes that flowed from working together while applying their knowledge of physics.

Concluding questions often say more about the quality of learning than anything else: What effect could the table not being perfectly horizontal have on your computations? How would that skew the result? Does the ball roll down or slide down, or is it a combination? How can you determine the coefficient of rolling or sliding friction directly? Which is more difficult to measure? How does the angle of inclination affect those variables? How would your prediction be different if it were conducted on the moon? How does the weight or size of the balls affect the horizontal distance from the edge of the table to the point of impact? If you had to repeat choices within the physical setup or your calculation process, what changes would you consider?

The discrepancy between each prediction and the actual result *is* the rubric. Success is dependent on applying theoretical physics, deciding context variables (choice of angle of inclination, distances, and steel ball), and making thinking visible through group presentations, and analysis of efforts/reflections. The individual queries/suggestions from the audience contributing to deeper understanding—a blend of quantitative and qualitative data.

Ellen Oliver Keene's tenth grade US history demonstration lesson in Charlotte, North Carolina, described in *Adolescent Literacy: Turning Promise into Practice* (2007) is related. The lesson was in response to local teachers' concerns that their students: 1) did not remember concepts almost immediately after being tested, 2) could not understand what they read, 3) refused to discuss ideas, 4) were unable to transfer ideas from one situation to another, and 5) were primarily focused on assignment length/what would be tested.

Her purpose was to "work with teachers who were interested in weaving *comprehension strategy instruction* into their content area coursework" (p. 28, [emphasis added]).

She began by demonstrating the use of 'way-in' texts—picture books and short pieces of text students can use to build background knowledge (schemata) that provide a way "in to understanding more abstract, concept- and vocabulary-laden texts" in preparation for student understanding of a series of complex essays marking the fiftieth anniversary of the *Brown v. Board of Education* ruling.

Using Toni Morrison's photo-essay book *Remember: The Journey to School Integration* (2004), where the author "writes from the point of view of the subjects in the photos," she began by sitting the students on the floor to create a sense of intimacy much like in elementary schools (not a small reason, I think, for the lesson's success). She then did *read aloud-think alouds* for the early pages of the book, while allowing students to see the photos. This is Madeline Hunter's classic anticipatory set—the purpose is to focus students' attention on the lesson, creating an organizing framework for the ideas, principles, or information to follow. It also fits with Hattie's surface information foundation for deeper thinking.

Her focus was *determining importance*. After reading a few pages, she *shared her sense of the most important concepts*, then invited students to state their opinions. She continued this process three or four times, "and before long, the kids had jumped into the conversation, making clear what they thought was important and defending their points of view with examples from the text" (p. 30).

Keene:

> These sophomores engaged in some spirited discourse about the notion of separate but equal and shed light on some aspects of school segregation I honestly had never considered. By the final stages of the conversation, I had become obsolete, removing myself to one side of the room as the students considered their interchange, now oblivious to the observing teachers. (p. 30)
> She then invited the teachers to debrief the lesson by asking the students questions. They wanted to know why the students were so actively involved compared to regular classes. Students told them they 'never truly understand' either the concepts they read about in class or listened to in teacher lectures; they described their experience as 'doing time', attending class, doing assignments and working for marks.
> They also explained why they wanted to discuss ideas in Keene's lesson: "After today, I finally get the whole Brown versus Board of Education thing. I mean, I didn't really know what separate but equal meant the way they define it in the textbooks, but those photographs were unbelievable—it wasn't separate, it was abusive. I wish I'd seen these photographs and read this book earlier." (p. 31)
>
> A teacher: "If teachers want you to get more engaged like this more often, what would you tell them to do?"
>
> Student: "Well, it seems like if we could just focus more on one thing and have time to talk about it, we'd really understand it more."
>
> Teacher: "Exactly what do you mean by *really* understand it?"
> Student: "You know, know it for longer than just the test." (p.31)

Keene's observations:

> Students were intoxicated with the intellectual nature of the conversation. They loved making and defending key points in the discussion. They were learning from each other's perspectives. They took the time to bring less-engaged students

into the conversation. They even related the cruelty of segregated schools to the dilemma faced by immigrants (legal and otherwise) in this country today. If they can engage and explore ideas like that occasionally, we must conclude that they are capable of doing it more frequently under the right conditions. (p. 32)

"Writing as a Mode of Learning", a chapter in Janet Emig's book, "The Web of Meaning: Essays on Writing, Teaching, Learning, and Thinking" (1983), compares successful learning strategies in general with those of writing—one strength being process and product in close correspondence. She observes that "higher cognitive functions, such as analysis and synthesis, seem to develop most fully only with the support of verbal language—particularly, it seems, of written language" (p. 123).

Writing is a powerful learning strategy; its availability as a medium for composing goes beyond all others. This uniqueness needs to be established/supported, she feels, "because so many curricula and courses in English still consist almost exclusively of reading and listening" (pp. 123–124).

Important characteristics of both writing and quality learning in general encompass immediate reinforcement and feedback, freedom to select, use of connections and propositions, hypotheses, and other summarizers. Emig sees three major ways in which we represent and deal with actuality (the contrast with intentions): (1) Enactive—we learn by doing; (2) Iconic—we learn by visualization; and (3) Symbolic or representational—we learn by "restatement in words" (p. 126).

The quality of feedback from writing is unique: "information from the process is immediately and visibly available as that portion of the product already written." (How they fit together). Re-scanning and review are instantly available. She describes clear writing as "that writing which signals without ambiguity the nature of conceptual relationships, whether they be co-ordinate, subordinate, superordinate, causal, or something other." All are characteristics of "engaged, committed, personal learning" (p. 127).

According to John Hattie's research, reciprocal teaching, a thinking/ learning comprehension strategy of summarizing, questioning, clarifying, and predicting abilities, is effective with second language learners, bilingual students, and those with disabilities.

This is an example of high-quality dialogue among peers with teacher support within cognitive acceleration. It also takes deliberate practice: Douglas Fisher, Nancy Frey, and John Hattie, in "Visible

Learning for Literacy: Implementing the Practices that Work Best to Accelerate Student Learning" (2016), suggest that comprehension strategies be practiced, then paired with subsequent strategies until students are proficient at all four.

This includes, in the beginning stages, assigning formal roles as summarizer, questioner, clarifier, and inference maker. In some schools, they report students using reciprocal teaching since grade three. Listening to group discussions provides valuable information for the teacher helping students choose what to look at next in their research.

More generally, Ritchhart et al. in "Making Thinking Visible: How to promote engagement, understanding, and independence for all learners" (2011) put forward the idea that understanding is not as low as listed in Bloom's taxonomy. "Today most educators would argue that understanding is indeed a very deep, or at least complex, endeavor…indeed, understanding is often put forward as a primary goal of teaching" (p. 7).

In retrospect, improving our capacity to learn is similar to the inclined plane—although we don't start in the same place, all of us, with hard work and support along the way, can accelerate our intelligence. The friction, obstacles, and resistance will not stand in our way. We are built for the long haul, so distance and time don't matter.

Chapter 5
Self-Regulation: Students as Independent Learners

Jennifer Katz in *Teaching to Diversity: The Three-Block Model of Universal Design for Learning* (2012), recognizes the confluence of academic success, emotional intelligence, and social learning:

> Ideally, all children would learn to be compassionate, kind, and responsible citizens of their communities, and the schools would have a role to play in this process. However, debate continues over the extent to which schools can, or should, devote time to social and emotional learning (SEL) while their primary responsibility is for academic learning. What is not recognized in this debate is the link between social and emotional learning and academic success. As research shows, strengthening students' sense of self in their school community actually increases their motivation to learn and their aspirations for greater knowledge and aca-

demic achievement. Zins, Bloodworth, Weissberg, and Walberg (2004). (p. 27)

Guy Claxton from *"Intelligence in the Flesh: Why Your Mind Needs Your Body More Than it Thinks"* (2015):

> We must begin by seeing our emotions as contributing to our ability to act intelligently, not as impediments to such action… There are times when we wish we had gone with our head rather than our heart. But reason and emotion are lifelong partners who occasionally tread on each other's toes, not sworn enemies. (p. 103)

We are seeking maturity: the ability to back off and face emotional, social, and cognitive threats with patience and thoughtfulness. This allows us to slow down, stay calm, and bounce back from failure. Previously discussed learning to learn attitudes, skills, and knowledge relevant here: gathering information, perseverance, working with others, learning from mistakes, responding to new situations, and reappraising thinking.

The teachers' role has changed. Ritchhart et al. from Making Thinking Visible: How to Promote Engagement, Understanding, and Independence for All Learners (2011):

> With the learner at the center of the educational enterprise, rather than at the end, our role as teachers shifts from the delivery of information to fostering students' engagement with ideas. Instead of covering the curriculum and judging our success by how much content we get through, we must learn to identify the key ideas and concepts with which we want our students to engage, struggle, question, explore, and ultimately build understanding. Our goal must be to make the big ideas of the curriculum accessible and engaging while honoring their complexity, beauty, and power in the process. When there is something important and worthwhile to think about and a reason to think deeply, our students experience the kind of learning that has a lasting impact and powerful influence not only in the short term, but also in the long haul. They not only learn; they know how to learn. (p. 26)

Cognitive conflict/dissonance, as stated, is used to describe psychological tension or perturbation created when individuals' expectations do not accord with their observations. They then seek to reduce this tension by reformulating their beliefs or by reinterpreting their observations. This can change their conceptual framework. In lesson design, cognitive conflict is engineered by the careful juxtaposition of information or experience.

Sequences designed to promote conceptual reorganization have three parts: an exposing event in which students are encouraged to describe their pre-existing conceptions and expectations, a discrepant event that generates cognitive conflict, and a resolution event in which students modify their conceptual understanding through individual reflection/discussion and debate with others.

The 2018 summer edition of *Canada's History* to its credit, exemplifies the above. The publication works with educators to actualize Peter Seixas' article, "Historical Thinking Concepts" (2017) of establishing historical significance (assessing relative importance, connections, and predicting).

Their goal is to bring life to the past and assist making the Canadian experience more meaningful and engaging to students by using primary source evidence, identifying continuity and change, analyzing cause and consequence, timelines, and considering historical perspectives that reference the social, cultural, intellectual, and emotional settings of the past (point of view, visualization, connections).

Another point of view: I recall a lecture theater with a professor making a presentation to teachers in Winnipeg MB. Stan Wilson, a Cree educator, sat next to me. For some reason, the professor mentioned Columbus discovering America. Stan immediately stood up and loudly proclaimed, "It's the other way around!" The professor looked confused, and finally looked in our direction. "It's the other way around," Stan repeated. "We found him on the beach!"

Excerpts from Seixas' article:

> For more than a century, democratic states have seen a tug-of-war between political demands to use school history to promote national solidarity, and a liberal educational vision of history to promote an engaged, literate, critical citizenry. (p. 1)

Historical thinking concepts are generative because:

> *They function, rather, as problems, tensions, or difficulties that demand comprehension, negotiation and, ultimately, an accommodation that is never a complete solution.* History takes

shape from efforts to work with these problems. Students' abilities to think historically can be defined in terms of their competence in negotiating productive solutions to them. (p.5, [emphasis added])

Seixas cites Graham Swift's 1992 novel, *Waterland*:

> The troubled history teacher and narrator, Tom Crick, lectures his resistant students who demand to know why they should be studying history, "*your demand for an explanation provides an explanation. Isn't this seeking of reasons itself inevitably an historical process, since it must always work backwards from what came after to what came before? And so long as we have this itch for explanations, must we not always carry round with us this cumbersome but precious bag of clues called History?*" (p. 106, [emphasis added])

Further support for student organization of curriculum content is offered by Tomlinson C. and Strickland C. (2005) through concept-based teaching:

> Concept-based teaching uses the essential concepts and key principles of a discipline as a primary way of organizing curricular content. For example, a history teacher might tell her students that history is full of 'CREEPS'. The acronym stands for Culture, Religion, Economics, Esthetics, Politics, and social issues. Students define each of the concepts in their own words, and these concept definitions give students a yearlong (and, in fact, lifelong) lens for viewing history. It also helps them make connections between their own lives, current events, and historical events. Principles that relate to each concept help students think more specifically about patterns in history. One key principle they might examine is, "People shape culture and culture shapes people." Students can see how this principle plays out in history and in their own lives. (pp. 350–351)

They discuss how culture-based differentiation affects our lives and how we may be unconscious of how it shapes us:

> It is easy to assume 'our way' is everyone's way. In education settings, this habit of thinking is particularly problematic

for students from minority cultures who attend schools shaped largely by the majority culture... Culture can affect how we relate to authority, whether we prefer contextualized or decontextualized learning, whether we feel constrained by time, whether we stress the individual or the group, and so on. There is a great variance of learning preference within each culture. The goal of culture-based differentiation is not to label or pigeon-hole students, but to understand and actively address the fact that a classroom that runs counter to a student's cultural norms and needs will impede that student's thinking. (pp. 350–351)

Schools expect students to learn without being taught how. The transition to self-directed inquiry with teacher guidance, the road less travelled, can improve the learning abilities of both teachers and students. We learn what we teach. Learning to learn attitudes, skills, and knowledge in teachers are expanded by teaching them to students. The learning to learn curriculum of Strang, Masterson, and Button (2006) emphasizes that importance. While teaching attitudes and dispositions are tough to teach explicitly, they stress the importance of students seeing them modeled by many teachers.

Classroom tips for students and teachers include making a conscious effort to use the language of thinking by using verbs such as 'extend', 'evaluate', 'justify', 'contrast', 'reinforce' as well as 'conditional'; phrases such as 'could be', 'might be', 'one possibility is', 'others think' or 'usually—but not always'. Naming thinking as it occurs also helps. For example, 'Brent is supporting Donna's ideas with evidence here', or 'Kevin is deciphering that strategy right now', or 'Cheri has laid out a thought-provoking comparison'.

It takes mindfulness to be totally aware of one's surroundings through hearing, touching, speaking, and tone. Questioning, according to Ritchhart (2011), is a good beginning. He insists the "What Makes You Say That?" routine requires the right tone—seeking information, but is not accusatory in terms of demanding evidence. Modeling such routines is a value-adding asset for any serious conversation/discussion where we wish to extend and clarify thinking.

Learning to learn principles:

Resourcefulness—selecting and obtaining resources to solve a problem or complete a task. Use of libraries, the internet, asking questions of others, creativity and intuition connected to prior knowledge, knowing what to do when stuck.

Reciprocity—having the right interpersonal and intrapersonal skills: examples are communication skills, learning from successful learners in groups as well as those who are less successful.
Resilience—self-discipline to be persistent in the face of distractions. *Response-ability*—to evaluate your performance and not repeat ineffective strategies/learn by doing.

Reflection—look back on experiences/past thinking with objectivity.

Descriptors of students who have learned to learn:

Self-confident, in charge of their own learning. Aware of the relevance of what they have chosen to learn. Access resources independently. See other students/teachers as partners. Set their own goals, self-assured, self-regulated. Demanding much of themselves as learners—not easily put aside. Doing the hardest things first. Know what they are learning and why.

Self-regulated learning, then, is students determining (with teacher help) what is to be learned, linking prior knowledge with the task at hand, filling in gaps with direct instruction/collaborative efforts with other students through connections, memorization, visualization, peer feedback, and new vocabulary; transferring understandings from one situation to another through comparison and contrast, summarizing the basics, practicing thinking routines, reading for a purpose, writing to learn, improving questioning, guided inquiry, and appreciating different perspectives from others.

Learning to bridge, the transfer of knowledge from one situation to another, will only be enhanced if it is part of the curriculum. As a subset, it needs instruction, practice, and reflection. According to Shayer, it is part of every learning opportunity. Each strategy/setting to be considered in other contexts. Explicit thinking in pursuit of such transfer can then be accomplished using student involvement routines such as visualization, think/pair/share, identifying thinking sequences, multiple causes and effects, false dichotomies, ascertaining variables, comparison and contrast, extensions, metaphoric thinking, and summarization.

For example, the term 'stabilizing' in fitness gyms describes the need to master and solidify specific routines/exercises before you increase weights/repetitions *or* add more routines. Early efforts to expand your choices/weight selection can lead to a deterioration of current capabilities. The same danger exists in schools. Too many changes, especially those not clearly linked to ongoing successful ones, can lead to backward slides. Too much is as bad as too little. Consolidating/stabilizing successes in schools, then, is critical for achieving superordinate goals.

In their book, *Spirals of Inquiry For equity and quality* (2016), Judy Halbert & Linda Kaser report that for years they have urged teachers to use *BC's Performance Standards* to assist in the transfer of learning ownership to their students. They observed that as teachers learned to use these effectively, students increased their ability to help themselves and others.

But they also report that after asking groups of teachers, "How many of you use the performance standards?" lots of hands go up. Then, after asking, "How many of you use the performance standards on a regular basis to co-create criteria with your learners?", *some* hands go up. And finally, after asking "How many of your learners use the performance standards on at least a weekly basis to coach themselves?", *few* hands go up (p. 58).

Evaluating teaching quality requires formative assessment designed and implemented by teachers: reflective self-evaluations along with regular input from students, principals, parents, and colleagues. Critical elements include how well teachers determine and support student thinking, function as part of a PLC, and make teaching choices/changes that improve student learning. As a joint endeavor, the process should not only assess teacher competency, it should generate it.

Judging the quality of teaching is no simple task—either by self-reflecting teachers, observations by other teachers, or their students. Ron Ritchhart (2015) draws our attention to its complexities when considering a study by Colorado researchers: "Controlling Teaching Strategies: Undermining Children's Self-Determination and Performance" (Flink et al. 1990), the object of which was to examine the effects of teachers having a *focus on learning* versus a *focus on performance/work*.

Two sets of teachers: one pressured to *maximize student performance*, the second told to simply *help students learn*. Student performance is assessed on the tasks initially taught <u>and</u> on a subsequent generalization task.

The results: (1) The combination of *work orientation* plus *controlling teacher behaviours* (more directive and evaluative) from pressured teachers *reduced* student performance on the follow-up generalization task, while (2) those teaching *with a learning orientation* did not. In fact, there was a small increase.

Pressured teachers attempted to maximize student performance in three ways: 1) control strategies and the absence of choice, 2) manipulation resulting in student feelings of tension, and 3) highly evaluative feedback (praise and criticism).

The study included nuances: The effect of competence information on students' achievement behaviours was found to be determined by whether information is perceived by students as an attempt to control behaviors versus providing information about skill level.

There was also a surprise: "Pressured teachers appeared significantly more interested, enthusiastic, and competent than their non-pressured counterparts. Finally, children taught by pressured teachers were rated as liking the teacher more" (p. 920).

In response, Ritchhart (2015) had this to say:

> One explanation for this rating is that there exists a widely held societal belief that pressuring students to achieve, providing highly structured support and evaluations of work, is a generally effective teaching technique and serves to enhance students' motivation and learning. (p. 54)

This has been the centrepiece of our educational history: demanding teachers getting results as *the* model of effective teaching. Also, belief in larger rewards (such as praise and recognition) as more effective than smaller ones, and that pressured students work harder and get better grades. But the overriding reason for controlling behaviour being detrimental, as Ritchhart states, is that *"fostering student independence exists as an important, worthwhile goal in its own right"* (p. 55, [emphasis added]).

Flink et al:

> From an applied perspective, this tendency for controlling teachers to receive high ratings has important implications. *Even though controlling strategies produce performance decrement, administrators and parents may highly evaluate teachers using such techniques because students may give*

> *the appearance of optimal teaching.* (p. 923, [emphasis added])

Another widely held society belief is natural ability over persistent learning. Angela Duckworth in her book, *Grit: The Power of Passion and Perseverance* (2016) reports Americans, when asked, "Which is more important to success—talent or effort?" they choose effort twice as often. Again, in psychologist Chia-Jung Tsay's study, participants, through questionnaires, endorsed "effortful training as more important than natural talent." But later, she discovered, after probing attitudes indirectly, "a bias that tips in exactly the opposite direction: we love naturals" (p. 23, [emphasis added]).

This and other studies led to Duckworth concluding that:

> What we say we care about may not correspond with what—deep down—we actually believe to be more valuable. It's a little like saying we don't care at all about the physical attraction in a romantic partner and then, when it comes to actually choosing whom to date, picking the cute guy over the nice one. (pp. 24–25)

Key elements of student feedback in aid of teacher improvement: rationale, specificity, guidelines, and respect. A team approach where teachers and students inform each other. Students to be forthcoming regarding their content or process thinking during lessons (one form of feedback) as well as assessing the quality of teacher support directly. The latter being a response to the first. This includes frank exchanges/hard conversations.

Feedback from students to teachers is relatively new. Hattie (2009), reflecting on such feedback:

> The mistake I was making was seeing feedback as something *teachers provided to students*—they typically did not, although they made claims that they did it all the time, and most of the feedback they did provide was social and behavioral. It was only when I discovered that feedback was most powerful when it is *from the student to the teacher* that I understood it better. When teachers seek, or at least are open to, feedback from students as to what students know, what they

understand, where they are making errors, when they have misconceptions, when they are not engaged—then teaching and learning can be synchronized and powerful. Feedback to teachers helps make learning visible. (p. 173, [emphasis added])

The improvement of the learning process is exactly that: making thinking visible—sets of strategies/routines seeking evidence, point of view, connections, assumptions, and relevance. This is part of a learning to learn curriculum advocating a sequence for students or teachers from what they know, to what they want to learn, and finally to how they want to learn it. It also addresses missing links in current teaching: activating prior knowledge and developing ownership/responsibility. Only after teachers know what students are thinking can they respond with quality support.

Both a fulcrum and a goal, *learning to learn* is a mix of *Unleashing the Positive Power of Differences: Polarity Thinking in Our Schools"* (2014) by Jane Kise where teacher support vs student initiative is exposed as a false choice, *and* Pearson & Gallagher's (1983) gradual release of responsibility, the progression from teacher modeling to independent application. Teacher progress is measured by how well students take responsibility for their own learning.

Common interim assessments, a subsystem of formative evaluations, define the success of professional learning communities. Appropriate data, both in terms of depth and timing, is essential to improving student achievement through better quality instruction.

The first step is PLCs determining a limited number of deep-thinking goals for each course by establishing transparent assessment methods at the beginning of the teaching and learning process, not at the end. Goals are defined by examples: if five teachers independently decide evidence for a particular outcome, we have five different standards, thus the need for a collective approach.

Effective feedback, as discussed, also requires building appraisal processes into every lesson. Where are the mistakes/strengths and how do we know what students are thinking? The difference between *common interim assessments* and *on-the-spot checking for understanding* is unit planning/strategic teaching aimed at improving progress toward year end results vs more immediate correctional responses.

Such responses take place minute-by-minute in individual classrooms. Bob Marzano, in *What Works in Schools* (2003), informs us that providing students with timely and specific feedback on their level of mastery accounts for higher gains than those provided by other school-based achievement factors, including parent and community involvement, safe and orderly environments, and collegiality in the schoolhouse.

Daily formative assessment is controversial. The consensus appears to be that comprehensive and timely assessment and feedback is possible, but demanding. And the reason is that teachers do all the work: collecting short written responses, mini tests, exit cards; reading them all, then categorizing the students according to mistakes is no small task. Other diagnoses of extensive writing, math problem solving, and scientific analysis, are just as difficult. All this in addition to creating models of expectations and rubrics.

Bill Ferriter, an eighth-grade science teacher working in a professional development community, begins an online commentary entitled "Is REAL Formative Assessment Even Possible?" (2011) with a conclusion: "timely feedback gathered and reviewed during the course of a learning experience that serves to *inform* both teachers *and* students and allows for the '*formation*' of new learning plans matters."
Important but daunting: in spite of the above, Ferriter was overwhelmed by the work and doubted if he could keep up the pace. An online response to Ferriter's comments from Chris Wejr (2011), another eighth-grade teacher, contains valuable advice:

> Students can self and peer assess as long as they understand the learning intentions and criteria. Many learning activities can be assessed through dialogue with students. You (addressing Ferriter) have done the three key things: clear learning intentions, clear criteria, and the use of descriptive feedback. Keep going with this and infuse a bit more each term/year rather than trying to do it all at once.

A related observation by John Hattie (2012):

> Many schools (especially high schools) resort to structural methods (for example, tracking/streaming, pull-out programs), but despite these methods all classes are full of heterogeneity (and this is more often or not advantageous, because students can learn much from each other). Teaching to these differences has become a mantra for some; in some cases *diversity is taken to extremes*—it merely means that all students are different. While there is no doubt that every student in the class is likely to be different, an art of teaching is seeing the commonality in diversity, in having peers work together, especially when they bring different talents, errors, interests, and disposition to the

situation, and *understanding that differentiation relates more to the phases of learning—from novice, through capable, to proficient—rather than merely providing different activities to different (groups of) students*. (p. 109, [emphasis added])

Jeffrey D. Wilhelm and Michael W. Smith, from their chapter in *Adolecent Literacy: Turning Promise into Practice* (2007), describe the "power of the flow" as contributing to students being fully engaged. They argue:

> *addressing individual interests* in an attempt to engage students, though doubtlessly valuable, can be extremely time consuming and is probably too difficult to achieve given the various students in each classroom and the many constraints placed on teachers. Situational interest, conditions in the environment generating focused attention that may or may not last, however, works for all students no matter their individual tendencies. (p. 233)

Note: "Situational interest is elicited by aspects of an object or a situation, such as novelty or intensity, or by the presence of interest-inducing factors contributing to the attractiveness of the situation" (Krapp, 1999).

The "power of the flow" is composed of sound principles. They set out its components: *Competence and control. Appropriate Challenge and Assistance to Meet the Challenge. Clear Goals and Immediate Feedback. Immersion in the Immediate. The importance of the Social.* (Beers K et al. (editors) of *Adolescent Literacy: Turning Promise into Practice* (2007), quote Robert E. Probst in *Tom Sawyer, Teaching and Talking* (2005), chapter 5, corroborating *competence and control*:

> The workshop model, presented so convincingly by Nancy Atwell and others, has demonstrated its effectiveness in eliciting hard work from students on both their reading and their writing. Allowing students some choice in their reading matter has encouraged them to read more widely and carefully. Giving them some respite from the five-paragraph theme and inviting them to write about matters of interest to them has kept them at the keyboard with a bit more enthusiasm. (p. 45)

In a studio atmosphere/workshop of quiet concentration, students and teachers whisper in deference to adjacent thinking and composing. Conferencing with individual students, stool in hand, the teacher moves quietly from student to student. Again, the focus is on increased learning ownership.

This workshop model fits between high schools' typical lecture followed by homework and the self-regulated learning approach advocated here. A move in the right direction as students become increasingly independent. All measured in terms of student choice, decision making, and results. A critical issue is the time for teachers to work with individuals and small groups. In this regard, Faye Brownlie and Leyton Schnellert (2009) quote West Vancouver teachers. Commenting on their students' laptop research project, they appreciated the level of student engagement:

> One of the surprises of this project has been how much more interactive time I have had with my students. They are so engaged with their work that I can move from student to student, coaching and providing specific feedback. I hadn't expected this. There are simply no management issues, and I have so much more time to teach. (p. 7)

The above are examples of formative assessments for all students. Each subject will have its own opportunities. For instance, guided content reading in social studies/science using a variety of texts with matching concepts but differing instructional reading levels similar to Nancy's workshop format.

Terry Roberts and Laura Billings in "The Paideia Classroom: Teaching for Understanding" (1997) on formative assessment:

> Traditional forms of evaluation stress the teacher's obligation to measure a student's knowledge and skill at key points during the year—at the end of chapters or thematic units, and at midterm and final exams. The teacher is the authority in the classroom and holds power over how and when students are "graded." This pattern often renders students passive, even resentful of classroom practice. A Paideia teacher does judge the relative quality of student work, but his or her classroom also features teacher self-and peer-assessment, and, perhaps most powerful of all, collaborative assessment by all involved of their common work… It is built on two as-

sumptions: that the teacher is a model learner and that students must learn to take responsibility for the quality of their own work. Ultimately, re-defining how they communicate with each other at every level—and that communication is, in the final analysis, the core of evaluation and assessment. (pp. 61–62)

Thought should be given to developing additional support for writing expertise: student helpers who love writing, learn the suggested practices above, and share the load with writing teachers. All within core modeling of writing/reading in all subjects as well as *analyze aloud-solve alouds* for math and science thinking. We learn what we teach.

Visible Learning for Literacy: Implementing Practices That Work Best to Accelerate Student Learning (2016) by Douglas Fisher, Nancy Frey, and John Hattie describes lesson planning as Backward Design; determining the steps needed to achieve outcome(s) by addressing surface information instruction and types of deeper thinking needed.

Acquiring and consolidating surface information requires such learning skills as repeated reading, distinguishing working memory from long-term memory, connecting concepts, mastering key vocabulary, summarizing information, note-taking on lectures, memorizing techniques, note-making on readings/videos, close reading, read-aloud/think-alouds, noticing/observation skills, annotating text, peer tutoring, memorization, and collaborative learning through small group interaction, write/pair/share, making thinking visible routines, and teacher support by direct instruction amid ongoing formative assessment.

Jonathan Bergmann and Aaron Sams, in their booklet, "Flip Your Classroom: Reach Every Student in Every Class Every Day" (2012), advocate moving away from teacher lectures to more diversified learning. They begin with the reflections of Jennifer Douglas, a Georgia high school teacher:

> Teaching under a traditional model is draining. I feel like I have to 'perform', which requires energy, enthusiasm, and a 'you are on-stage' effort at all times. I remember last year driving to work, thinking: "Man, I feel like just being a student today. I wish I could go in and let someone else do all the work—be in the passenger seat for once."

> When I switched over, I felt free. I was able to go in and watch my students work. I don't mean that I sat back and drank coffee—I stayed busy interacting one-on-one; working with kids who were struggling; addressing questions that students had that I never had time for before; really getting to know my kids. It is just that the burden of learning had traded hands. And you know, really, it had to be passed on. I can't force someone to learn—they have to accept that responsibility for themselves. This method allows them to clearly see that-and give them a structured environment that ensures success. (p.17, [emphasis added])

Flipping replaces traditional teacher lectures followed by homework with students viewing teacher-made videos before coming to class, then engaging in diversified learning at school. The videos in support of the direct instruction/pre-emptive learning of surface information. Instead of a classroom packed with teacher talk and relatively few student questions, the expectation is that teachers have more time (as Jennifer reported) to work with students one-on-one or in small groups.

Recognizing direct instruction as separate from "lectures and other forms of passivity," Oakley et al. (2021) has suggestions for turning lectures (videotaped or otherwise) into direct instruction:

> The teacher chunks carefully thought-out nuggets containing the key ideas of a lecture into short snippets. These brief golden nuggets of information are then interspersed with plenty of retrieval, practice, small-group discussion, and other ways of allowing the students to work more actively with the material than just listening and watching.
> The reality is, learning complex, biologically secondary material is not a spectator sport—it demands that students actively grapple with the material. The grappling can be as simple as reviewing notes with a partner after a five-to seven-minute presentation. (p. 100)

Classrooms, nonetheless, including those that are flipped, require a tandem focus on *teaching students how to learn* and *gradual release of responsibility*. Ground-breakers that seem to have escaped flipping enthusiasts. That and the need for collaborative learning communities—also never mentioned.

Wagner T. and Dintersmith (2015) agree: They concluded that flipping, *"while a modest advance in efficiency, falls far short of the degree of innovation we urgently need"* (p. 199).

It is still possible flipped classrooms can increase the appeal for self-regulated students working through problems and engaging in collaborative learning with teacher guidance. These benefit learning because the learner is actively generating meaning instead of passively receiving information. In the flipped classroom, this classroom learning is guided by teachers; such support is not available during homework.

Some thoughts on the use of videos (in or out of school):

1. Teacher-made videos are aa valuable part of direct instruction.
2. Motivation is enhanced through increased student choice.
3. One drawback is that not all students have access to online teacher videos or computers at home/access to the internet. The use of school computers after school is one answer. Even better is providing take-home computers along with textbooks.
4. PLC's videotaping meetings as models for student collaboration in the classroom.
5. Support for students missing school.
6. Pausing videos/ repeating sections to think over what was said/demonstrated.
7. Teacher/student modeling/demonstrating learning outcomes.
8. Group presentations for school assemblies.
9. Support for community members/parents taking courses without full attendance in classrooms.
10. Student demonstrations of achievement.
11. Demonstrating/documenting effective student improvement plans.
12. Modeling visible thinking routines.

The article, "The Flipped Classroom: Pro and Con" by Mary Beth Hertz (2015), summarizes the situation:

> So, in the end, why should we care so much about the flipped-classroom model? The primary reason is because it is forcing teachers to reflect on their practice and rethink how they reach their kids. It is inspiring teachers to change the way they've always done things, and it is motivating them to bring technology into their classrooms through the use of video and virtual class-

rooms like Edmodo and similar tools. As long as learning remains the focus, and as long as educators are constantly reflecting and asking themselves if what they are doing is truly something different or just a different way of doing the same things they've always done, there is hope that some of Dewey's philosophies will again permeate our schools. We just need to remember that flipping is only the beginning. (p. 1)

The Power of Making Thinking Visible: Practices to Engage and Empower All Learners by Ron Ritchhart and Mark Church (2020) confirms MTV strength through impact evaluations. They contend that combining core academic competencies with the interpersonal and intrapersonal abilities of collaboration, communication, and decision-making results in improved student confidence.

They emphasize how teachers reach kids:

> They become curious about their students' learning, how they are making sense of ideas, what they are thinking, and what ideas engage them. MTV both allows and asks teachers to know their students in a different way. Traditionally, we have known our students by their academic performance and the skills and knowledge they possess. Many school systems rely on end-of-school comprehensive exams to define students through a single reductive score. When we focus on students' thinking, we see them as much more. We become interested in how they come to know what they know, what questions they have, and what challenges they face. We no longer see these challenges as deficits but as interesting opportunities for exploration. This curiosity in our students' thinking further drives our efforts to make their thinking visible as a mechanism for better understanding them and providing more responsive instruction. (p. 11)

Schools comparing past achievement with post *Making Thinking Visible* data after several years:

Washington International School ranked 73rd as the most challenging high school in the United States by the Washington Post saw significant gains for average students over the previous year. Such gains were especially dramatic for students in the Second Language English classes, "where average scores went from 5.2 (on a 7-point scale) to 6.07" (pp. 13–14).

Universidad Technologica de Chile (University of Technology of Chile) in Santiago, where 152 students taught thinking routines out of 833 business students taking a core Cost and Budgeting course scored 1.3 higher than the rest on a 7-point scale—a 19% advantage over 32 different courses sections and three campuses.

Ritchhart's own research, although not directed at test scores, showed a significant effect on students' mega-strategic knowledge—awareness of strategies available to them as thinkers and learners. The effects are wide-ranging. Ritchhart and Church offer testimonials from elementary, secondary, and special needs teachers on their changed roles as teachers, improved formative assessment, and impact on students with disabilities.

From a grade three teacher in Michigan:

> To really focus on making thinking visible fundamentally changes the role of student and teacher. As I utilize thinking routines and document our learning, I notice my students speaking up more and guiding our learning. Focusing on students' thinking places the power in their hands and fosters a teacher-student relationship built on mutual trust and respect. (p. 5).

Secondary school teacher in Sydney, Australia:

> When I make my classes' thinking visible, it's like putting in a dipstick in to check the oil. I can immediately see what they do and don't understand. It's a cue to what I need to do next in my teaching. This is probably the biggest way that my teaching has changed since I started teaching 25 years ago. I'm now much more responsive to my students' thinking. (p. 5)

Secondary Speech and Language Pathologist in Rochester, Michigan:

> Witnessing nonverbal students with moderate cognitive impairments shift from struggling to answer assigned reading comprehension questions to proudly displaying their thinking has forever changed my view of supporting learners with neu-

rodiversity. Making thinking visible practices offer these students a path previously untraveled, giving them a voice, a purpose, and a sense of pride. I see a <u>huge shift in attitudes regarding the learning outcomes and thinking abilities</u> of these learners across our school. (p. 5)

The above is empirical evidence from the classroom: teachers' observations/evaluation on debriefing students, deeper thinking, reflections, and local assessments. You might note the emotional growth/positive dispositions that accompany improved cognitive growth—another testament to the confluent nature of thinking, feeling, and improved attitudes toward learning.

As a mathematics teacher at Assiniboine South School Division in Winnipeg, Manitoba, my principal asked if I would permit a group of district principals to observe a lesson. Their observations, relayed to me later, included special interest and appreciation for the lesson's debriefing.

As usual, ten minutes before the end of our seventy-minute class, we pushed tables aside and arranged chairs in a circle. The format was simple: students sat where they placed their chairs and spoke at their own volition. Same reflection sequences every day: they shared what they learned, spoke on thinking/feelings during the lesson, reflected on what they could do better, and projected what might come next.

Such reflections were often personal: going beyond feelings/thoughts on how they were doing in class to other concerns: disappointments, being judged by others, supporting and gaining support from friends, slowing things down when pressured, getting organized, the importance of physical health, and success in one area of your life as reassurance of capability in others. Piggy backing on ideas was common. For some, getting high marks was important while others focused on relationships.

At the time, I was involved with confluent education, a Manitoba ministry of education project aimed at connecting emotional and intellectual growth in schools. I recall sharing and demonstrating stress-reducing strategies with my students; we had a saying, "Lose your mind and come to your senses." Also, mindfulness or "staying in the now", a focus on awareness but not judging: breathing, body pressures, sight, taste, smell, listening, and touching—an appreciated break from thinking, hoping, worrying, remembering, and regretting.

Learning to learn was not a topic in schools at the time, but I consider the positive reaction of the principals the result of students' participation, respect for each other, thinking out loud, considered reflections, listening skills, and quality of questioning as we learned together.

Elmore (2008), based on extensive lesson observations, sees many teachers working too hard:

> The students were engaged and amused, and they were certainly weren't complaining. But when you looked at the classroom as a setting for *student work* it was clear that not much was happening. A straight transcript of classroom discourse, for example, would reveal that, in order to keep students' attention focused on the front of the room, teachers were asking predominately factual questions—questions that could be answered literally by the student pulling the information straight out of the text on the desk in front of them. When teachers did ask questions that required higher levels of cognitive demand—interpretation, argument, analysis—the overall pace of previous questions meant that waiting even a short period of time for a student response seemed like ages, so the teacher quickly moved on to the next question before the students could fully engage the previous one. (p. 240)

The traditional physical setup for learning in high schools has its drawbacks. Getting students to question or even answer questions is more than difficult, often reduced to teacher telling and a few top students responding. Sharing thinking among students is zero. Students questioning other students for evidence, point of view, relative importance, or a host of other perspectives doesn't exist. With such classes, Think-Pair-Share still works, but getting a wider range of participation doesn't happen.

We also have the advice/experience of Brownlie and Schnellert (2009):

> "In a classroom that focuses on assessment for learning, teachers' questions are open-ended and invite reasoning. Teachers listen in a respectful way, intent on understanding the students' thinking and in engaging in real discourse. Students are invited to question themselves, to use their questions to guide their learning, and to kindle their curiosity. Questions are not used for control or for quick guess-my-thinking games. All students are included in the discourse, so strategies such as no-hands may be used—that is, students do

not raise their hands to answer a question. Rather, we pose a question, students discuss possible answers with a learning partner, and then we call randomly on different students to answer the question." (p. 28)

My experience is that the best physical arrangement for class discussion is the circle; each student sees colleagues face to face, the teacher sitting in one of the chairs. If a teacher mini-lecture is needed, and it is at times (along with retrieval, practice, and small-group discussion), then we move from circle to horseshoe.

Elmore points to another problem. While some high school students prefer to have their teachers do their thinking for them, teachers have a similar issue when considering how to achieve important student learning goals; his observations concluded that teachers were generally shying away from new thinking: doing what they already knew rather than what was needed to produce results.

This reminds us of John Holt and the need to know what students are thinking before we can help them improve. Seeing the thinking is important. If mistaken thinking is not recognized as such by the student, there is no chance of replacing it with better thinking. Formative feedback is based on precise information on what is happening. Especially the thinking in students' heads.

Ritchhart (2011) holds that making thinking visible: 1) fosters deeper learning, 2) cultivates engaged students, 3) realigns the roles of students and teachers to mutual support, and 4) enhances formative assessment practice. Synonymously, it 5) accelerates learning (even when measured by standardized tests), and 6) escalates positive dispositions to think and learn. He stresses that routines need to be tried, reflected upon, and then retried. All within a culture of teachers learning from each other and their students.

Summit Educational Group, a private tutoring company, is in tune with self-differentiated learning. They call it "Individualized Pathways"—students progressing in separate learning paths but all working toward shared goals. Students choose which resources to review *and* the environmental conditions. Some might learn independently, others in small groups. Some require tutoring from a peer or teacher. Students take assessments when they feel ready. Learning is stressed over pace. There is no limit on the number of times a student can take an assessment, but this does not mean abandonment—if a student fails an assessment, help is available.

To consider self-differentiated instruction in current high schools, visualize a classroom of thoughtful students. Some at tables working alone or with a partner; two students, side by side, one reading to the other; another pair at a whiteboard putting together a concept map; some writing at computers or searching for information; others reading with pen poised over a notebook.

A group of three are conversing in chairs with another classmate videotaping them; two students are returning from the library in close conversation; another pair is teaching themselves vocabulary with flash cards: the word in one quarter, its opposite in another, a definition in the third, and a hand-drawn picture for the last. A nearby parent is listening to a student summarize a piece of non-fiction, both oblivious to the rest of the class.

Over in a corner, a pair of students have paused their teacher-made video presentation to discuss the content. In another, the same teacher is on a stool, back to the rest of the class, quietly listening to a student, her notebook resting on her lap. A few students are examining previous students' work on lesson outcomes taped to a wall: some completed, some not. The largest group of six students are seated in a semicircle facing a student doing a read aloud-think aloud from a textbook.

Another wall, titled Learning Outcomes, carries examples of learning products with the headings: Beginnings, Progression, and Proficient. On the opposite wall is a mini-banner: *What do I know related to the new learning? What should I learn first? How will I learn it? How will I know I have succeeded? What kinds of thinking will help me? What thinking routines might help here? How can I work with others?*

Also included is a concept map identifying kinds of thinking pertinent to learning choices: strategies, thinking routines, and learning to learn skills, dispositions, and knowledge. An ongoing summation of thinking as the class learns how to learn. Another is a visual of *the history of class thinking/learning categories that* assists students when up-dating documentation of their lesson thinking and reflection portfolios.

Developing quality instruction that adjusts lessons for different groups while having the same learning goals defines district success. Gail Boushey and Joan Moser's classroom research in "Daily 5" (2014) instills routines for students as independent reading, writing, and mathematics learners thus allowing teachers time to focus on re-teaching individuals or small groups:

> Looking back on our teaching practice, we see a definite progression in the way we have managed our literacy block. We began with a teacher-driven model that relied on busy-work, workbooks, packets, and inauthentic reading and writ-

ing activities, which resulted in low student engagement. We progressed to centers, then to a workshop model, and finally to where we are now. The Daily 5 is designed to teach children to build their stamina and independence in each of the Daily 5 tasks so they can fully engage in meaningful, authentic reading and writing for an extended time. The Daily 5 tasks are steeped in choice, which increases motivation and student intellectual engagement. While they are engaged in this authentic reading and writing, we are then able to work with children, conducting individual conferences and working with small groups based on their needs as a result of our assessments. (p. 11)

Although developed for elementary classes, let us consider their 10 steps for fostering student independence and success as applicable to high schools:

1. Identify what is to be taught (learned)
   Totally relevant to high schools: clear examples, non-examples, and rubrics (developed *with* the students). Illustrations of how the learning might fit within a deeper thinking continuum. Students often need learning intentions to be explicitly taught along with success criteria.
2. Set a Purpose and Create a Sense of Urgency
   What's in it for me? Secondary students also need to know why learning outcomes are useful. Clearly coincides with fostering student involvement/motivation.
3. Record Desired Behaviours
   We need to be as exact about desirable learning behaviours in high school as in elementary schools. Expectations should be visible to everyone. We should determine positive behaviours/ attitudes/ dispositions *with* the class and *why* they contribute to everyone's success. Chalktalk, one of Ritchhart's thinking routines, builds a class concept map starting with small groups where comments and suggestions are shared. Another example of the inductive organizational development principle discussed earlier.
4. Model Most-Desirable Behaviours
   The changed role of the teacher fits here. Teacher to model listening, kindness, and honesty in addition to thinking strategies, reflection, sequence, planning, and noticing. Discarding general praise in favour of recognizing specific accomplishments based

on effort, not intelligence, can be a positive step in developing students' confidence.

5. Model Least-Desirable Behaviours, then Most-Desirable Behaviours Again

   Exaggerating unhelpful behaviours, an awareness strategy within confluent education, works by drawing attention to their bad effects. For high school students, clearly identifying choices is an important part of the learning process. Desirable demonstrations include such positive attributes of group learning as active listening, summarizing, being specific, and staying on topic.

   What happens beyond the classroom is also critical. What students say, feel, or text away from school should be addressed. Again, inductive reasoning starts with gathering student concerns, identifying required strengths, and setting plans for students to support each other. Teachers courageously sharing past mistakes and how they led to improved learning helps students do the same.

6. Place Students Around the Room

   Offer high school students suggestions, not placements. Determine the right options through whole class planning. Possibilities include quiet spaces, computer availability, out of classroom choices such as libraries, computer rooms, outdoor areas, and space for group presentations. These increasingly available as student ownership grows.

7. Practice and Build Stamina

   Self-efficacy and increasing disposition for hard work comes to mind along with teacher observations and feedback. Student awareness of stamina escalates with reflections by individuals, groups, and the teacher. My class debriefings described previously would fit here along with individual learning journals shared in small groups. Keeping track of their own most desirable/worst behaviours is another good suggestion from the Daily 5.

8. Stay Out of the Way

   This is just as important in high schools. Too many students in the past depended on teacher approval for motivation. Teachers should stop praising students, then step back and observe. We want students to be able to choose the kind of thinking required. This is how ownership is built—teacher suggestions as a last resort.

As with the Daily 5, this is extremely important at the beginning of students' choices and during the transition from teacher led instruction to student ownership. The new teacher role in pursuit of student ownership means listening for student understanding, coming up with helpful questions, deciding how to support the next step in a student's thinking, connecting learning to lesson outcomes, and shutting up.

9. Bring Students Back to the Gathering Place
Not an everyday necessity but identifying successes/concerns/reflections on their learning is important in a diversified class dedicated to learning from each other. Getting people together to assess/share next steps works. I don't believe this is true—I know it.

10. Conduct a Group Check-In ("How did it go?") should be combined with point #9. Reflection/debriefing not only speeds individual learning growth, but students also learn from each other (sixth theorem). High school students, even before they reassemble as a class, need time for journal reflection as preparation for whole class reflection.

Confluent education used learning routines focused on learning from each other—Think/Pair/Share as one example—the opposite of classroom practice at the time. We learned to incorporate these into lessons. The biggest effect was improving the involvement of students in their learning. So far from the 'teacher talk-student listen' of most high schools.

Much of this, compatible with student choice and ownership, is teachers practicing conversational strategies that capture and promote student thinking. This includes clarification requests, confirmation checks, repetition, and recasting previous thinking. Interactional feedback as students write or speak also includes noticing and evidence, the teacher mediating the students and content.

One on one conversations that uncover student thinking demand more teacher curiosity and less looking for correct answers. Asking for evidence, elaborating, and posing questions that shift thinking, requires teachers to set aside evaluation. Ritchhart (2020) cites English, Hintz, and Tyson's "educative listening" as mandatory where the teacher listens/pays attention to the student's "struggles, challenges, and confusions" (p. 26).

We need more overt reasoning, sharing, and elaborating across many learning activities. Context is important. Connections to previous interactions, thinking routines, and learning outcomes make the most out of student discourse. The challenge of teacher and student questioning is to choose questions that are of genuine interest and *that open doors to new considerations*.

Beyond content outcomes, we want to build learning autonomy, advanced citizenship, motivation, collaborative skills, thinking abilities, concern for others, strengthened belief in one's learning capacity, and a forward-looking inventive disposition for future learning of any kind. Clearly, not too much to ask.

The plan to make a plan. So how do we help the class analyze how they will learn given outcomes with maximum participation/ownership rather than just giving them our ideas or, even worse; having more whole class sessions with the teacher asking questions and a few students responding?

One consideration is allowing students who are ready for deeper thinking to do just that, either alone or with others, while also being open to helping fellow students. Again, whole-class involvement is needed in the plan. How does direct instruction connect with student independence? Think the same way as previously: visualize steps in thinking; base knowledge followed by deeper thinking. Growing student autonomy/ownership along with teacher role reformulation, as mentioned, will not be welcomed by all. Thinking for oneself is harder work than letting others, especially the teacher, do it for you.

Expect persistent resistance from some teachers, students, and parents. The pull here is emotional intelligence gains, improved mind-muscle strength, social growth, fewer lonely people, and physical connections to thinking/feeling along with a growing conviction that you can learn just about anything.

Bridging the gap between what each student already knows and can do, and the expectations for each learning outcome also requires teacher investigation of such past variables as: (1) previous teaching strategies, (2) general trajectory of success, and (3) self-efficacy (how do students see themselves as learners). All key to accelerating intellectual growth for everyone.

Written tests can give teachers information on the impact lessons have on students mastering particular learning outcomes, but it is not the only way. One option is student presentations where the emphasis is not only showing how well you know the subject, but how it was learned. Others are one on one interviews, drawings/diagrams, role-play, videos, interviews, and written reports.

The most important learning to learn strategies are reading, writing, speaking, and listening. It is imperative that schools respond when students don't learn. Solutions require systematic processes of intervention, Later Literacy being one, to ensure students receive timely support for learning according to a school-wide plan. That being said, a cautionary note from Elmore (2008) that current remediation often *"consists of putting students in place for longer periods of time, on the theory that it was the students who failed rather than the teachers who taught them"* (p. 226, [emphasis added]).

Later Literacy, a one-on-one reading program for students in the upper grades, is a proven intervention. Instead of *"learning to read"*, students *"read to learn."* Characteristics: miscue analysis, running records to analyze student thinking while reading, feedback designed to grow student independence with forty minutes of daily instruction for forty lessons, a writing component, evening reading assignments backed by parental support, and direct vocabulary teaching.

First introduced by Joyce McDonald of OISE (Ontario Institute for Studies in Education), LL certification depends on being taught by an OISE qualified LL teacher of teachers over a school year. As principal of Horsefly Elementary/Junior Secondary School in Cariboo-Chilcotin SD #27, I completed the program along with three other teachers from our school and one teacher aide. The total number of volunteers from the district (serving more than four thousand students) was six.

Besides our qualified Later Literacy teacher of teachers, the district provided a teaching behind-the-glass facility where we were observed by our teacher and colleagues as we worked with a volunteer student. The results for Later Literacy across Canada predicted a reading growth of 2 years after approximately 2 months instruction. Our experience in BC was about the same. This learning to learn program was successful, not only because students improved reading/writing skills, but also because of the accompanying growth in student confidence.

I also taught LL over the years I was principal of BC High School SUIS in Shanghai. My first student was Jack Z, the student at the beginning of this book, who scored at the grade 5 level. I tested him individually, along with the other grade ten students in the fall of 2010.

At the end of his first year, after participating in our LL program, Jack scored at the grade 11 level of reading comprehension and went on to become a highly successful student in all subjects. After graduation he enrolled as a biology major at McGill University after turning down a $25,000 scholarship from the University of Alberta, Edmonton.

I didn't have the time to respond to all students who needed help. So, I cheated: although I am a certified teacher of LL, I am not a qualified teacher of teachers; I trained Chinese language support teachers and a few Canadian teachers anyway. This included observing my lessons.

Later Literacy students improved their reading comprehension—much of their success was due, I believe, to growing confidence; they (and their parents) clearly appreciated the close attention; there was nothing like it, I don't think, in the Chinese school system. An important signal was classroom teacher comments on improved performance almost immediately after a student began working in LL.

The average reading grade improvement for Later Literacy students the first year in Shanghai was 5.5 grades as compared to the 2.0 grade improvement average back in Canada. A further advantage is that the program supplied teachers with strategies they could take back to their classrooms to help other students improve.

Success for all students means installing comparable programs in today's high schools. Unfortunately, whatever presence Later Literacy had years ago in various locations across Canada seems to have disappeared. Perhaps the main reasons were the program assigned to resource teachers with ratios of 300:1 and the perception that 1:1 instruction, no matter its effectiveness, is unaffordable.

Yet without such a program so many students will lose out. Making this a priority could include the following:

1. Hiring a district Later Literacy teacher trainer with the added responsibility of supporting Teacher-Leader Professional Learning Communities interested in providing school wide LL programming.
2. The same PLCs to model/support Later Literacy principles in regular classrooms through small group/whole class guided reading.
3. Find time in each school for teacher-leaders to create/support a cadre of Reading Helpers from peer tutoring student volunteers, senior centre community members, and interested community readers.
4. Principals/vice-principals/resource teachers to teach LL during activities period.

A concern: reading instruction in high schools is often restricted to either "the most disabled readers" as Kylene Beers describes in the introduction to *Adolescent Literacy: Turning Promise into Practice* (2007), or "ongoing in-class coaching by subject teachers aimed at further development of critical literary skills" for those who read at grade level.

She concludes, "We see too many schools that offer remediation or intervention for those students who read far below grade level and nothing for anyone else" (p. xv). To address this need she sees a daily intensive intervention class with a qualified teacher for students to develop the basic skills of "fluency" (word recognition, automaticity, and the ability to read with the expression needed for a text to make sense), vocabulary, and comprehension.

That's not all; she also suggests a different course for those "with skills learned but not yet mastered." The time required could be a semester or less: these students would work with their assigned textbooks to improve their reading rate or vocabulary skills. These are students "who can read with understanding…but have trouble organizing what they've read in their minds so they can retell it with coherence or write about it with clarity" (p. xvi). Again, a qualified teacher is required.

Another improvement is reading support in regular classrooms with subject teachers. This will require individual coaching, reading strategies for particular texts, writing to learn, and developing vocabulary, all aimed at understanding more challenging texts.

For those students who "have a strong command over a variety of reading strategies and use them almost without thought as they read increasingly more complex texts," she sees subject teachers with the ability to "model comprehension, vocabulary, and fluency strategies whenever needed" (p. xvi).

A one-on-one mathematics program could follow LL guidelines. A family commitment for one half-hour of deliberate practice each evening; a forty-lesson program in addition to regular math classes, with a sequenced mathematics remediation program spanning basic computation, number sense, factoring, rational numbers, powers and radicals, solving algebraic equations, and applications—a graduated problem-solving approach based on student readiness.

Amidst all of this is student choice. Comparable choice for teachers means PLCs investigating their own teaching through reflection, seeing each other teach, videotaping lessons for common observation, critiquing, and concluding. Determining what thinking routines work best for what subjects and then referring to them by name builds a higher level of professional discourse.

An example of a *"one size fits all"* conundrum: in 1995 parents within the Richmond School District of Greater Vancouver proposed direct instruction, based on the work of Helen Raham, the executive director of *Teachers for Excellence*, as being more effective than indirect methods. As reported by Charles Ungerleider, former Deputy

Minister of Education for the province of BC, in his book *Failing Our Kids: How We Are Ruining Our Public Schools* (2003), the parents' demands were denied as the board, after months of deliberation, perceived it as antithetical to the BC curriculum. Another example of unrecognized false dichotomies.

Past experience in attempting to teach all students in a positive and effective manner deserves our attention. It's a reminder of an intermediate set of researched approaches aimed at curbing the deleterious effects of long-term groupings.

One is the parallel timetabling of three or more subject classes. This allows redistributing students on the basis of need: re-teaching, more practice, or enrichment using short-term flexible groups. This suggestion reveals aspects of the isolating/limiting culture of current high schools as teachers prefer the fewest lesson preparations possible with all grade level classes getting the same lesson.

Encumbrance, then, is teachers confined to a single subject in one grade, thus eliminating temporary redistributions. An accompanying second bad effect is the absence of teacher experience with previous or succeeding grades: two examples of lost opportunities to improve teaching and learning; both attributable to a culture that is unconscious of serving teachers ahead of students. As Richard North Patterson warns: *"teachers to not serve themselves."*

Tracking, the current stand-alone high school strategy for addressing student differences, has failed. Disadvantaged low-end classes perform dismally while top-end students are subjected to bigger carrots and sticks, little choice or voice, an increased volume of teacher talk/memorization, worse homework, and little collaborative learning.

Lower-level classes fail to improve student performance because of teachers who drew the wrong straw, teach the way they were taught, or were themselves sorted by past performance. Control concerns, repetitive teacher telling, *finishing* courses, permanently sorting eagles from mud hens, and teaching below the middle replace high expectations for all.

According to Gamoran's article (1992), "The variable effects of high school tracking", *American Sociological Review's* research indicates that higher-track teachers were more enthusiastic and took more time preparing lessons. Teachers in low-track classes, he concluded, spent less time on instruction and more on behaviour management.

Evidence from Jo Boaler (2019):

> A study in Britain showed that 88 percent of students placed into tracks at the age of four remained in the same track for the rest of their school lives. This horrific result does not surprise me. Once we tell young students they are in the lower-track, their achievement becomes a self-fulfilling prophecy.
> "The same is true when teachers are told which tracks students are in; they treat students differently whether they intend to or not." (pp. 24–25)

These results surprise no one: with fewer opportunities to learn from classmates (again—students learn from each other, not just the teacher) and curricula focused on knowledge and little else, the downward slide gets steeper. Witness ongoing evidence/experience that failed high school students repeating the same course taught in the same way rarely do better.

Addressing such concerns is a combination of "Backward Design" where the same deep-thinking goals for everyone are broken down into sequenced steps progressively leading to goal attainment, followed by common, regular, formative assessments. Students require differing supports: re-teaching, extra practice for students who need it, or enrichment for students who have mastered the concepts. This would allow the same pacing through the curriculum with no disadvantage to students in lower groups.

In their book, *Common Formative Assessment: A Toolkit for Professional Learning Communities at Work*, Kim Bailey & Chris Jakicic suggest differentiating students, but only for necessary outcomes and for a limited time. They believe flexible grouping supports specific learning needs without exposing less-able students to the negative outcomes of grouping them into a 'low group'. They also recommend teachers consider other flexible groupings such as student interests/concerns.

Adam Gamoran (ibid) defines *tracking* as specific courses (in BC, English 12 vs Communications 12) with differing levels of learning/thinking outcomes while *streaming*, refers to different graduation routes such as university preparation, commercial, general course, or vocational.

His summary:

> I conclude that grouping and tracking rarely add to overall achievement in a school, but they often contribute to inequality. This finding is most consistent for high school tracking, but it is not uncommon in other forms and at other levels. Typically, it means that high-track students are gaining and low-track students are falling farther behind. But the effects of ability grouping are not the same in every context, and we need to discover how they come about in order to improve productivity and reduce inequality. (p. 4)

The word "streaming" is not used in most Canadian high schools. But the practice is still there. Charles Ungerleider (2003):

> Whether officially sanctioned (as it is in Ontario), Canadian high schools are de facto streamed as a consequence of having parallel, but not equivalent, courses in mathematics and English at the same grade level. Given the way high school timetables are constructed, once students are streamed in mathematics or English, they are streamed in most of their remaining courses. (p. 96)

Some parents see lower tracks as dead-ends. Parent Leslie Gavel, in her book, "Dropout: How School is Failing Our Kids (And What We Can Do About It) (2017)", gives credit to the Canadian Education Association for standing up against streaming because "studies on ability grouping show inequitable outcomes and social consequences." (p. 173)

She cites Harvey Krahn and Alison Taylor of the University of Alberta comparing the availability of post-secondary options open to them. Saskatchewan leads with 87%, British Columbia at 66%, Ontario at 64%, and Alberta at 59%.

Research, at times, claims higher ability students do better in tracked high school classes than in mixed-ability classes. But the price is high: lower leveled students, often heavily comprised of racial minorities, immigrants, and children of poverty do far worse.

This point is emphasized by Tomlinson and Strickland (2005):

> A student whose first language is not English cannot feel integral to the group when he can never read the text, understand directions, or make a real contribution to the work of

groups to which he is assigned. The teacher in this must see the link between communication and belonging and develop multiple ways for the learner to have a voice in and make a contribution to the class.

A student from a minority culture feels anything but central to the operation of the group when all of her cultural peers are consistently placed in low-achieving groups and are assigned work that looks dull. Belonging is not a reality when the teacher is more likely to call on, chat more affably with, and make eye contact with students from cultures other than your own. Your importance diminishes when the teacher shows she expects less of you by settling for incomplete work, overlooking missed assignments, or failing to coach you on how to enhance the quality of a product. (p. 13)

Given the above, the conclusions of Harvey Daniels et al. in 'Rethinking High School: Best Practice in Teaching, Learning, and Leadership' (2001) are no surprise: "The full inclusion of special education students is one system that enhances community in our school. The other half of the process in the formal school program is to eliminate tracking.

American high schools, they state, divide students according to ability. Usually 'basic', 'regular', and 'honors'. They then tack on "special education" below these, and "advanced placement" at the top. Parents in most districts can request that their children be moved up or down a level, but in practice, once students are placed in a track, they are likely to stay there for their entire high school career.

They go on:

To place students in lower academic tracks signals that it is acceptable to look down on others. Students who divide into cliques are often simply mirroring the divisions initiated by adults…research delivers conclusive statistics on tracking: students in low-ability tracks receive lower-quality instruction, covering less content, with more rote drill, and teachers preoccupied with classroom management. Tracking consigns the lower ranks to a lesser level of learning from which most never escape. The worst news is the racial inequity that tracking begins. (p. 67)

Referring to Wheelock and Lynne (1997, p. 8) are suggestions on detracking:

* developing a culture of de-tracking—helping students and teachers to believe that having everyone work together in a school is valuable and can support learning
* involving parents—helping particularly the parents of already successful students to understand that de-tracking will advance all students in the school and not lower teaching and learning levels for their kids—otherwise, parent opposition can destroy the effort
* providing professional development for teachers—introducing strategies and curriculum for working with diverse students in the classroom, and facilitating the planning needed to reorganize the school
* phasing in change gradually, so that changes are supported and problems are addressed
* rethinking other aspects of the program, such as ways to deliver extra help for those students who need it without using pull-out activities that implicitly label the 'pullees' (pp. 69–70)

Wheelock and Lynne advise additional support: summer workshops for teachers on a range of teaching strategies, planning time in schools, peer coaching, and teachers given time to observe each other teach and work with university partners.

Best Practices High School in Chicago, however, according to Harvey Daniels et al., did little of the above. They report:

> We simply started without tracks, and nobody seems to miss them. We've heard no complaints from parents. The teachers all routinely conduct classes using workshop and small-group activities, conferencing regularly with individual students. Some kids work harder and achieve more than others, though the teachers continue to encourage everyone. A number of students have requested the option to do extra work and receive honors credit for it, but they are adamant that they don't want to be placed in a separate class. Through their electives, juniors and seniors pursue a few topics of their choice at more challenging levels… What can we say? It works. (p. 70)

More evidence from Jo Boaler in her book, *Mathematical Mindsets: Unleashing Students' Potential Through Creative Math, Inspiring Messages and Innovative Teaching* (2022):

> Research has shown what happens when schools and districts decide to de-track. One important study showed the impact of de-tracking in New York City's school district. In New York City, students used to be in middle schools with regular and advanced classes. Then the district decided that they would remove advanced classes and teach advanced mathematics to all middle school students. Researchers were able to follow three years of students working in tracks and then three years when students were working in heterogeneous classes. The researchers followed the six cohorts of students through to the end of high school. They found that the students who worked without advanced classes took more advanced math, enjoyed math more, and passed the state test in New York *a year earlier* than students in tracks. (p. 113)

De-tracking, then, confers important benefits for students of all levels within a heterogeneous classroom. Improvement is then apparent, not only in student relationships but test scores.

Tieso (2005) found that *top students in such classes demonstrated significantly higher achievement than high-performing students who were taught using textbook curriculum/whole-class instruction*. She concluded that revising/differentiating the curriculum, along with creating purposeful flexible grouping, may significantly increase students' mathematics achievement, especially for gifted students.

Gamoran (1992) advocated two other steps: (1) reassess students' capabilities and take new information into account when making assignment decisions, and (2) enable students to make up curricular material they may have missed—for example, in tutorials during the school year or the summer—so that those who are ready to advance are not held back by a lack of curriculum coverage.

The latter requires investment not just by schools but also by students, who must undertake extra work to catch up. Flexible grouping systems also mean rotating teachers so that all students have opportunities to learn from the most effective teachers and to prevent the loss of morale that sometimes occurs for teachers who are assigned low tracks year after year.

Within a month of teaching the lower-level Math 101 course at Frontier Collegiate in Cranberry Portage, MB, I decided to run two groups: a continuation of Math 101 as well as its university stream counterpart, Math 100. I offered the choice to all thirty students, and, to my surprise, they all opted for the more demanding course. The last pleasant surprise was their motivational level: average effort in Math 101, these kids had something to prove to their classmates, their friends in other sections of Math 100, themselves, and perhaps even to me. Good exam results across the board.

Students should make course decisions, not schools. I recall Arnold Dysart, an OEC (Occupational Entrance Course) student from South Indian Lake, who dropped out of Frontier Collegiate for the remainder of his first year to go trapping with his grandfather. Shortly after his return, he requested a move to the General Course.

As principal, I faced teacher opposition based on nothing more than moving students between streams was disruptive/bad precedent. I moved him anyway. Within a month, Arnold approached me and asked to move again: this time to the University Entrance program. More opposition, but he persisted, and I reluctantly agreed.

He graduated with the rest of the university entrance stream, earned his B. Ed from the University of Manitoba, became a principal in our school division, and was eventually promoted to Area Superintendent. Years later, I was hired as the high school consultant, and in some ways reported to him.

An aside comes from Dr. Riffel, former head of administrative studies at the University of Manitoba while discussing this book. Based on a study he carried out within Frontier School Division, he concluded that students who left the system, upon their return, often did better than those attending more regularly. Their success related to the emotional and social support of family and friends during their time out.

Tomlinson C. and Strickland C. *Differentiation in Practice: A Resource Guide for Differentiating Curriculum, Grades 9–12* (2005), contrast differentiated practices to past/current high school culture:

> Yet too many teachers cling to the comfortable patterns of the past. Despite abundant and mounting evidence to the contrary, our high school classes still evince the belief that teaching is telling, that the teacher is the teller, that learning is repeating, that curriculum is coverage, that students are unmotivated and dependent, that assessment happens at the end of large blocks of teaching, that grades serve the purpose of "separating the sheep from the goats," and that 'classroom management' is just a synonym for control. At the least, high

> school teachers fear if we don't 'teach like the colleges do'—primarily through lecture and independently completed assignments—our students will be ill-prepared to succeed at the college level. (p. 2)

As my father jokingly described teaching, "First, you tell them what you are going to tell them, then you tell them, and then you tell them what you told them."

The entrenchment of such practices is also described by Ritchhart et al. *Making Thinking Visible: How to Promote Engagement, Understanding, and Independence for All Learners* (2011):

> Teachers in such classrooms are rightly stumped when asked to identify the kinds of thinking they want students to do because there isn't any to be found in much of the work they give students. Retention of information through rote practice isn't learning; it is training...
>
> The opposite side of this same coin is a classroom that is all about activity. In the often-misunderstood notion of experiential or inquiry-based learning, students are sometimes provided with lots of activities. Again, if designed well some of these activities can lead to understanding, but too often the thinking that is required to turn activity into learning is left to chance. Other times, the activity itself is little more than a more palatable form of practice. (p. 9)

The challenge of achieving differentiated instruction in high schools is explored in Duane Kiley's comprehensive, informative study: "Differentiated Instruction in the Secondary Classroom: Analysis of the level of implementation and factors that influence practice" (2011).

He determined that differentiated practices are well-defined, but that not much interest exists among secondary teachers. He thinks there may be a good reason for this: *adapting traditional teaching to accommodate individual differences may be too difficult.* What is really needed is differentiated instruction within a wider set of guidelines.

The study looked at teachers' willingness to implement differentiated instruction in high schools. Teachers reported, somewhat surprisingly, that neither the number of students or classes taught per day, nor the amount of planning time available, nor the quality of administrative support influenced a teacher's decision to carry out differentiated instruction. The only significant factor was how much teachers valued it as a practice.

These teachers also saw little benefit from traditional workshops that failed to model the differentiation they sought to achieve. Lecturing a diverse group of teachers about addressing individual differences was seen as hypocritical. What they valued was the input of colleagues: brainstorming, creating, implementing, and reviewing results. They were also aware of what motivated their efforts—achieving success for an increased number of students.

Kiley:

> Teachers described administration as promoting the practice but indicated that there was no follow through with training and structure which would effectively continue differentiated practices in the classroom. The training that they had experienced was described as minimal, not always effective, and sometimes missing the mark. A frequent complaint was that training examples for differentiated instruction were usually not at a secondary level. *Teachers also expressed dismay and some humor in the fact that the professional development did not utilize the same differentiated practices that the training espoused.* (pp. 62–63, [emphasis added])

Success, however, is possible. Kiley's summary of the effects of a *six-year study of differentiated instruction in Colchester High School based on standardized test scores:*

	1999	2006		1999	2006
Reading Understanding	53%	63%	Writing Effectiveness	58%	82%
Reading Analysis	51%	78%	Math Skills	33%	68%
Math Concepts	44%	52%			

In addition to score improvements, Colchester High School experienced the following improvements where the number of students achieving "Honors" status on the NSRE exams rose in every subject, often dramatically: (for example, from 17% to 29% in writing conventions, from 19% to 46% in math skills, and from 15% to 25% in math concepts).

Disciplinary interventions dropped by 42%. Expulsions declined from 7 to 1. The dropout rate decreased from 6.9% to 1.03%. Quantitative measures document significant improvement in *school climate* for teachers. (pp. 33–34)

My father taught seventy farm students from grade one to grade ten in the rural community of Lidstone, Manitoba. And he wasn't alone: at the time, a high number of one-room schoolteachers across Western Canada were in similar wheat fields. How did teachers, let alone the students, survive? Answer: students learning from each other by watching/participating in lessons taught to other grades or by observing students "*at the board.*"

Two examples of support for individual differences: (1) the clearly defined Later Literacy individualized reading/writing program, and (2) incorporating supplementary materials at different reading levels but with the same curricular content. At the same time, the right reading level may not be as important as the interest generated. Alfie Kohn (2011): "Researchers found that children's interest in a passage they were reading was *thirty times* more useful than its difficulty level for predicting how much of it they would later remember" (p. 4).

Self-regulated learning is not easy nor quick, but worth the effort. The success of a high percentage of our high school population depends on the progressing ability of teachers to insert differing classroom materials, methods, and products into their classes—a collaborative approach where differentiated teaching/learning is available to all.

Faye Brownlie and Leyton Schnellert (2009) advocate lessons that allow for self-regulated learning—gradual release of responsibility for individual students, collaborative groups, and the entire class is founded on transparent outcomes, assessed readiness, potential learning sequences, and teacher support.

Key principles: 1) Clarify/model key concepts from learning outcomes 2) Relate learners' interests and prior knowledge/experience 3) Work backward to determine starting points/learning chains 4) Use multiple ways to acquire and consolidate surface information 5) Identify the deeper thinking required 6) Explicitly teach support strategies; making thinking visible routines/collaboration skills; and 7) Align formative and summative assessments

Visible learning not only clarifies learning outcomes but routines, habits, and thinking processes required to achieve those outcomes. All backed by teachers facilitating emotional engagement through anticipatory sets/cognitive dissonance, quality direct teaching, split-screen lessons, modeling, and student choice. This confidence building is paired with collaborative learning, purposeful action, and reflection supporting students as independent learners.

In order for students and teachers to become viable partners, Hattie, in *Visible Learning: A Synthesis of over 800 Meta-Analyses Relating to Achievement* (2009), concludes that:

> Visible teaching and learning occurs when learning is the explicit goal, when it is appropriately challenging, when the teacher and student both (in their various ways) seek to ascertain whether and to what degree the challenging goal is attained, when there is deliberate practice aimed at attaining mastery of the goal, when there is feedback given and sought, and when there are active, passionate, and engaging people (teacher, students, peers, and so on) participating in the act of learning. It is teachers seeing learning through the eyes of students, and students seeing teaching as the key to their own ongoing learning. The remarkable feature of the evidence is that the biggest effects on the student learning occur when teachers become learners of their own teaching, and when students become their own teachers. (p. 22)

Dispositions are important. Our overall goal is student confidence and willingness to engage in rigorous problem solving, overcome uncertainty, search for evidence, and serve others. All under the light of a democracy where freedom and responsibility go hand in hand.

Recent observations/research from icons Michael Fullan, Ron Ritchhart, and John Hattie, as stated earlier, show *deeper thinking benefits lower achieving students the most*. One reason, I believe, why Fullan insists on including higher thinking skills almost immediately in lesson planning. Love of hockey won't happen without playing the game. Perfecting your shot against a stationary washing machine in your basement is not the game. Real goalies can play too.

Some secondary teachers feel they don't have time to foster deep thinking *and* drill enough into students for success on examinations. They are wrong; students remember more, not less, information through connections or visualizations after deeper thinking. Such thinking increases the capacity to remember through those connections.

An experiment described in "Building A Better Teacher", (2014) by Elizabeth Green accentuates the point. Noticing that which doesn't fit with one's prior knowledge and experience captures our attention. We form generalizations, patterns, and systemic information throughout our lives. Such noticing/evidence, then, where the patterns are violated, is part of remembering experiences that, in themselves, would otherwise be forgotten.

Children watched a toy car placed on a model train track that rose to a hill. Then, a larger car rolled down the hill and struck the car. The car was pushed a certain distance. After repositioning the car, an even larger car was rolled down the hill and the small car was pushed further than the first time. The last time, again after repositioning the car below, a car smaller than the rest was rolled down and struck the car. And this time, the car at the bottom rolled back the furthest.

The children's attention was determined by the time they fixed on each trial. The last trial held their attention the most. The lesson was that even at a young age, people can apply experience/past learning to every situation. The children were six months old.

Chapter 6
Activating Allies: Parents and Students as Partners

Reforming high schools: "Teachers, students, and parents starting where they are, using what they have, doing what they can."
Modified fridge door sticker

From her book, *Dropout: How School is Failing our Kids (And What We Can Do About It)* (2017), by Leslie Gavel; a Calgary, Alberta parent, Jiddu Krishnamurti: "Action only has meaning in relationships; without understanding relationships, action on any level will only breed conflict. The understanding of relationship is infinitely more important than the search for any plan of action."

Without participation and leadership from students, parents, and community at both the school and district levels, high schools will not improve. Pressure and support from these groups are indispensable for change.

This view is reinforced by Hattie (2012) in a study of five New Zealand schools. They found that teaching parents to "co-understand the importance of deliberate practice, concentration, the difference between surface and deep knowing, and the nature of learning intentions and success criteria" as well as language about learning in today's classrooms pays dividends.

Parents learned how to help their children attend and engage in learning by speaking with teachers and school personnel. This led to "enhanced engagement by students in their schooling experiences, improvement in reading achievement, greater skills and jobs for the parents, and higher expectations, higher satisfaction, and higher endorsement of the local schools and the community" (p. 188). On Hattie's scale of effective impact, the results were medium to high.

A sidelight was the recruitment of retired teachers as home-school liaison workers. These were people who taught parents the language of schooling needed to advance their effectiveness when interacting with school staff. Such a role for veteran teachers, by having an official capacity within the school/district, opened the door to parents working more closely with teachers.

More evidence at Roosevelt High School in Dallas, Texas. As reported in the book, *Rethinking High School: Best Practices in Teaching, Learning, and Leadership* (2001), by Harvey Daniels et al., their parent involvement program introduced "curricular and structural reforms that led to striking increases in student achievement" (p. 263). State tests showed an improvement from the 40th percentile to the 81st percentile in reading comprehension and from the 16th to 70th percentile in mathematics, while attendance improved by 11 percent.

One study reported in the same book found that schools encouraging parent participation was more effective than "family characteristics such as parental education or socioeconomic level, in determining whether parents actually become involved" (Dauber and Epstein, 1993, p. 265).

The goal was parents becoming an integral part of the school. Contributions included parents on committees planning school change, tutoring, conducting special projects, or raising funds. Parents lobbied for needed school infrastructure, attended school run courses on supporting students at home, developed computer skills and written communication, and audited high school classes.

Here in Canada, Paul W. Bennett (2020) sees parents currently having little say in decision making. He makes the following points:

1) Parents feel unwelcome to approach schools with questions or concerns.

2) Although school principals appear to want partnerships with parents, this is severely restricted.
3) Parents quickly find they have little influence and "find themselves marginalized or become frustrated and drop by the wayside." (p. 20)
4) School administrators/principals are skilled at limiting parental involvement and influence across the system.

He views democratic schools with students, teachers, and parents in close control/ownership as essential for improving student achievement:

> Decentralizing education is a means to an end and not the end in itself. Thirty years after the first wave of school-based management initiatives, it is abundantly clear that self-managed schools, by themselves, are not enough to produce dramatic improvement in the quality and vitality of public education. The devolution of decision making to the local school and community level carries with it significant benefits, but two problems remain to be solved to fully realize the vision of more democratic and effective schools. First of all, real authority, in far too many cases, is still invested in ministries of education and/or regional school administrations, limiting the freedom of action of school governing councils.
>
> Second, when decentralization is implemented, it usually applies to the management structure and process (such as site-based budgeting) but does not really impact the day-to-day teaching and learning that exert a bigger influence on school improvement. Decentralization, then, is only the first piece in the overall strategy to make our schools more democratic, responsive, and accountable to parents, teachers, students, and communities. (pp. 229–230)

"Relations with Parents", a subsection in Charles Ungerleider's (2003) book, examines the role of teacher unions and some teachers in suppressing parent involvement in schools. He is far from optimistic about the chances of parents becoming a fundamental part of improvement efforts.

From his experience in a number of leadership roles (including Deputy Minister of Education in British Columbia), he sees teachers having lost their moral and professional authority because (1) "a better educated public defers less to them", and (2) "the organizations that represent them have *resisted regulation in the public interest, opposed heightened accountability, and refused to accept greater parental and public involvement in schooling*" (p. 228, [emphasis added]).

John Goodlad (2004) spoke to polarization on the role of parents in school decision making:

> The debate over public schools as we have known them versus parent-run schools has an either-or tone, and this has led, I believe, to an unfortunate and unproductive polarization of views. It stems in part from superficial interpretations of what parents want. Polls and surveys show that they would like a greater say in the affairs of their schools. But this does not mean that parents want to take over the schools. Some do, but most don't. Rather, they want to be kept informed in as clear a fashion as possible, especially about their children's progress and welfare. Further, they want the decisions and those who make them to be visible. They would prefer to leave the running of the school to the principal and the classroom to teachers, and, if possible, to hold them accountable. (p. 273)

Bryk and Schneider, in *Trust in Schools: A Core Resource for Improvement* (2002), while probing what kind of relationship teachers should establish with students' families, stress the importance of judgments we make of others' intentions:

> These discernments appeared to be shaped by the degree of vulnerability individuals felt toward others. A focus on principled behavior that we eventually came to term *integrity* became another key concern. In this regard, individuals pursuing their own self-interests and having little regard for the academic and personal welfare of the students were seen as not trustworthy. (p. 153, [emphasis added])

They advocate the following: Teachers working closely with parents to meet students' needs. Parents invited to visit classrooms to observe the instructional program. Schools regularly communicating with parents about how they can help their children learn. Discussions with parents about support needed to advance school outcomes. Encouraging feedback from parents and the community. The principal pushing teachers to communicate regularly with parents. Teachers attempting to understand parents' problems and concerns. Parents greeted warmly when they call or visit the school.

They are also concerned with power imbalance:

> In the context of power asymmetry, the burden generally falls to the most powerful party to initiate actions that reduce the sense of vulnerability experienced by others. Given the significant power imbalance between poor parents and school professionals in most urban contexts, it is incumbent on school professionals to take the lead. During our field research, we observed a variety of initiatives aimed at this problem. These included starting a parent centre at the school; designing instructional support activities that parents can do at home to assist student learning, and developing parent and family programs in response to local needs. (pp. 130–131)

Other comments from their book:

"Little in their professional socialization or formal training prepares them (teachers) for working with parents and other adults in the community" (p. 139).

"Our research suggests that effective urban schools need teachers that not only know their students well, but also have an empathetic understanding of their parents' situations and have the interpersonal skills needed to engage these adults effectively" (p. 139).

"As parents perceive a wide range of behaviours intended to make them feel more comfortable, they come to understand that school staff hold a genuine regard for them and really care about their children" (p. 131).

"This willingness of teachers at Thomas [School] to reach out to parents, to listen to their concerns, and to go the extra mile for their children was much appreciated by parents, and they reciprocated by extending strong support to teachers" (p. 69).

"Another parent spoke of how one teacher conducted workshops for the parents to demonstrate her instructional techniques and help parents become better educators of their own children. 'She made me feel welcome since my daughter started school'" (p. 69).

"Teachers at Thomas recognized parents' sense of vulnerability and actively sought to make them feel more comfortable. How best to accomplish this, however, remained uncertain. The head of the Parents Center explained that child care and coffee were made available at parent activities to promote attendance" (p. 70).

"A lot of people, and I was one of them, tend to put a lot of people up on pedestals because they have a title, and it doesn't have to be that way. I think what this is, you need to spend time with these people to realize they're just people" (p. 139).

Online comments from teachers in the Vancouver BC area:

> "I really believe we need to make research and literature available to our school communities. This will also help educate parents of students so they can walk beside us as we make schools better. We could do this at assemblies—invite parents to assemblies. This is not in any way saying that we should not value what our school communities now bring to the table."

> "As educators, we should have a thorough and up to date knowledge of what works best for kids in classrooms. For parents, they should have a strong understanding of how we can do the best for their child. If we can bring those elements together, schools will be better for all."

Online student concerns/suggestions from a BC school district:

"I often find myself wondering what I could do to improve. Maybe once a month a student and a teacher could meet, much like parent-teacher interview for students, for the parents cannot heed the advice for the students."

"Free blocks we could study, have time to do more work and when we can help other students in that class if they needed us."

Comments from parents on recent BC Curriculum Changes:

"Rarely are students asked what they think the problems are in their schools while most educators still act as though vocal parents, standardized test makers, and college admissions committees are the customers that matter the most. Students are much more frequently thought of as the recalcitrant 'raw material' from which quality products must be fashioned."

"Students will be asked to set their own learning plan, and then to self-evaluate on their progress. In theory, goal setting and allowing students to determine what they want to focus their learning on—based on their strengths, interests and aspirations—is promising. But my concern is whether teachers will be able to deliver this in the classroom while they still have to meet set learning objectives within each subject area and grade."

"The line up to speak to your child's teacher can be very long. I have had to wait up to an hour for 2 teachers each. There should be a way to make it more efficient. What if there is an appointment schedule—where you have fifteen minute booked appointments per child/parent?"

Parental involvement in schools, regardless of form, correlates positively with student success. The difficulty is often poor participation at the high school level compared to lower grades. A common complaint of high school teachers: "I never see the parents I need to see."

Reasons are parents feeling less knowledgeable about subject content, meetings with four or more different teachers each semester, teenagers asserting newfound independence by discouraging parents from getting involved, and schools offering open-ended school invitations rather than specific appointments.

Alexandra Pannoni of US News quotes Megan Penrice teaching at Pottstown High School in Pennsylvania on why few parents show up for their parent-teacher conferences:

> "I'm not sure if it's that the kids are to the point where they are more self-sufficient and independent—so parents don't necessarily think they need to—but I think it's really important that they do."
>
> "Penrice says that for every sixty students she teaches, probably four or five parents attend parent-teacher confer-

ences—a much smaller turnout than when she taught elementary school."

"We looked at the data about parent-teacher conferences at our district's ten high schools and found that parents were using only eighteen percent of available conference slots. The schools were setting aside ten hours for conferences, but on average, teachers spent only two hours actually talking with parents. Those eight unused hours represent a full day of instructional time. We had to consider eliminating conferences."

Things are no better elsewhere. One district's website in Greater Vancouver forcefully reminded parents that interviews with teachers are limited to nine minutes—not eight, not ten, but nine minutes. Failed school and district leadership in black and white.

As the newly appointed principal of MBCI (Margaret Barbour Collegiate Institute) in The Pas, Manitoba, a grade nine-twelve high school with over seven hundred students, I did the math. Each teacher taught an average of 104 students per semester, some many more. If every parent showed up, and each meeting took as little as fifteen minutes, the time for each teacher would amount to twenty-six hours. That's over five full school days of interviews each semester.

It took a few minutes to sink in: high schools do this because it fails. A high percentage of parents would break the bank. An example of a cultural/historical process so ingrained that failure is perfectly acceptable. The sadness of this situation exacerbated by its passive acceptance by principals, students, teachers, and parents.

MBCI had a teacher advisor system as an advocate for each student, but it didn't include parent-student-teacher advisor meetings. Our School Management Team recommended the following changes: (1) students to choose their teacher advisor from among all certified teachers including administrators, (2) subject-teacher reports to be expanded and copied to teacher advisors, and (3) teacher advisors scheduling (with student help) parent-student-teacher advisor meetings each semester.

Should parents wish to meet subject teachers, the teacher advisor would arrange it. These subject teacher meetings were infrequent; perhaps the reason was that most parents didn't want a discussion about mastering quadratic equations or cohesive paragraphs. They wanted to know about motivation, relations with classmates, character development, what their daughter or son needed to succeed across all subjects, plans to support their child, and what they could do to help.

Parent turnout was a few points off 100%. Meeting times ranged from twenty minutes to over an hour based on student need. Because meetings were by appointment and numbered less than twenty for each teacher advisor, any rescheduling was easily arranged.

The three determining factors for our success, I believe, were: 1) student choice of teacher-advisor (such freedom of choice is both motivational and rare in high schools), 2) all students required to participate in the meetings, and 3) scheduled meetings as compared to parents wandering around the school in search of teachers. As well, not all took place in the collegiate; a considerable percentage of my meetings were across kitchen tables in my students' homes.

Each year, it is important to allow students to choose advisors from across the school, not necessarily subject teachers. It is the relationship that is important, not the role. Restricting choice to subject teachers could eliminate principals, vice-principals, guidance counsellors, and resource teachers. One strength of student-chosen advisors is the high percentage of students with the same advisor throughout their high school career. In my own experience, keeping track of the ups and downs, goals and aspirations of 15–18 students were not an issue; time was on my side.

The quality of teacher reports is critical; important for helping students create learning plans that work for them. In our BC High School in Shanghai, we spent time on their improvement. One guideline being concrete examples backing teacher observations. Writing such expanded reports also improved our thinking. As a classroom teacher, my reports substantially increased my reflection/ability to improve learning supports for my students.

Close to 100% of parents working with students and teachers in developing student learning plans has an additional benefit. It increases capacity for change: *all parents* becoming increasingly aware of both the school's learning support system *and* its current limitations; a critical step toward parents becoming full partners in school improvement.

Accelerating collaborative opportunities, teacher advisors personally invite parents to become an integral part of the school: daily advisories, whole-school assemblies, ad-hoc inquiry groups, audited courses, no-fee credit courses (full or part-time basis), tutoring, after-school activities period, staff meetings, professional learning communities, and leadership credit courses.

Such opportunities, in fact, should be afforded all citizens, thus moving toward the landscaped collaborative learning of school and local communities discussed in Chapter 7: Building Social Capital: Team Building.

At MBCI, my perception was that the new system was appreciated more by parents than teachers, but later, teacher attitudes became increasingly positive. Reluctance was not due to having to learn something new; beyond requiring students to be at the meetings, they had all written student reports previously (although never seen by fellow teachers); they had all participated in teacher-parent conferences—some had included students at those conferences.

No, perhaps the reason, as described by John Goodlad in *A Place Called School* (2004), was the shift from subject specialists to school improvement representatives; the change from a more isolated role to new responsibilities (including facilitating/monitoring a student-driven learning plan) toward students, parents, other teachers, and their school.

While superintendent of the South Slave Divisional School Board in the NWT, the two high schools had the same results as MBCI: Diamond Jenness Secondary School in Hay River and PW Kaiser in Fort Smith, both enrollments in the 300–500 range. Closer cooperation with all parents and students contributing toward an improved graduation rate across the district.

Evaluative comments on teacher-student-parent conferences from other jurisdictions:

"Colorado River Union High School Districts had their first parent-teacher conferences of the school year last week and once again, students led the process. 'We changed the format of the traditional parent/teacher conference a few years ago,' Frei noted. 'Student-led parent/teacher conferences are incentives for the students and their parents to take ownership of their education process. We've seen the positive results as our test scores and graduation rates continue to improve, and the number of our graduating students attending college remains higher than both the statewide and regional averages."

"The conference can also cut through adversarial posturing—especially, perhaps, if it takes the form of a three-way conversation: teacher, parent, and kid. Such conferences should be the rule, not the exception. And not just for older students. I have seen 6-year-olds talk about themselves at a conference with insight and discernment."

"From a teacher's perspective, conferences are useful because they push you to reflect on each kid and her schoolwork. To go through a child's portfolio with her, and talk together about her academic progress and behavior would be all the more meaningful."

"Kinney says that overall, such conferences were a very positive experience at her school—and parents seemed to agree. 'When we started, we had 40 to 45 percent attendance rate [for traditional parent-teacher conferences], but when we moved into Student Led Conferences, it shot up to 90 percent,' she says."

"The student-led conferences had many positive outcomes, Maddy said. Not only did it increase parent attendance and involvement, but it also increased student accountability. Organizing the conference also increased students' interpersonal communication, organizational and goal skills. Parents also seemed to enjoy the experience. 'I enjoyed the student led conferences,' said parent Angie Langen, 'It was a new and enjoyable experience for my daughter to be able to tell me where she is at in school.'"

To emphasize, student learning assessment/planning at such meetings is important in a number of ways. It is through such meetings that all parents become aware of needed changes in both school and district—an important support for parents becoming part of the change team.

Learning plans start with each student's concerns: What am I doing well? What needs to be improved? Where do I need help from particular teachers, fellow classmates, or home? What kind of help is available? How do I find the time required to learn—in and out of school? Have I become more aware of local community issues/problems? Do I really understand both the content and learning to learn outcomes in each lesson? What help can my TA be to me? How much choice do I have during advisories? How do I build trust with subject teachers and other students? Have I made my thinking visible to others? Reflecting on my strengths/areas in need of improvement, have I learned from my mistakes?

How do I become an effective school citizen? Am I aware of how others are becoming better learners? Is the school getting better overall? Is my writing and reading improving? Is my learning portfolio up to date? How have I supported fellow students and my teachers? Have I learned how to give specific, honest, and helpful feedback to others? Is the Ladder of Feedback automatic now? Is deliberate and sustained practice a part of who I am? How have I progressed in each of the seven theorems?

Student owned improvement plans with the support of the student's self-chosen teacher advisor, classroom teachers' input, and direct parent involvement are consistent with the 'personal mastery' discipline described by P. Senge et al. in *Schools That Learn* (2012):

> The practice of developing a coherent image of your personal vision—the results you most want to create in your life—alongside a realist assessment of the current reality of your life today. This produces an innate tension that, when cultivated, can expand your capacity to make better choices and to achieve more of the results that you have chosen. (p. 7)

Just as the school requires clear learning goals, expanded leadership opportunities, collaborative expertise, deeper thinking, self-regulation, extended and improved relationships, and transparent accountability, so does each student, teacher, advisory, and classroom.

As a teacher advisor at BC High School SUIS in Shanghai, improvement plans for a few of my students included them gathering subject teacher comments from every class with a follow-up teacher advisor-student-parent meeting every Friday. Those parents never missed a meeting.

Sue Sackstein from *Teaching Students to Self-Assess: How do I help students reflect and grow as learners?* (2015) submits the following advice to teachers:

1) Make room for students to practice reflection during classes—this includes portfolios with specific feedback from teachers and fellow students. "What are students doing well? What could they do better?" Teachers to "highlight particular portions of students' reflections and offer strategies or ask probing questions to help them add depth" (p. 4).
2) Reflection questions everything. Make questions an important consideration in all entries to learning portfolios.
3) Make reflection a part of every learning experience. Include journal and teacher modeling of reflection on content, learning skills, and teaching methods.
4) Focus on actual learning/thinking; not simply liking or not liking content or activities.
5) Encourage students to reflect in different ways: writing, face to face conferences, videos, or artistically. She advocates reducing

the emphasis on marks by using reflection as a tool for both student and teacher learning evaluations.
6) Offer ways for students to share reflections with other students or social media websites—thus helping "teachers connect students' learning to the larger world outside school" (p. 5).
7) Teachers should model reflection on their own learning.

Expanding this last point, Senge P. (2012) references Stephen D. Brookfield's book, *Becoming a Critically Reflective Teacher* (1995):

> Teacher/learners at any school level and across disciplines can learn to improve their teaching through the practices of reflection he describes. Brookfield suggests that teachers view their practice through four different lenses: their own, their students' eyes, their colleagues' perceptions, and theoretical literature. Those without much experience in social science may be surprised at how valuable educational theories are in helping them improve their own teaching. Educational institutions across all levels are notoriously unsupportive of critically reflective teaching, and Brookfield offers some suggestions for creating a more supportive culture. (p. 267)

The goal is self-regulated learning. Students putting together learning plans through others' lenses: day-to-day feedback from teachers and peers. Data to be combined with subject teachers' regular assessments on academic progress/social-emotional learning. As recognized by Brookfield, the same guidelines for teachers—using student surveys, focus groups, and colleague feedback to develop their own improvement plans.

It is important that feedback from subject teachers goes beyond marks. Marks are a curse because they allow students, teachers, and parents to easily compare students. No better criticism of the use of marks can be found than that of Neil Postman in *Technopoly: The Surrender of Culture to Technology* (1993), "If a number can be given to the quality of thought, then a number can be given to the qualities of mercy, love, hate, beauty, creativity, intelligence, even sanity itself" (p. 13)

A deeply felt concern from parent Leslie Gavel (2017):

> And I, like everyone else in the school apparatus, was fixated on test scores and grades as well. How else do you measure students' achievement? Grades have been with us for so long, embedded in our notions about learning, that it's made it almost impossible to imagine another way. (p. 131)

The research is unequivocal: ranking students hurts kids. A sordid fact when you consider that by far the majority of high school tests/exams are confined to who did better than whom. Professional formative assessment determines how a student's thinking is improving and where the student needs help or enrichment. The only comparisons that make sense indicate how a student is progressing against learning goals.

Isolated marks, at times, do motivate some students. But because of the collateral damage, prompt written or verbal feedback along with marks is better, and specific feedback without marks is often best. That same information for students is also an incentive for teachers on how to teach better. How are student errors impacting our teaching?

All of the above points to advancing parent and student ownership/leadership. Leaders without titles as essential for distributed leadership means opportunities for leadership are all around us—but they need awareness and promotion. At Jiaoke campus in Shanghai, our high school included formal credit courses in leadership as well as informal teacher-led efforts during our daily activities period.

Some were led by teachers and some by students. Not all lasted, but that's not always bad—a part of learning. Regardless, such activities offer opportunities for teachers to advance learning to learn attitudes, skills, and knowledge based on student choice. Also, time for students to breathe easy with self-chosen teachers and (dare I say it—comrades).

I taught a leadership group of about twenty students from grades nine to twelve during activities period, a forty-minute block (or much longer) after regular classes. I was assisted by a parent volunteer (Peter's father) whose consulting business advised companies in Shanghai with an emphasis on collaboration between employees and management as compared to Chinese companies' traditional top-down approach. Our focus on opportunities to practice/improve leadership attitudes, skills, and knowledge in and out of school.

We began by gathering thoughts on leadership behaviours, qualities that influence others, whether a person had to be titled to lead, helpful skills, and their past experience when influenced by others.

We also looked at how we might help each other improve our skills, attitudes, and understandings. Brainstorming opportunities for practiced leadership included student government, family responsibilities, helping others do better in school, community service, presentations at parent assemblies and after-activities/sports teams.

Beyond our after-school meetings, I responded to questions, reflections, and concerns through e-mails. The real evaluation of student progress was in their leadership/work *outside the class* and their reflections on that experience. It was the difference between learning about a subject, and learning through real life experience/opportunities.

Advisories, a daily time allotment of forty minutes at the beginning of each day as suggested in Chapter 7 of this book, are an important feature in building quality relationships: "Advisory is really the backbone of the secondary experience," says education consultant Tom Vander Ark, the CEO of "Getting Smart", a Washington organization focused on school design, coaching, and professional learning. He goes on to say, "At the heart of advisory is a simple, research-based concept: that students are more likely to thrive when they have stronger relationships—especially with at least one adult in the school building"

According to and Rachel A. Poliner and Carol Miller Lieber, authors of *The Advisory Guide: Designing and Implementing Effective Advisory Programs in Secondary Schools* (2004), educators build programs tailored to the needs of their students. Some schools incorporate student leadership and government, but all programs should allow students the opportunity to mentor or support each other or plan activities that impact the broader school.

Online comments on advisories:

> "Academically we have discussions about how they're doing in their classes and what are some strategies they use to overcome some of the challenges they have in their classes."

> "My role is primarily academic counseling, whether it's reviewing for and giving feedback from an exam, or specific intervention strategies in order to get the students focused and to help them pass their class."

> "Advisory is my central concern. This will define our school culture and community. We need to focus on building this program first, and then our team goals, values, and dynamics will emanate from advisories."

"The purpose of an advisory session should be to work on developing, both individually and in a group context, the inquiring habits of mind that mark a scholar. Socratic seminars, book discussion groups, debate on school and community issues, and philosophical investigations might all augment one-on-one coaching in this model of the advisory relationship."

"In the student focus groups, 98% of students responded affirmatively when asked, 'Do you think advisory helps you academically?' Students responded that their advisories helped them focus on their studies, receive critical academic support, strategize about classes and teachers, set academic goals, and belong to a group of peers striving for success."

Teachers know that relationships with students are vital in creating a sense of community. As one teacher commented, "Advisory is a place for students to know an adult." Another teacher described how *"developing relationships with advisees allows teachers to work more effectively with their subject students."* ([emphasis added]) "They report having a 'bank'. It helps them to be able to be more honest with students and for students to be honest with them… It's hard to receive criticism or any words that are disciplinary if a relationship hasn't been built."

Activating allies is achieved through deeper involvement with the goals of the school, observable and workable trust as underlying success in every collective endeavour, and recognizable action on behalf of student achievement/wellness.

Advisories consolidate a caring relationship between high schools and students. As Jaqueline Ancess discusses in *Beating the Odds: High Schools as Communities of Commitment* (2003), teachers must build on student interests/concerns. And although all students benefit from having at least one school person they feel they can trust; the children of the poor are more likely to be advantaged both for personal growth opportunities and academic counselling.

The transition from subject classes to advisories could be a concern for traditional schools where teacher-directed learning is the norm, *but not for schools moving toward self-regulated learning.* Advisories bring additional opportunities for students to extend their regular class self-reliance/ability to work with others while advancing school citizenry, student government, and school improvement.

Through gradual release of responsibility, students take the lead, thus creating more opportunities for teachers to assess learning abilities, coach individuals, and provide process support. At forty minutes per day, this is considerable time—the equivalent of a full credit course each year of schooling devoted to reflection, leadership, and parent-student-teacher partnerships.

Monitoring student improvement plans, fostering relationships between advisees and other teachers, improving school-parent communication, academic counselling, meeting students' needs for personal guidance, promoting students' perception of the school as a caring institution, building interpersonal and social skills, raising awareness of geo-political issues, and analyzing national and local community concerns are all available through advisories.

Differences between regular classes and advisories: students' choice of teacher advisors, flexible curriculum based on a particular group's readiness, no compulsory exams, no grades, descriptive evaluations, and students' concerns to carry the day.

An advisor's blog comment: "We never came up with a cohesive curriculum which is what I was told would happen during the interview. I would love long term curriculum advising so I could see what someone has done [with their advisory session] over the course of the year."

Another's comment: "As students get closer to adulthood, schools often become more isolating and impersonal. Advisory programs offer the structure to meet students' developmental needs because it is the one place in school where students are intimately known as a 'whole child'."

An eighth-grade boy: "Advisory gets you into the state of mind that school is not only about work, but that it is a place where teachers really know you and understand you."

"Creating a Culture of Connectedness through Middle School Advisory Programs" (2009), an article by Sarah Brody Shulkind and Jack Foote concluded the following:

1. Advisors keep track of each advisee: awareness, inquiry, and follow-up.
2. Students believe advisories help improve academic progress. Advisories helped students focus on their studies, receive academic support, strategize about classes, set academic goals, and belong to a group striving for success.
3. Advisories become learning communities.
4. Students gravitate toward one another for p*eer tutoring or study groups.*

Developing quality advisory classes will take time. One important support group for advisories is PLC meetings where each subject teacher is also a TA. As suggested in Chapter 7, this amounts to three hours per week.

Advisory functions:

1) Extending/reinforcing self-differentiated learning in the classroom,
2) Building/monitoring individual student learning plans,
3) Providing a safe haven for all students to organize presentations/reflections,
4) Promoting student/parent leadership for school improvement/after school activities,
5) Welcoming parent participation
6) Time for teachers: lesson plans/thinking or learning for regular classes,
7) Tutoring each other,
8) Deliberate practice, planning, collaborative skills, resiliency,
9) Building trust while advancing collaborative skills/attitudes,
10) Observing other advisories,
11) Providing time for internships/community service.

Such functions grow/sustain student leadership for school initiatives such as assemblies that teach, school-wide student *learning to learn* conferences, and pupil lesson observers providing feedback to the school on the quality of lessons according to district-wide criteria as well as finding processes for measuring and *communicating those results to students, parents, and* communities.

Guy Claxton et al. in "The Learning Powered School: Pioneering 21st Century Education" (2013) describe students at North Oxfordshire Academy:

> Students are being trained to act as coaches to each other. They are learning how to respond to another person's needs, to evaluate their levels of skill and motivation, to listen and question to unearth understanding, and to enable others to reach their goals. As they develop their skills, they are being given opportunities to learn how to coach teachers too.
> Self-evidently, the creation of a culture in which students know how to give perceptive but respectful feedback to their teachers, and in which teachers are willing to listen to stu-

dents and take seriously what they hear, does not happen overnight. It takes time, coaching, and support on both sides, and there are often hiccups along the way. But we have yet to visit a school that has dared to move in this direction and regretted it. On the contrary, they universally agree that the journey has been hugely worthwhile. (p. 141)

Guided inquiries by student government, advisories, and ad-hoc groups instigate change by gathering both quantitative and qualitative data: interviewing teachers/students, studying school/district information, and making classroom observations. Examples are PLC effectiveness, teacher workload detracting them from their primary role of improving student achievement, degree of self-regulated learning in classrooms, effects of streaming, quality of writing feedback, technological supports for learning, school rules, disciplinary practices, and determination of grades. Groups/individuals then present findings at school assemblies open to parents/community.

Instead of time controlling us, we need to take control of time. Wood, G.H. in *Time to Learn: How to Create High Schools That Serve All Students" 2nd edition* (2005) sets out flex time typically shorter than a regular class period. While the format might vary from school to school, the purpose remains the same: to give students a chance to follow their own interests/receive extra support and take charge of their own learning.

Flex Days: A weekly flex day may be an early release day, where students have the freedom to do work based on their individual needs, interests, and community goals. Students work independently or in groups, across grade levels, on interdisciplinary projects or activities. Some schools with flex days work with students to take part in internships or community service opportunities off campus.

Students volunteering to work with teachers can have an impact. At the simplest level, I recall, back in September 1967, as principal of Frontier Collegiate Institute in Cranberry Portage, Manitoba, looking to provide audio-visual learning support for teachers. I approached five grade twelve students who only needed one or two courses before graduation the following June. They were more than happy to volunteer—too much time on their hands.

They would, after some help, learn how to run a 16 mm film projector, a filmstrip projector, make overhead transparencies, as well as volunteer for any other chores/supports teachers felt would be helpful. By any measure, this simple teacher-student collaborative effort was a success.

Later, as principal of MBCI in The Pas, Manitoba, teachers brainstormed ways to make our student assemblies more effective. Seating more than seven hundred students and teachers was a problem. In the past, they had used bleachers in the gym. Instead, we wanted students in organized rows of chairs with individual classes and their teacher sitting together, facing the stage. But how could we quickly set up seven hundred chairs at the beginning of the day?

The answer was student support. Twenty students from all grades volunteered to become part of the "Chair Brigade." They set up all the chairs for the students prior to assemblies and stacked them away at their conclusion. I was surprised when they asked permission to sit together in the front row. They also requested T-shirts with "Chair Brigade" on them. No other favours, except in June, when the brigade and I took a half-day and went out into the country for a picnic.

Another level of students as allies set out by Juliet Strang et al. (2006) is student participation in learning conferences, management teams, teacher hiring, lesson observation, school change credit courses, and staff/PLC meetings.

And all following "gradual release of responsibility": this guiding principle not only for self-differentiated learning in subject areas, but for school wide ownership, leadership, democratic-making, and peer support programs.

Teaching democracy in some parts of the United States, although uncommon, includes *student participation in school board meetings, running for board membership, civics classes, participation in district planning, community support for schools, and school evaluations.*

Generation YES, a nationwide technology program, infuses *students to teach teachers technology* as a powerful way to engage students in learning as well as promote classroom efficacy, with some educators enthusiastic about this learning model. In Annapolis, Maryland, the local school district has engaged students as full voting members of the school board for more than 25 years. In Oakland, California a group of students recently led a district-wide evaluation of their teachers, curriculum, facilities, and students. Here in Canada, Ontario allowed a student trustee to attend school board meetings. No vote, but still a voice for students.

Ground level collaborative learning communities such as PLCs and advisories support and extend Ritchhart's (2015) eight factors of cultural improvement: 1) teacher expectations for growing intelligence, 2) common language and use of language to support interactions, 3) a new view on the use of time focused on thinking/learning, 4) holistic modeling by teachers, 5) exacting thinking routines in and *out of the classroom*, 6) seizing curricular opportunities that engage students at every level, 7) proven interactions that spread respect for others and ourselves, and 8) learning environmental factors.

These behaviours, orientations, and attitudes will not spread by themselves. It is through the collaborative efforts, leadership, practice, modeling, research of students, teachers, and parents in assemblies, classrooms, advisories, and learning communities in and out of school that we develop the enlarged culture we seek.

A related statement by Steinberg S. and Kincheloe J. within *Students as Researchers: Creating Classrooms that Matter* (1998) on learning from each other:

> In the same manner that we don't want to take flying lessons from an instructor who can't fly an airplane, students can only learn to become researchers from teachers who are capable of doing research. Teachers must model research and share their own research with their students. (p. 16)

Roland S. Barth (1990) referring to Donald Graves (1980):

> There is no better way for adults to impart the importance and skills of writing than to be writers themselves. Graves reasons that we cannot expect a teacher to practice the craft of teaching writing who does not practice the craft of writing itself. (p. 99)

Pursuing the point:

> I am convinced that adults who write well in school, and make their writing visible, teach students as much about writing as those who deliberately set out to teach writing. And I have found that writing about practice is immensely helpful in speaking about practice. The skills and ideas exercised in writing are easily, if not automatically, transferred to speaking. Most teachers and principals are regularly called on to display the latter skills even though they may not appear to need the former. I find that prior experience writing about a topic contributes to command over the spoken word. (p. 99-100)

As the unknown student in Chapter 2 implored, schools characterized by "a healthy amount of challenge to encourage learning in a safe and friendly environment" dedicated to student welfare should rule. The same is true for teacher welfare: they too need the freedom to learn within safe, mixed learning communities of teachers and students where shared moral purpose and collective response-abilities outweigh notions of 'winners' and 'losers'.

House and Lapan's (1978) research in *Survival in the classroom* under the chapter "Credibility with Students", reports five questions summarizing student concerns when evaluating a teacher. (Yes, students evaluate teachers constantly, compare notes, and share opinions).

How free are we to decide what we learn and how we learn?
How qualified are teachers? Do they know what they are trying to teach?
Can they explain things in different ways we can understand? Can they teach?
How clear are their expectations?
How fair are they in evaluating us? Do they have favourites?

Doug Fisher et al. in *Visible Learning for Literacy: Implementing the Practices that Work Best to Accelerate Student Learning* (2016) report students using a mix of trust, competence, dynamism, and immediacy as criteria for teacher credibility. Teachers who don't keep their word, show incompetency in their subject, or seem detached from student learning are seen as untrustworthy. Fairness is critical. Repairing relationships through displaying student work/thinking, class achievements, speaking to the growth of all students, pride based on evidence, and a focus on improvement can go a long way in building trust/long range relationships.

If what is good for students is good for teachers, then let's assume teachers have similar concerns:

- How free are teachers to decide what they learn and how they learn?
- Do principals and district administrators have the quality knowledge/ leadership platform needed to improve teaching and learning?
- Do they know what they expect teachers to learn?

- Can they teach teachers—explain well, model, and use good examples/ methods? How clear are their expectations?
- How fair are they in evaluating teachers? Do they have favourites?

These are lessons for teachers, principals, and district administrators. If teachers want respect, collegiately, expertise, clarity, and fairness from administrators, they should take a hard look at students' concerns. And if principals empathize with students' concerns, they should reflect on their own thinking/behaviour when working with teachers.

A respectful, collaborative approach by principals/district personnel that pays off when solving teaching problems with teachers also works for teachers working with students. I offer the example of Stephanie, an inexperienced teacher in Shanghai teaching computerized Creative Design (drafting) to grade eleven Chinese students.

Because she was told only bad teachers sent misbehaving students to the principal, she suffered through Mary's interruptions, refusal to quit chatting with her neighbours, and bad manners to Stephanie over months. Finally, she tried something besides admonishments. She asked Mary to stay behind after class.

Without reviewing Mary's behaviour, Stephanie told her that she didn't know what to do; told her she liked Mary personally, but had no idea how they could work together. She knew Mary was capable of doing better; she got along well with her fellow students, but learning in the class was suffering.

On the road to Damascus—another epiphany. Not only did Mary improve, but she supported Stephanie for the rest of the year. They became friends founded on mutual respect. Mary's behaviour and lackadaisical attitude disappeared, she became a more serious and successful student with all her teachers.

Nobody is saying one-on-one conferences with disruptive students are quick fixes, but a mix of honesty, concern, and respect for a student is a powerful foundation for improvement. In general, I don't see self-regulated learning getting very far without clear, effective, and self-disciplined interactions taking hold. This is so important. Student responsibility and ownership founded on students learning to respect each other and teachers without close supervision.

There are no easy answers. Students are people, not robots. Reflect on how you were feeling about yourself as a teacher or your planning when a substantial number of students act as if they would rather be anywhere else. There are reasons behind every action. Using punishment is not only bad, it shows how little you are willing to invest in students—and they know it.

Contrast the traditional view of classroom management with the reflections of a highly regarded teacher (Mr. K) I worked with in Shanghai. When asked for his main area of improvement:

> Biggest area of improvement? Classroom management. When to be more indulgent and understanding (as often as possible), when to use tough love, when to inject flexibility into standards and deadlines (almost always, as needed) and how to appreciate what students are realistically capable of doing in class, given their individual talents and backgrounds. This latter, of course, is a critical part of ongoing differentiated learning.

Comporting with the above, insistence on polite, respectful behaviour requires teachers modeling personal and professional commitment to others. Behaviour management, a synonym for rewards and punishment, has been, despite its prevalence, a colossal failure. Behavioural skills don't happen through a hands-off approach waiting to see what happens, but through insistence on correct behaviour through everyday interactions between teachers and students.

School-wide behaviour planning includes students. To be frank (my middle name), it has little to do with writing one-sided contracts for students listing ways to suspend/expel. Quality planning is recognizing social skills students are lacking and addressing them, as with any other learning, through clear expectations, direct instruction, deliberate practice, cooperative thinking, teacher modeling, concern for others, and gradual release of responsibility.

Chapter 7
Building Social Capital: Team Building

"The future is not some place we are going to, but one we are creating. The paths to it are not found, but made; and the activity of making them changes both the maker and the destination."
– Peter Elly

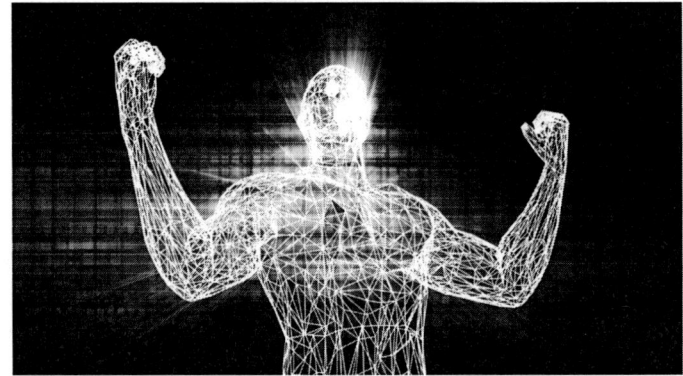

Sir Ken Robinson and Michael Fullan see a movement on its way to becoming a revolution, overturning a culture of compulsion for a culture of choice as difficult, but doable. Self-regulated learning, a combination of student choice, learning to learn, and gradual release of responsibility, is part of that revolution. Other "right drivers", according to Fullan, are a clear sense of direction, coherence, interwoven policies and strategies, and an embedded culture of improvement.

The British Columbian student crying for help is not alone. Patricia H. Hinchey and Pamela J. Konkol (2018), quote American students attending a prestigious, affluent high school asking the administration to address their high stakes/high academic pressure climate:

> At [our school] there is one path to success. This path is made clear from the day high school anticipation begins, and is reiterated until graduation. From the age of 13 every perspective [name of school] student understands that this path makes no exceptions, and those who wander off or fall behind are left for failure. Everyone here understands that there is no worse fate than failure.

It ends with an entreaty:

> And you, the [name of school] administrators, must work with us. Stop teaching us there is only one way to be a student. Stop treating community colleges, trade schools, and apprenticeships like failing destinations. Stop paving the one true path to success…and start treating us like people, not GPA's or test scores. Start letting us choose how we wish to be defined. Start helping us to find our dreams, and give us the tools we need to achieve them. Start understanding our priorities instead of implementing yours. Start defining success as any path that leads to a happy and healthy life. Start teaching us to make our own paths, and start guiding us along the way. (p. 60)

First, agreement on inter-connected goals, then collaboration on starting points, followed by collective accountability (internal and external) for the results. All based on local information, focused research, distributed leadership that includes students and parents, considered practice, and ongoing feedback.

This requires bottom-up and top-down trade-offs at every opportunity. One long standing source of discord within high schools is teachers focused on academics and refusing to spoon-feed students, while others see the need to support the whole child. This bifurcation mirroring polarized conflict between progressives and conservatives on such issues as national health care, economic inequalities, publicly funded childcare, government for all, systemic racism, gender equality, climate change, and prison reform.

Howard Gardner, in his book, *The Unschooled Mind: How Children Think and How Schools Should Teach* (2011), sees the major purpose of school as "access to the products of the major disciplines." He cautions that "disciplinary knowledge and understanding are entirely different from the memorization and regurgitation of factual information that characterizes 'subject matter' knowledge—and that continues to be foregrounded in most educational circles" (p. xxi).

He believes that "every person on the planet ought to have access to the products of these disciplines, or he or she will continue to hold views that are in significant measure unfounded or even nonsensical." (P. xxi)

Consequently, it is the logic of mathematics and science, deeper thinking in all subjects, recognition of false assumptions, unveiling of self-serving dogma, rule of law, learning opportunities afforded by language, willingness to work with others, assessment of evidence, and concern for the less fortunate, that will allow the survival of democracy.

Producing a General Purpose Statement (GPS) can assist in avoiding the extremes of both traditional teaching and progressive education, what Jane Kise (2014) calls the false dichotomy of academic achievement vs whole child education. Reconciliation, she states, starts with recognizing the other group as partners in achieving common goals, a necessary condition for whole-school collaboration/alignment.

The more carefully you set the foundation, the less likely it will fail. As Kise puts it, we need to "listen to the reasoning of those with whom we disagree, validate their needs and fears, and vow to work together, no matter how difficult it is" (p. 4).

She sees intellectual conflict as an asset, not a liability. One concern: the GPS is not the usual mission statement so vague anything is justified; to be effective it must infer processes, guidelines, and subgoals that focus and align district resources, roles, and decision making at all levels.

In the case of traditionalists, possible negative results are: immature students left to sink or swim, learning squeezed into a fixed timespan, competition as the only method for judging success, marks as the sole motivation, isolated student learning, teaching methods centred on teacher talk, failure to gather data on student engagement and motivation, restricted student choice, academic achievement stressed over personal growth, failure to heed research on the value of arts/hands-on problem solving, superficial preparation of students for science and other challenging subjects, memorizing as evidence of thinking, emphasizing external exams over other learning goals such as creativity; narrowing the academic curriculum, limited support for students becoming lifelong learners, students dreading asking (or answering) questions for fear of appearing inept, confining differentiated instruction to technology, sorting students through leveled courses or outright streaming; and teachers defined solely as subject specialists, not language teachers, nor student advisors.

Information on student engagement and motivation from underperforming students is rarely gathered. Underachieving students from Kise's book:

> "The smart kids get to learn new things. We're stuck with the same stuff over and over."
> "Teachers need to be fair and give compliments to everyone. Compliments are something you'll work hard for."
> "Teachers need to work with you until you get it. I can't get help at home. The worst is when you don't get it and they say, 'Didn't you listen?'"
> "No teacher should be telling me I can't do something. If I want to try a harder task or read a harder book, let me do it!"
> "Teachers and students look at me like I'm backward. Once in a while, tell me I'm doing a good job."
> "The smart kids have all been a teacher's pet at some time."
> "I learn when teachers listen and ask questions, trying to understand what I'm saying." (p. 49)

Over-zealous progressive educators have their own downsides/unintended consequences: weaker students falling further behind due to a lack of academic emphasis, unclear achievement criteria, confusing low expectations with caring, replacing academic challenges with more popular games, attributing low student success to poverty/home situations, time for academics reduced in favour of teaching social skills, personal growth, nutrition, or personal finances; reduction in students challenging themselves because of being over-protected, students failing state/provincial examinations, poor preparation for university, low expectations for thinking abilities, downplaying the importance of mastering academic disciplines/deeper thinking, underestimating the ability of students to overcome adversity, confusing enjoyment with learning, and repetitive test opportunities encouraging lack of focus/ownership.

At the school level, the following organizational development routine is helpful for achieving consensus. It is aimed at increasing communication, finding common ground, improving relationships, and reducing misunderstandings and polarization under Theorem 6 (learning from others). Each group meets separately and builds two lists: 1) thoughts, attitudes, and perceptions of the other group, and 2) predictions of what the other group is saying about them.

The two groups meet and share their lists—the interactions restricted to clarification. The groups then retire to separate rooms to 1) discuss what they learned about the other group and themselves, and 2) make a list of issues that need to be resolved.

Together, the two groups share what they learned, prioritize issues, and lay plans for improved collaboration. Also on the table: ongoing formative assessment of progress, needed supports from the school/district such as time for visiting the other groups' classrooms, and ways this routine could be transferable to one on one, or group to group student learning.

Finding common ground is a challenge in and out of school. The polarized conflict between progressives and conservatives within nations has a long history. Further concerns are contained in Sapolsky R. M.'s book, Behave: The Biology of Humans at our Best and Worst, (2017):

> Starting with Theodor Adorno in the 1950s, people have suggested that lower intelligence predicts adherence to conservative ideology. Some but not all studies since then have supported this conclusion. More consistent has been the link between lower intelligence and a subtype of conservatism, namely, right-wing authoritarianism (RWA, a fondness for hierarchy). One particularly thorough demonstration of this involved more than fifteen thousand subjects in the UK and the United States; importantly, *the links among low IQ, RWA, and intergroup prejudice* were there after controlling for education and socioeconomic status. The standard, convincing explanation for the link is that RWA provides simple answers, ideal for people with poor abstract reasoning skills...
>
> In one study conservatives and liberals, when asked about the causes of poverty, both tended toward personal attributions (They're poor because they're lazy). But only if they had to make snap judgments. Give people more time, and the

> liberals shifted toward situational explanations (Wait, things are stacked against the poor). In other words, conservatives start gut and stay gut; liberals go from gut to head…
>
> Liberals and conservatives are equally capable of thinking past gut personal attributions to subtler situational ones— when asked to do so, both are equally adept at dispassionately presenting the viewpoints of the opposite camp. It's that liberals are more motivated to push toward situational explanations…
>
> These findings suggest it's easier to make a liberal think like a conservative than the other way around. Or, stated in a familiar way, increasing cognitive load should make people more conservative. This is precisely the case. The time pressure of snap judgments is a version of increased cognitive load. (pp 446–448, [emphasis added])

Sapolsky's research goes beyond relevance for achieving consensus on change in high schools; its considerations also critical when promoting democratic citizenship within the school system and elsewhere. Unchecked right-wing authoritarianism, spiced with conspiracy theorists and freedom without responsibility, not only has the capacity to suppress high schools, its adherents threaten democratic ideals across nations.

A pertinent letter to the Bangor (Maine) Daily News (October, 1964) entitled "Democracy is Destructible" from E.B. White (2019) describes "the classic pattern of authoritarianism and the police state":

> Discrediting the court, intimidating the press, depicting the federal government as the enemy of the people, depicting social welfare as the contaminant in our lives, arguing that the end justifies the means, slyly suggesting that those of opposite opinion are perhaps of questionable loyalty, and always insisting that freedom has gone down the drain.

He concludes by reminding us that democracy is destructible: "It is, indeed. It can be destroyed by a single zealous man who holds aloft a freedom sign while quietly undermining all of freedom's cherished institutions."

There are other obstacles to school/district consensus. Jennifer Abrams (2016), notifies us that finding common ground has challenges, not simply because of disagreements within professional learning communities, school staff decision making, or new roles for supporting student learning, but as a result of challenging the culture of the organization.

She sees hard conversations as less effective when the issues are on a bigger scale, such as conversations with a group, a district, or with supervisors. This is the result, not of different perspectives, but of the culture as a whole.

Her warning:

> Hard conversations don't happen in a vacuum. They happen in a system of relationships. Teachers, busy with students, don't always have the mindset to think about the politics at play in the current system as much as they should. They're busy focusing on the students. It's understandable. And yet, if you want to make systems change as a teacher leader or administrator, it's critical to be aware of what is going on from the 'balcony point of view'. There are explicit *and implicit* norms at play all the time. (p. 41)

Abrams refers to Dr. Robert Marshak's work, *Covert Processes at Work: Managing the Five Hidden Dimensions of Organizational Change* (2006), from which she learned not only to pay attention to working well with others but organizational change effects. What is the ripple effect on the rest of the organization, she asks, when honest feedback, hard conversations, and agreement between individuals or groups occur? She challenges us to look at the proposed changes not only through the eyes of individuals or groups, but the organization as a whole.

Her practical questions:

1. Who are the stakeholders with interests related to the change, and based on their needs how might they perceive this change?
2. What sources of power or influence do these stakeholders have to impact the change?
3. How will you deal with each critical stakeholder to ensure support for the change?
4. Will you need to modify your proposal to gain enough support from those who could block your plan?

5. How will we continue to monitor shifting needs, interests, and political processes as change unfolds?
6. How will we work with the covert processes at play during this change? (pp. 42-43)

For this last question, she gives examples such as "the old boys network at play in the hiring of administrators", or discussion of someone "who took away someone else's job 30 years ago" (p. 43). These, Abrams states, are personal baggage carried over to the professional present.

Possible Goals in a General Purpose Statement (GPS):

⇒ High academic results.
⇒ College/career/citizenship readiness.
⇒ Equity as responding fairly and proportionally to the needs of individuals, redressing disparity and acknowledging systemic discrimination/ removing barriers.
⇒ Enhancing communication capabilities through reading, writing, and speaking instruction in all high school courses. Decreasing rewards and punishments and increasing intrinsic motivation through gradual release of responsibility.
⇒ Moving away from a narrow definition of school success (witness the American students above) toward student creativity/choice on a variety of learning/career opportunities. Collaboration with parents/community to meet physical, social, intellectual, emotional, vocational, and safety needs.

There are more:

⇒ Local teacher/PLC freedom to explore and inspire with accountability.
⇒ Different teaching strategies such as direct instruction *and* guided inquiry as appropriate. High levels of student engagement and motivation.
⇒ Democratic participation and ownership of education by students, parents, and community. Seeing other points of view: old enemies becoming new friends, false dichotomy recognition, and appreciating the multicultural and plural landscape of society.
⇒ Love of learning, learning to learn, enhancing creativity, lifelong learning, making thinking visible, deeper thinking, and nurturing intelligence.

⇒ The ability to work with others.

⇒ Personal growth as a blend of intellectual, physical, emotional, and social learning; all contributing to happiness at any age.

⇒ Time for students/teachers/administrators for collaborative thinking, learning, and planning.

These goals overlap, support each other, and are almost all sub-objectives for such interconnected goals as *high academic results for all students, the ability to work with others, love of learning, learning to learn, enhanced creativity, lifelong learning, making thinking visible, deeper thinking, raising general intelligence, and democratic citizenry.*

A reminder: George H. Wood, in his book, *Time to Learn: How to Create High Schools That Serve All Students 2nd edition* (2005), connects participating in a democracy with ability to learn:

> Passivity and low expectations are not only the enemies of learning, they are also enemies of democratic life. A democracy requires that its citizens be engaged, think for themselves, be willing to take action, and tolerate ambiguity. When the final part of a young person's public education is to passively consume sometimes trivial information, they are not learning what it means to be a self-directed thinker or citizen. (p. 45)

Behaviors/thinking of self-directed citizens:

Use evidence as the basis for voting/decision making. Know how to research issues. Collaboratively work with others to solve problems. Become knowledgeable of the history, short and long, of recurring issues at home and abroad. Understand systems of government including local, territorial, state, provincial, and federal responsibilities while recognizing, at times, the need for change. Advocate for the collective good while respecting the rights of individuals. Recognize false dichotomies as well as the need for compromise, kindness, and balanced approaches to societal issues. Employ and consolidate learning to learn abilities such as listening, reading, writing, speaking, and working with others. Identify differing points of view. Fight racism in all its forms. Support environmental, social, and governance values.

As an example of voters addressing research/evidence, Andrew Coyne, in a Toronto Globe and Mail article, July 22, 2022, when discussing federal support for improved health care, had this to say:

> The key to understanding any party platform is to read the part that is written in invisible ink: There is what it says, and then there is what it does not say, which is usually far more significant. But since neither of them (Liberals or Conservatives) can actually control how the provinces spend the money, it amounts to free cash either way–just enough to allow the provinces to put off reforming their health care systems, without making them accountable for the results. If experience is any guide, higher compensation for providers, but no shorter wait times.

Democratic participation/ownership of education by students, parents, and community is a force for change. Witness the following comments from the Greater Vancouver School Board website (March 2021):

"At the senior level, I would love to see 'mark chasing' and 'system gaming' disappear. I would like my own kids to enjoy school and recognize its value."

"Get rid of mandatory courses. Let students pursue their interests without restraint."

"[VSB needs to] understand and communicate the real true meaning of education."

"All the research shows that an increase in physical stimulation and outdoor play, at all ages, is very beneficial. We'd like to see initiatives that increase the opportunity for this in our school."

"[We need] community cohesiveness [and] social responsibility. The public schools must focus on ensuring [that] children are educated for the future of our nation, not just academically... [and] to ensure [that] all children are able to see that they belong in this world [as] part of a greater community."

"[We need to] work [on] closing [the] gap between Aboriginal students and families."

"[There is] poor utilization of valuable public facilities. Schools should be the centre of the community, but cannot be when the doors are locked..."

"[I hope for] a community of schools that are closely connected and feel like part of a whole group instead of separate schools."

"The sense of community at our school makes our entire neighbourhood seem a safer, more welcoming place for our kids to grow. I love the integration of school and community."

"Schools set the tone for a neighborhood. If the school is doing well, a lot of people will care about other aspects."

"Multi-age classrooms encourage diversity [within] students and abilities and foster authentic community."

"Teachers [need] more educat[ion] on how to support their transgender students."

"[We need to] continue to provide opportunities for VSB staff to increase their own knowledge of Aboriginal culture and traditional knowledge to decrease racism within the schools."

"[I hope for an] inclusive atmosphere, coupled with the direction of scarce resources towards students most in need."

"In these trying times, the district's teachers, administrators and support staff have been the glue holding [the system] together. Under incredibly challenging conditions, their collective will have been tireless in ensuring that the institution that is public education, continues to set the standard for what is possible."

"Our kids' teachers have been amazing, and resourceful in dealing with ever increasing funding shortfalls. We also appreciate the advocacy that some VSB trustees have been doing for appropriate funding, seismic upgrades, and [the] maintenance of neighbourhood schools."

"Parent communication from the VSB has improved since 2013— would love to see this continue and see that parent voice is heard during this process."

"There have always been a small number of incredibly dedicated teachers who give many extra hours after school and in the evenings...these self-sacrificing 'super' teachers should be recognized much more...most of their impact was made in their 'volunteer' capacity, not their paid professional capacity. Please find ways to recognize these special teachers and make their stories (and impact) known."

Online summative statements on student comments:

"Students are most concerned with the education that they are receiving as well as the environment in which they are learning. They are appreciative of what now exists within the VSB system but want more flexibility and diversity in what they are learning, and all of it in a safe, inclusive and stress-free environment so that they can actually enjoy learning."

"There are particularly notable references by students to advocate for a value-shift that would move towards an education system that focuses less on grades and exams. Sexism came up as an issue within the student stakeholder group. In particular, describing the perceived sexism that females face when it comes to dress code and conduct."

We need visible public discussion on how to move forward. At the local level, this suggests a District Learning Support Committee (DLSC) as a forum: superintendent, district staff, principals, union representatives, local citizens, school board members, community representatives, parents, teachers, and students. Meetings to be held, fishbowl fashion, with a standing invitation for other community members including local newspapers/radio/TV.

Its purposes first, to *model* an inclusive, transparent process for learning communities in the district. Second, to *support* coalitions of teachers, students, parents, and community focused on student achievement by reducing distractions, assisting with formative data/information, reallocating resources, helping organize communication amongst schools, and providing expertise/research when requested. Third, to *monitor* district progress by aligning individual responsibility and collective expectations/accountability; and fourth, to *find consensus* on a GPS (General Purpose Statement).

In establishing a DLSC, facilitators might begin by gathering information from potential members. Interviews do more than gather information. Done well, they model communication skills, make thinking visible, appreciate different points of view, reveal potential challenges, build credibility/trust, identify collective and individual strengths, and emphasize local ownership of challenges and solutions. Possible interview questions for serving on a District Learning Support Committee:

> Why did you decide to serve on this team? Have you participated in collaborative work in the past? Under what circumstances? How should this committee work together? What skills, knowledge, or attitudes are needed? What do you see as its purpose? What kinds of school/district support will the DLSC require? How will the District Learning Support Committee hold PLCs/schools accountable for student achievement? How will it support schools, professional learning communities, student initiatives, and parent input? How do you think district goals influence decision making in your school now? What concerns do you have? What strengths are available to deal with those concerns? How will the DLSC assess its impact? What are you prepared to do to make the team successful?

The winning process for substantive change, M. Fullan insists, depends on finding "right drivers": *a clear sense of direction, coherence, interwoven policies/strategies, and an embedded culture of improvement.* The GPS or General Purpose Statement, hopefully, provides the *clear sense of direction.* Attaining *coherence* through *interwoven policies and strategies* is next, all pulling and pushing toward *an embedded culture of improvement.*

The District Learning Support Committee to provide pertinent information related to its role of supporting PLCs and schools. To that end, along with heading off resistance, Abrams recommends the district roll out a publicly available *Frequently Asked Questions* sheet with *answers* to expected concerns prior to planning. Examples:

1. How will the district support understanding the need for change and how it might affect role expectations? Who will lead the charge? How will we all support their credibility?
2. Why is this change needed now? What is the data/research on the status quo that provides the evidence? How will we explain benefits to students, teachers, principals, district staff, parents, and the community?

3. How will the district explain how the decision for change was made? In what way can others be involved in future decision making as we move ahead?
4. How do we address the concern of teachers with work overload? What is coming off the plate? What district supports in terms of funds, time, resources, and coaching are planned?
5. How do we handle conflict between past methods and newer expectations? How do we explain that we aren't dismissing all the old ways in their entirety? It is not a complete either-or situation. How do we demonstrate appreciation for current teachers and administrators along with the case for an improved learning culture?
6. How do we address failure fears and assure teachers they will not be judged immediately on their lack of success? This is a long-term growth endeavour.
7. How is this change different from past efforts? How will we know if the goals for our students are being realized?

Questions for School Wide Practices: 1) How do we maximize the number of high school parents participating in school improvement? 2) What input from students, subject teachers, parents, and community leadership will consolidate a good school improvement plan? 3) How do we include student input in evaluating teachers? 3) What should or should not be part of student assessment reports? 4) How do we integrate parental expertise with school curricula? 5) How can school assemblies support student ownership? 6) What school support is needed for effective student improvement plans?

Questions for District Leadership

1. How do we develop district wide benchmarks for requisite student learning outcomes?
2. How do we support a common advisory/learning to learn curriculum?
3. How do we reduce time spent by principals on administration in order to concentrate on teacher and student learning?
4. How do we cut time on meetings to increase district staff interactions in schools/classrooms?
5. What are common professional standards for district wide lesson plans?

6. How does leadership learn to confront individual and group behaviours through hard conversations based on empathy and student needs?
7. How do we inculcate distributed leadership across the district?

Improving any school demands the ability of the teaching staff to work together. But one overriding concern can often prevent widespread cooperation by blocking whole-school change. The first step, then, might well be the removal of that concern, not only as an obstacle; but as proof the staff can get past major differences and move forward.

These include expectations based on ethics, role responsibilities, welfare of students, offers of support, precedents, collaborative initiatives with others, and bottom lines on what is professionally permissible. These are two-way conversations; determining the whole picture/context as necessary for quality decision making.

False polarities described by Abrams include: clarity and flexibility, work *and* home priorities, teacher as lecturer *and* facilitator, needs of students and needs of teachers, centralization and decentralization. But perhaps the most pertinent false polarity is advocating district-wide improvement vs appreciating the performance of current teachers.

Examples of *standard professional expectations* in Abrams' book critical to the development and proficiency of professional learning communities of teachers, principals, and district staff are:

> We speak positively about the district and each other at work and in the community. We take personal responsibility for personal and group decisions; therefore 'We versus They' does not exist, we do not blame or make excuses. Everyone has a responsibility to communicate concerns and possible solutions to the appropriate person… It is our responsibility to participate as a team member in a collaborative environment using ideas, resources, and information to achieve common goals. Think well of yourself, and take pride in your professional dress, personal appearance, and personal health. (p. 9)

The matter of trust cannot be overemphasized. Working together, teams have the ability to resolve problems, generate increased capacity for change, and achieve common goals. Professional learning communities of teachers, over time and properly supported, are essential for improving instructional expertise and learning for all students. Diversity in our student population is not a weakness, nor a problem; it is a major opportunity for increasing everyone's capacity to learn.

Policies and Strategies Directed at an Embedded Culture of Improvement

1. Professional Learning Communities
2. Learning to Learn/Deeper Thinking/Making Thinking Visible /Time to Learn
3. Self-Regulated Learning/Gradual Release of Responsibility
4. Language across the Curriculum/Learning to Learn/Deeper Thinking
5. Teacher/PLC support of Principals/District Staff
6. Leadership and Motivation
7. Parents and Students as Allies/Advisories/School-Community Integration
8. Formative School/District Assessments

These topics are described in this book. The sequenced content is based on the need for change, demonstrated leadership, widespread ownership/ collaboration, district support, democratic inclusionary practices, action research, student ownership, formative assessment, outreach to parents, local community participation, partnered school districts and recognized accountability.

These guideposts are roughly comparable to achieving goals by local governments, municipalities, counties, provinces, state departments of education, the U.S. Department of Education, territories, and nations as they are within classrooms, schools, and districts.

Foundational beginnings are those elements most immediately accessible: PLCs learning to learn together, students and parents as partners, a focus on quality teaching and learning in and out of school, student self-regulation/gradual release of responsibility, and language for learning in every class.

Success is dependent on teachers and students' everyday support for principals, district staff, parent inclusion, advisories, community integration, and accountability. These combined with the ever-present theorems of 1) learning how to start, 2) learning what we teach, 3) teaching the whole person, 4) learning by doing, 5) learning how to lead, 6) learning from others, and 7) learning to be accountable.

This book is not a set of instructions. It does provide, however, valuable conclusions, clues, signposts, deductions, structures, and research based on the experience of myself and others. The change *you* are after will be assisted by its considerations as you and your colleagues, students, and community partners find choices that work for you.

Clarifications:

Point 5: Supporting principal/district leadership is a mutual benefit. Without reciprocal support from the principal, vice principal, resource teachers, counsellors, and district staff in terms of time, advice, and shared information, PLCs are severely handicapped.

Point 6 is also leadership, but with the view of extending it to include students, parents, and the community. The model is familiar in hockey: lead by example, support others, practice resilience, and assert confidence in the rest of the team. Take a listen to NHL captains during post-game interviews—win or lose.

Point 7 is personal involvement/support from parents such as teacher advisor-student-parent meetings for building change: students reflect on their progress, assess the availability of school supports, integrate school and out of school learning, determine roadblocks and opportunities, and plan for self-improvement. Formative school/district assessments, point 8, as previously stated, are needed for improved collective learning on the go: all pointing to ever-increasing capacity and accountability.

One outgrowth is students contributing to the effective functioning of schools. In Shanghai, a group of students, without being asked, and cognizant of the Chinese principal's decision *not* to replace our school secretary took over a good portion of the secretary's responsibilities. Investigating opportunities for students to directly contribute to their school falls under opportunities/responsibilities for student government.

Parents are a critical part of the mix. Beyond participation in the DLSC, parents help plan school change, tutor, conduct special projects, and raise funds. Parents lobby for needed school infrastructure, attend school run courses on supporting students at home, and develop computer skills/written communication along with auditing high school classes.

The rules for teachers appear to be these: 1) start with what you know, become the best professional teacher/PLC member you can be, 2) look for allies with an open arms approach—students, parents and the public, 3) look upward and collaborate with principals and district personnel as part of the team, 4) use student success as your prime aim/proof for change, and 5) view school and community as opportunities for student leadership under another rule—the gradual release of responsibility.

As Fullan and Gallagher (2020) concluded, the devil is in the details. What works in one school, district, or class may be less effective in others. This suggests, as described in other organizational development processes, regular gathering of inside information through questionnaires, conversations, interviews, focus groups, and observations as essential for improved ownership and motivation.

Spirals of Inquiry for Equity and Quality (2016) by Halbert and Kaser, with their focus on improving student engagement, student achievement, and equity for minority groups, has the same message. They see inquiry teams employing key stages: the first is *scanning*, described as checking "that our learners are at the heart of what we do," while focusing on "thoughtful evidence from direct observations", followed by *"How does this matter?"* to ensure the importance of the inquiries, then engaging in new professional learning *action*, and finally checking that *"enough of a difference has been made."*

Such spirals to be inculcated as a system changer for teachers, professional learning communities, schools, districts, state and national departments of education, and provinces. These teams "always coming back to the experiences of the learners we serve" thus keeping us motivated to "move forward in our own learning." They describe collecting evidence that goes beyond quantitative data, state/provincial assessments, and "office behavior referrals" to determine a more complete picture (p. 48).

Halbert and Kaser's four questions seek evidence of intellectual and social engagement:

> Do young people report that they find their learning meaningful, relevant, and important? Do they know two adults within the school who believe they will be a success in life? Do they feel a sense of connection with their peers? Are they engaged in activities that give them a sense of community? *(*p. 49)

They point out that such scanning includes *teaching practices* along with *formative assessment systems.*

Halbert and Kaser arrived at seven conclusions from 'The Nature of Learning: Using Research to Inspire Practice', as set out by the 'Organization of Economic Cooperation and Development' in partnership with the 'Centre for Educational Research and Innovation' in their study of Innovative Learning Environments (ILE). The effort is an attempt to answer the question, *"How can today's schools be transformed to become learning and teaching environments that develop lifelong learners with the attitudes, skills, and knowledge required in the knowledge society?"* (p. 27).

An innovative learning environment:

1) Makes learning central through encouraging learner engagement and developing self-regulation.
2) Involves learning that is social and often collaborative.
3) Is highly tuned to the key role of the motivations and emotions of learners.
4) Is acutely sensitive to the individual differences among learners, including their prior knowledge.
5) Is demanding for each learner but without excessive overload.
6) Uses learning-based assessments that are thoughtfully constructed with a strong emphasis on formative feedback.
7) Promotes horizontal connectedness across activities and subjects—both in and outside the school—with active community involvement. (p. 28)

They also include advice on professional learning and improved student outcomes. Focused efforts require time—one or two years. In their experience working with BC schools, they see schools finding additional time for professional learning communities, staff meetings devoted to learning issues, professional book study groups, early morning sessions, or reaching out to other schools and districts.

An additional nuance based on the work of Helen Timperley, is "that whether participation in professional learning is voluntary or mandatory is not the key issue. What matters most is that the learning is of the highest possible quality and that it is deeply engaging." (p. 56)

Accessing expertise is stressed whether found inside the school, the district, online, within a local university, or another school in the province. They suggest that having a "trusted and well-respected colleague from another school help facilitate the learning can shift long-term norms within a staff group" (p. 56).

The existence of well-respected teacher-leaders and their importance within and across schools is described by Andy Hargreaves in the forward to *Developing Teacher Leaders* 2nd edition (2009) by Frank Crowther:

> All teachers in schools know who their leaders are—the ones who teach well, work hard, are prepared to stand up for what they believe, are able to work with and command respect among diverse colleagues, and are in it for the children rather than themselves. Teacher leadership often paradoxically requires confident but low-key principalship in order to prosper, but in some systems like Finland it is a defining feature of how the system operates. (p.xi)

Effective strategies are not primarily suggestions or structures—they are about extending relationships: building trust, resolving conflicts, learning to learn while teaching it to others, freeing students from past restrictions, building confidence through tiny victories and large celebrations, and welcoming parents and communities as partners. Tone is important—a combination of intelligence, confidence, humbleness, persistence, and kindness; no better combination can be found.

Jacqueline Ancess in *Beating the Odds: High Schools as Communities of Commitment* (2003), describes three researched high schools that promote student achievement through such characteristics as:

> Teachers are available. They take students' accounts of their problems seriously. They respond to students' personal and academic problems. They persist in efforts to help students personally and to meet educational obligations. *Students are intentionally connected to school adults with whom they have rapport.* The relationships are used for the achievement of students' expectations and the school's expectations for them. There are also opportunities and support for students to transcend self-imposed personal and educational limits. (p. 85, [emphasis added])

By preparing split screen lesson plans for content objectives *and* learning to learn capacities *with* students, we effect change well beyond our classrooms. Demonstrated student learning through quality writing, clear explanations, persuasive speech, creative responses, self-reliance, and integrity of character is the success needed to expand the movement. Our students are our ambassadors. More and more parents will appreciate, applaud, and support change after witnessing their children's accelerated interest and enthusiasm for learning in and out of school.

Pulling people on board depends on more than hope or even good teaching and learning. Parents, especially those who often feel disconnected from schools in the past such as minority groups, parents of children with learning disabilities, and those with a history of failure, are warmly welcomed as both observers and participants in advisories, classrooms, school assemblies, professional learning communities, after-school activities, professional learning days, and staff meetings.

Enrolling parents in courses is another option. One group could be young parents who enroll their pre-school children in a high school's child development/childcare course similar to the one we offered in Fort Smith. Progress in achieving self-regulated learning for students and parents is also helpful as it allows for parent time schedules and other responsibilities.

Schools need to keep track of previous dropouts, and as the school's capacity to serve a wider range of needs grows, it should invite those students back on a full or part-time basis. Knock on doors of dropouts if you have to, as we did in Grand Rapids, MB; offer hope/improved support, and welcome them back.

Another example from Mississippi by Nicholas Kristof:

> The school superintendent in the town of Hollandale, Mario Willis, told me his high school graduation rate was 97 percent, and he explained how his school fights to keep kids. The other day, he said, he had a call from the high school principal about an 18-year-old senior who was dropping out. The student lived in poverty and had a single mom who was unemployed, so the family's economic situation was desperate. Not seeing a way out, the young woman left school and took a restaurant job.
> That's when the school went all out to bring the student back. School officials repeatedly visited the young woman at home. They spoke to her mother, and they talked her employer into arranging work hours for her after school. So now she is back in school, on track to graduate. New York Times article, May 31, 2023

Students as change partners: 1) sharing their progress/learning in advisories, 2) small group presentations at school assemblies with parents/community members in attendance, 3) class websites for parents/community with student writing, comments, and reflections, 4) peer tutors/interested *future teachers* (doable with self-regulated learning) as part of helping students in both their own and elementary schools, and 5) student government leadership within the activities period, the community, and throughout the district. There are two kinds of time: time for teachers gained from student self-regulated learning within scheduled classes for them to observe, coach, and give formative feedback to individuals/small groups, and secondly, scheduled time for collaborative planning.

Students as school ambassadors includes school progress presentations to Lions Clubs, Town Councils, Band Councils and other community organizations that emphasize school success in reaching agreed-upon goals as well as continuing obstacles. They appreciate teacher, parent, and community support along the way, share mistakes as building blocks, and respect those with opposing opinions. Conflict resolution and collaboration skills are not only learned in classes, but also demonstrated as an integral part of such outreach.

Without time for collaborative learning and planning, improved student achievement is unlikely. Grant Lichtman, in his book, *#EdJourney: a Roadmap to the Future of Education* (2014), examines the issue under the title "Time for Adult Collaboration":

> Most teachers desperately want more time to work with their colleagues and to learn about new teaching practices, to try out new ideas, to constantly develop themselves into better teachers. It is one of the marvelous common threads of the profession: Most teachers got into teaching because they really care about kids and want to do whatever they can to be the best teachers they can be. Teachers tend to be eager to learn, just as they are eager to promote a love of learning in their students. But few schools allocate significant chunks of time for professional development. (p. 16)

Lichtman, while working with students and faculty at St. Andrews' Episcopal School in Fort Worth, met students who offered a solution. The students pointed out that adults needed time by themselves to learn, just as they did. They recognized that many of the classrooms at all grade levels were becoming project-based, and good projects are designed to include time for student collaboration, research, making, designing, building and creating. The students asked:

"What if say, every other Thursday for a half-day, all or many classes at the school had 'project time'? We need time to work on these projects together and don't really need teachers hovering around at those times. A few adults could supervise a large number of students during these collaborative work times, releasing the rest for large, frequent blocks of professional growth time." (p. 18)

Evidence for such changes: Kuhlthau et al., in *Guided Inquiry: Learning in the 21st Century* (2007), describe lack of time as *the contributing factor inhibiting success in instructional teams*. They reassumed traditional roles *"because they lacked the appropriate time to be more inventive"* (p.51, [emphasis added]).

A cautionary note from Andy Hargreaves in his foreword to *Developing Teacher Leaders*, 2nd edition, (2009):

> Under confident, outstanding, yet strangely low-key principals, some schools were able to energize the collective leadership of their teachers as they collaborated together to make improvements that benefit their students. They were able to develop what I call strong cultures of collaboration. But other principals tried to drive collaboration through their staffs, telling them where and when to meet, with whom and for what purpose. In this context of what I called forced collaboration or contrived collegiality, many teachers actually started to collaborate less. (p. viii)

The suggested timetable below is one answer to the question: Where is the time for comprehensive teacher collaboration, advisories, assemblies that teach, after-school learning activities, PLC meetings, staff meetings, and student government? But what is really needed is a full-scale inquiry using the ideas of local administrators, teachers, PLCs, students, parents, and community members of each school.

Time for PLCs, Advisories, Assemblies, Activities

Tuesday and Thursday		Monday, Wednesday, Friday
8:30-9:10	Advisories/Assemblies	8:30-9:10
9:10-10:25 Period 1		9:10-10:10 Period 1
10:25-11:40 Period 2		10:10-11:10 Period 2
11:40-12:30 Lunch		11:10-12:10 Period 3
12:30-1:45 Period 3		12:10-1:00 Lunch
1:45-3:00 Period 4		1:00-2:00 Period 4
3:00-4:00 Staff Mtgs/Student Activities		2:00-3:00 PLC Mtgs
Official School Day ends at 3:00 pm		2:00-4:00 Activities

Assumptions: that shortening classes to an average of sixty-six minutes is compensated through a combination of *forty minutes per day of small group social/academic support in advisories, school assemblies that teach, a daily activities/learning period for student choice, and three guaranteed hours of PLC action research each week.* Quality over quantity. Moreover, PLC planning time not at the expense of individual teachers' daily one-hour preparation. Saturdays and Sundays are open to student/community use.

How do teachers get to visit other classrooms? What planning is needed here? Expanding the district teacher-on-call budget beyond illness to include teachers observing colleagues' classrooms is one solution. Another is PLC members teaching the same course simultaneously. Students in one teacher's class re-distributed amongst others based on differentiated learning opportunities.

Another benefit of teaching the same course would be teachers gaining experience in all grades. Self-regulated learning, where students manage their own time through widened space—libraries, computer rooms, or classrooms with minimal teacher/parental supervision—also provides flexibility for teachers.

Classrooms divided by a folding wall allow teachers to be freed up to observe other lessons. All based on GRR—gradual release of responsibility in the use of time, planning, resources, and reciprocal learning. This opens other doors (no pun intended) for short term groupings of students for enrichment/remediation, extended practice, re-teaching, and peer tutoring.

Reflection on student capacity is found in *Time to Learn: How to Create High Schools That Serve All Students* (2005), by Principal George H. Wood:

> Because schools take too much responsibility for student behaviors, they seldom give kids *the chance to manage their own time*. Fearful that kids will choose inappropriate behaviors for which the school will be blamed, we choose instead to tightly control kids while they are under our supervision... We tend to be too afraid of failure in schools, wanting everything to be perfect and students to perform flawlessly... Instead, schools should be places where kids can fail with the minimum amount of fear or penalty. In failure we can see where the next lesson should be taught. (p. 135, [emphasis added])

This does not imply that all student behaviour is acceptable. There is no freedom (covid or non-covid) without responsibility. And this includes <u>what you shouldn't do</u> *and* <u>what you should do</u>. Those who behave badly/disrupt others' opportunities to learn (or live) can have their freedom temporarily curtailed. Leadership from senior students can be especially helpful. We don't expect all students to be on task 100%, but continued behaviour that is disrespectful, intolerant, or wastes the time of others necessitates guidance, planning, modeling, teaching, hard conversations, school supports, and at times, short-term consequences.

In BC High School Jiaoke Campus in Shanghai, our staffroom was unlike any I experienced back home—the result of knocking out a wall separating two regular classrooms—teachers' desks arranged along the walls. The school secretary also had a desk. A printer with nearby tables for sorting materials served everyone; each teacher's laptop connected to the printer.

The staffroom was open door. It was a rare moment without students or parents. The Chinese homeroom teachers, who taught supplementary/adjunct classes in Science 10/Social Studies 10 and were indispensable for home-school communication, had their desks interspersed among the Canadians.

Canadian teachers at SUIS had seventy minutes of preparation each day—considerably more than teachers in BC, where they average half of that—often one prep period of seventy minutes in one semester and nothing in the other. As an aside, BC teachers still lag behind every other province in Canada in preparation time. It makes more sense that this should be our main target, not lowering far less meaningful high school pupil-teacher ratios.

In China, students, during breaks between classes, lunchtime, and beyond regular school hours, were often at teachers' desks—for extra help or to visit. The staffroom served as an important resource for building relationships amongst students and teachers, parents and teachers, and teachers and teachers. What became increasingly clear was how physical setups influence such opportunities.

My office and the vice-principal's office were both within fifteen feet of the staffroom. I spent my time with teachers, students, and parents in that staffroom, teaching two classes of physics, tutoring two Later Literacy students, observing/participating in classes; hosting a student leadership course in activities period, leading stretching/isometrics sessions for students before school, attending parent support groups by grade level in an adjacent meeting room, or leading/attending our parent/student assemblies in the lecture theatre. This along with a learning community mix of Chinese and Canadian teachers three times a week.

The more ways we demonstrate we are in this together, the better off we will be. Warren W. Fabyen, in his master's thesis, "A Study of Secondary School Assemblies in Massachusetts," (2014), determined general assemblies to be an important vehicle for developing a sense of unity. Assemblies model thinking routines in large groups, underline the value of cooperative effort and action, and boost school morale. He describes assemblies as enhancing citizenry, showcasing cooperation for the "pleasure of the whole" and bonding school and communities together.

In the timetable above, assemblies are the first part of each day. Without a lecture theatre, this provides for early placement of chairs/tables, microphones in aisles, and whatever else is needed. As stated, the MBCI Chair Brigade, T-shirts and all, would do this in short order.

We wish to grow student citizenry inside and outside the school. As an example: Sicamous, BC, an attractive summer resort community (where I live) is situated on a channel between two lakes—Mara Lake to the south and Shuswap Lake to the west. We are a five-hour drive away from both Calgary and Vancouver.

Alberta ownership is everywhere. At least 50% of the residences (my neighbours) are owned by Albertans. A high percentage of local businesses and workers depend on Albertans for their livelihood. The controversies over the pandemic year (2020) in our town are the same as for a multitude of BC communities within reach of Albertans. Local biases, however, existed long before the pandemic.

Each year, from April until September, there are more Alberta license plates than British Columbian. Their trucks and boats (easy to spot—they have only one license plate) are gas-guzzling noise polluters; the grocery store is full of Albertans running down aisles the wrong way; they throw cigarettes on the highway, stones at electric vehicles, and plug up our beaches.

This has only worsened with the pandemic, according to yearlong residents, due to the higher rate of infection in Alberta. They are also judged as not smart enough to follow *any* guidelines let alone complicated ones (like 2 metres) needed to protect lives. As a past Alberta resident, I apologize for failing to notice such deficiencies in myself, former Albertan teacher colleagues, and family members in Edmonton, Red Deer, Calgary, and Medicine Hat.

That was not the only challenge. We also have the home-grown version of Albertans. My haircutter related an incident where a local man refused to wear a mask, swore profusely about government running his life, and finally left when she threatened to call the RCMP. Freedom to infect others his priority in assessing democracy.

Our grocery store employees have, at least at the beginning of the pandemic, experienced similar outbursts. There are also conspiracy theorists who call the virus a government hoax, believe vaccines are the cause of autism, and resist anyone, for whatever reason, telling them what they should do.

The mayor has asked for tolerance. *The Eagle Valley News* has articles from businessmen concerned about health guidelines that don't fit the level of incidence here in Sicamous. Not only are businesses suffering, but some workers have restricted hours or lost their jobs. People are hurting financially. In the local high school, one case of the virus was discovered. One death in the community to date.

Democratic values in public schools, student achievement, and effective citizenship are intrinsically linked. Enhancing citizenry in our students, building school and community partnerships, and using high school assemblies to collaboratively address community concerns all start with purpose. Using the pandemic as an example, we consider the following: What do we need to learn as individuals, as a school, and as a community? And how can we help each other learn?

There are many places to start. One is formulating goals through small group discussion in advisories. We begin with questions, not answers. *What do we want to learn? How will we learn it? How will we know we learned?*

Possible Investigations/Questions:

- What are the different points of view among the community?
- What evidence supports each POV? How do we judge evidence? Who do we trust, and why?
- What does citizenry mean in terms of government vs individual behaviour? In terms of health concerns, how does this differ with age?
- Where are the false dichotomies?
- How do individual decisions affect fighting the virus?
- What good has come out of this pandemic?
- What democratic rights, responsibilities, and evidence were demonstrated, attacked, or ignored?
- How do we avoid inter-personal conflict? Beyond health and the economy, what negative impact has the pandemic had on our community, province, nation, and the world?

- How do we form good questions?
- How do we analyze others' thinking?
- Reflection—what have we learned as individuals? Individual families? A school? A community?
- What information is needed? Where do we get it? What kind of thinking is required here?
- How do stereotypes/prejudices begin? What is their purpose? What lasting damage do they do to the subjects, their detractors, and the community as a whole?
- How do feelings help in your investigations? How do they hurt?

This last point is described in Michael S. Roth's online article: "A Focus on Critical Feeling", March 17, 2021:

> Through history, literature and the arts we make connections to worlds of emotion, creativity, and intelligence that take us beyond our individual identities and our group allegiances. The exercise of critical feeling should make us less susceptible to demagogic manipulation and to the misleading politics of resentment. It should make us more understanding of why other people care about the things they do.

The above questions are mine, but it is the students' concerns and *their* questions, as required for quality ownership, that count. For this, advisories are the right forum. Led by their advisors, and each other, students formulate questions that promise to move their investigations forward while reflecting their concerns. Later in this chapter I suggest extending such student research into the school, local community, learning support, and opportunities for change.

Whole-school involvement could be difficult during the pandemic. But starting with students' questions and looking to involve the community, we might begin by asking community members such as the mayor, local physicians, other health specialists, businessmen, senior centre representatives, town council members, RCMP, Alberta based residents, and conspiracy theorists to present their views, then respond later to students' questions/concerns through school assemblies open to the public.

During such presentations, students make notes on types of thinking: point of view, evidence, assumptions, relative importance, relationship to student questions/concerns, cause and effect, and other connections for group analyses in advisories.

Advisories take time to respond. Preparation for students to include readings/study on *what constitutes evidence* where dyads/small groups practice close reading, reading responses, summarization, formulating questions, while applying group learning skills. The learning to be supplemented with feedback from others/family, plus reflection.

During return engagements, and using the Ladder of Feedback as an aid to quality criticism, we have advisories: 1) requesting clarification 2) offering appreciations and agreements on specific points 3) stating disagreements/ alternate views, and 4) thanking the presenters.

An additional step is student researchers presenting their conclusions to the community in summaries that include suggestions/short- and long-range plans for community leadership consideration.

Physical space for these presentations plus responses might not be available in some high schools. But it is within most communities. In Sicamous, the Red Barn has room for students and allows public use; the Senior Centre and Legion Hall are others. These are available in most communities across Canada and other countries.

And for those of us who remember people contracting polio prior to Jonas Salk's vaccine and, as a result spent a lifetime on crutches, the conspiracy theorists exhibit a different kind of sickness. But for that, unfortunately, there is no vaccine.

School/community collaborative learning need not be occasional. In their chapter within *Networks for Learning* edited by Chris Brown and Cindy Poortman (2018), "A Professional Learning Network for the entire local Education System", Tulowitzki P. et al. describe collaborative teaching/learning in Germany on a more permanent basis. Instead of Professional Learning Networks with teachers working together, their expansionist term 'local educational landscape' encompasses extensive cooperation between schools, informal learning organizations, and other community resources.

Tulowitzki P. et al. (2018):

> While improved teaching and learning is also an aim of educational landscapes, *the learner, not the school nor the teachers, is front and center of the concept.* This results in educational landscapes often not only comprised of teachers and school leaders, but also of social workers, educational consultants, and facilitators, volunteers who work with children or young adults as well as local politicians linked to matters of education and/or youth…

> The lifeworld of the child is considered as the starting point and permanent background of all formal and non-formal learning activities. Thus, horizontal cooperation focuses on enabling a child's developmental opportunities in all areas *and aims to integrate school-based learning and out-of-school learning settings.* (pp. 117–118, [emphasis added])
> Landscapes can be viewed as applying the idea of a Professional Learning Network to an entire local educational system. They can also be attributed to a desire to do away with patchwork and piecemeal solutions and instead develop one coherent approach around the needs of the learner...
> A possible path could be to take the more focused notion of a Professional Learning Network and *slowly widen it to gradually encompass more agents,* leaving out aspects of local educational management altogether. Looking at Professional Networks, a gentle expansion toward the notion of educational landscapes could provide for a more comprehensive change of practices and deeper learning for those involved. (p. 130 [emphasis added])

A fictional instance of expansion is the novel *Evening Class* (1996) by Maeve Binchy. An Irish school in Dublin offering a combined learning experience for community members, high school students, and teachers. Their purpose to learn to speak Italian in preparation for a trip to Rome. The teacher is a former resident who spent years in Sicily. If ever there was a complete example of quality lesson preparation, collaborative learning, learning by doing, learning from others, social skills, modeling, and growing confidence in how to learn, this is it.

The power of choice in self-regulated learning is verified in extracurricular activities. "The Benefits of Participating in Extracurricular Activities", a study by Claudette Christison of Brandon University, Manitoba, published in the BU Journal of Graduate Studies in Education (2013), concluded they add to student success in the following ways:

1. Leadership, time-management, and willingness to accept constructive criticism
2. Self-esteem and resilience
3. Social development
4. Community involvement

She established that students understanding the benefits of extra-curricular activities helps them identify activities that support their academic and personal development. Duckworth (2016) came to the same conclusion: "Countless research studies showing that kids who are more involved in extracurriculars fare better on just about every conceivable metric—they earn better grades, have higher self-esteem, are less likely to get in trouble" (p. 225).

Claudette cites the work of Margo Gardner et. al (2012), "who followed eleven thousand American teenagers until they were twenty-six years old to see what effect, if any, participating in high school extra-curriculars for two years, as opposed to just one, might have on success in adulthood."

Beyond a year resulted in students more likely to graduate from college, volunteer in their communities, have a job, and earn more money. Developing resilience had one important variable: it didn't matter what activities students engaged in, but how long they stuck to it. Signing up for something for more than one year and making "some kind of progress" was critical.

Deliberate practice is a mainstay in pursuit of resilience, one of the key principles of learning to learn. Duckworth's basic requirements: 1) a clearly defined stretch goal, 2) full concentration and effort, 3) immediate and informative feedback, and 4) repetition with reflection and refinement.

Her suggestions:

1. Know the science of practice.

    We put together self-guided lessons, complete with cartoons and stories, illustrating key differences between deliberate practice and less effective ways of studying. We explained that no matter their initial talent, great performers in every domain improve through deliberate practice. We let students know that hidden behind every effortless performance on YouTube are hours and hours of unrecorded, invisible-to-outsiders, challenging, effortful, mistake-ridden practice. (p. 138)

2. Make it a habit.

    Figure out when and where you're most comfortable doing deliberate practice. Once you've made your selection, do deliberate practice then and there every day. Why? Because routines are a godsend when it comes to doing something hard. A mountain of research studies, including a few of my own, show that when you have a habit of practicing at the same time and in the same place every day, you hardly have to think about getting started. You just do. (p. 139)

3. Change the way you experience it.

From a swimming coach:
Deliberate practice can feel wonderful. If you try, you can learn to embrace challenge rather than fear it. You can do all the things you're supposed to do during deliberate practice—a clear goal, feedback, all of it—and still feel great while you're doing it. It's all about in-the-moment self-awareness *without judgment*. It's about relieving yourself of the judgment that gets in the way of enjoying the challenge. (pp. 140–141)

How do teachers model deliberate practice? Collaborative learning communities to demonstrate persistence through clearly defined goals, criteria for success, practice with feedback, and reflection with refinement.

Staying in the *now*, as the swimming coach suggested, is just as applicable to writing, deep thinking, public speaking, running, relationships, gym work, isometrics, and accomplishing any goal—large or small. Focusing on breathing and posture while doing planks eliminates pain. Deliberate practice in this book alone has been recommended for improving skills/ knowledge/ perseverance in such contexts as reciprocal teaching, direct instruction, social skills, visible thinking routines, observing lessons, self-differentiated learning, leadership skills, modeling read-alouds/think-alouds, collaborative skills, lesson planning, asking quality questions, and guided reading.

More advice on deliberate practice is Harvey Schachter's *Globe and Mail* newspaper article December 7, 2023, referencing Rob Dial's book, *Level Up*: "More generally, the hardest part of doing what we don't want to is breaking the cycle of inaction and getting started. After recognizing what it is that needs to be done, he recommends counting to three and then just doing it. Train yourself not to negotiate with your mind. Act."

In the beginning days of Frontier Collegiate Institute in Cranberry Portage, Manitoba, the semester system had not arrived. Instead, we had yearlong courses at 37 minutes/class. The teachers were young, enthusiastic, and activities such as reading club, photography, soccer, and student government took place after school hours. They were important as vehicles for students and teachers to get to know each other better/enhance personal relationships. But, again, time was an issue. Some town students had other responsibilities; teachers had children expecting them at home; we needed scheduled time for all.

On Fridays, we shortened each class by seven minutes, thus allowing fifty-six minutes for clubs/activities. It wasn't the only time these groups met, but it guaranteed time for an expansion of such activities. It was popular—all students signed up for a range of collaborative learning activities with their chosen teachers, many continuing after the official school day.

At BC High School in Shanghai, we simply added an hour to the school day. Not so easily done in Canada. Chinese and Canadian teachers created activities on their own or in partnership with other teachers. The size of groups ranged from a few students to thirty or more. They included academic interests, physical education, hobbies, and special interest groups.

Examples: yoga, meditation, reading club, school newspaper, strength training, computer club, musical theatre, chess club, student government, drama, guitar, seeds, cooking, leadership course, touch football, table tennis, soccer, volleyball, school yearbook, movie club, crafts, exercise club, international mathematics competition preparation, photography, dance club, writers club, drawing, and art—wholly the result of the personal interests and knowledge of students and teachers.

In the timetable above, we scheduled an hour each day for such activities, a number of them led by volunteers—again, as in the above examples, students and parents organizing and supervising themselves. Many of the groups, as indicated, were focused on enriched academics as outgrowths of school subjects.

This is an extension/assertion of the self-regulated learning goal and process during the school day while advancing independent expertise—gathering information, collaborative learning, resilience in the face of unexpected challenges, and response-ability as learning by doing, and individual/group reflection—all key for achieving any district goals. These important student choices dependent on their acceptance of responsible leadership, space, time, and funding.

The timetable described above creates time for professional learning communities, advisories, and assemblies. It also allows for parent/community involvement and leadership in student learning through after-school activities. These while advancing and sustaining an embedded culture of improvement along with PLC collaborative learning time within teachers' contracted day. Staff meetings, as part of the mix, however, are traditionally beyond the 3:00 pm instructional deadline.

In their book, *Rethinking High School: Best Practice in Teaching, Learning, and Leadership* (2001) by Harvey Daniels et al. the forward-thinking "Best Practice High School" in Chicago also determined a timetable for supporting learning to learn, democratic citizenry, student learning independence, collaborative learning, and parent/community partnerships.

Leadership from Chicago Public Schools encouraged student voice, integrated curriculum, internships around the city, and students as citizen volunteers, along with the Quest Center of the Chicago Teachers Union providing start-up funding. The school, unlike the timetable I suggested, has internships built in:

Best Practice High School

	Monday	Tuesday	Wednesday	Thursday	Friday
	Regular	Block	Internship & Flex time	Block	Regular
1st period	8:30-9:20	8:30-10:13	8:30-12:00		8:30- 9:20
2nd period	9:23-10:13			8:30-10:13	9:23-10:13
3rd period	10:16-11:06	10:16-11:59			10:16-11:59
4th period	11:09-11:59			10:16-11:59	11:09-11:59
Lunch	12:02-12:32	12:02-12:32	12:02-12:32	12:02-12:32	12:02-12:32
Advisory	12:35-1:05	12:35- 1:05	12:35- 1:08	12:35- 1:05	12:35- 1:05
5th period	1:08-1:58	1:08-2:51	1:39-2:51	1:08-2:51	1:08-1:58
6th period	2:01-2:51				2:01-2:51

Students meet in each of their classes three times per week—two singles and one block—about 50 minutes less than the previously suggested timetable. The introduction of internships as a half day per week for half the students in the school means more planning time for teachers—sorely needed in British Columbia at least. Grades nine and ten in the morning and grades eleven and twelve in the afternoons.

Seven Oaks Met School in Winnipeg, Manitoba also integrates school and community learning. Its "One Student at a Time" philosophy is based on the premise that students learn best doing something they are passionate about in the real world. Met Schools work with community partners, businesses, professionals, and organizations to provide opportunities for students to explore their interests and career goals with mentors.

Online information: "Internships (in-person/virtual): Met student interns are typically matched one-on-one with mentors and spend two days a week on site conducting special projects and providing help to their mentors and staff as needed. Back at school, their advisors worked closely with students to develop the skills necessary to succeed at their internship sites. As part of the Met School's One Student at a Time philosophy, each internship experience will be unique to the student, mentor, and workplace."

One way or another, finding time within the high school schedule for internships such as those in the Seven Oaks School Division, or the Chicago version, can be done. If a half-day/week as in Chicago were to be realized, that time might need to be replaced—this could be done by adding about six minutes to the rest of the classes in the weeks having internship—in Chicago it lasts twenty-four weeks, so overall it would mean around three minutes increase per class.

The benefits of such planning are large. Not only do internships enhance each student's learning, but they are also another bridge to the community, an important objective in itself. Another benefit, again, is extended planning time for individual teachers. For those twenty-four weeks at least, it is three hours per week. Again—quality over quantity. Self-differentiated learning applies to PLCs as well as individuals—a collective formative approach/reflection.

At Margaret Barbour Collegiate Institute in The Pas, Manitoba we connected with Keewatin Community College about six blocks away. For interested students, compulsory courses were timetabled in the morning; afternoons for attending the college. Students could choose carpentry, mechanics, or electrical—these programs qualified as high school credits. The bonus was completing the first year of a two-year program leading to journeyman certification. Another connection was the community swimming pool located within the high school—more opportunities for school and community to collaborate in the interests of our students, teachers, and the general public.

Ted Dintersmith, in his book, *What School Could Be* (2018), describes a high school in Iowa in 2012 where sixty-five adults, including community leaders, attended school for one day and were treated as regular students. Regardless of their differing backgrounds their conclusion was unanimous: "We can do much better". Their school, Iowa Big, started with just twelve students. Funded by three neighbourhood school districts, the school has no building or curriculum. All of the students attend their regular high school except for a number of hours each day at Iowa Big.

Each student takes part in two to five projects per year, which they either choose from a project pool or create themselves with the Iowa BIG teaching staff. Students first look through the project pool to choose the projects they are most excited about. Then, the choice is mediated through three filters: Does the student really love the idea? Is the project itself interdisciplinary, so it creates an opportunity for learning across multiple fields? Is there an external audience with a vested interest, not just in the product but also in the project?

As described in this book, social capital extension can be summarized as *inward* as teachers increasingly view themselves as fellow learners/more capable of meeting the needs of all students, *upward* in pursuit of improved administrative, district, state, and provincial supports/cooperation; *across* in working with parents and the community as allies, *outward bound* as they collaborate with sister schools, other districts, states, provinces or territories, and *downward* as they build confidence, independence, and leadership in their students.

Chapter 8
The Distributive Property: Student Achievement/ Accountability

Concept Map 3

The Distributive Property
(A+B+C) (D+E+F) =AD+AE+AF+BD+ BE+…

(Relationships + Language + Collaborative Learning) (Student Leadership + Incentives/Supports + Student Achievement)

The first three factors differ from the other three, not only as more immediately accessible but as prerequisites for students becoming change agents, acquiring incentives/supports, and realizing success. The reverse is also true: over time, improved relationships, advanced language capability, and expanded teams are the result of student leadership, supports, and assimilated student achievements.

Additionally, the first two factors in each grouping impact the third. Relationships and improved language skills are essential for collaborative learning while student leadership and system incentives/supports are steps toward student achievement.

Relationships

This give and take is evident in the seven theorems. The second theorem (we learn what we teach) sees learning as a two-way street. While determining where others are starting from in theorem 1, we compare and contrast our own context. This also applies to social and emotional factors in theorem 3, action choices in theorem 4, leadership considerations in theorem 5, collaborative opportunities in theorem 6, and individual and group accountability in theorem 7.

Reciprocal learning relationships are the result of the thinking routines, guidelines, habits, suggestions, and structures described throughout this book: teachers observing each other teach, hard conversations, mutually defined roles, ladder of feedback, effective professional learning communities, advisories, the link between writing and speaking, and conflict resolution capabilities.

Others are decision making focused on expertise over hierarchy, modeling, mentoring, group work skills, determining and appreciating different perspectives, finding humour within our own contradictions, critical feeling, making thinking visible, student based research on their own high school and others, teacher focus on students' thinking, recognizing false dichotomies, school and community learning partnerships, freedom with accountability, writing to learn, reading as thinking, and active student leadership.

Additional key components (large and small) for improved relationships/achievement levels are student-chosen advisors, considered risk-taking, parents as daily partners, future teachers, students as ambassadors, community service, open door school assemblies, reciprocal teaching, jigsaw, read-alouds/think-alouds, recall, double-entry journals, guided practice, need for playfulness, information circles, dictogloss, strategic tutoring, diverse texts, peer tutoring, activities period, student internships, reading response, distributed leadership, gradual release of responsibility, democratic values, and cognitive acceleration.

Change, according to Richard F. Elmore (2008), depends on the instructional core: the relationships between teachers and students and the organizational practices that support those relationships. Relationships are evident in the physical nature of classrooms, student groupings, teacher accountability, teacher collaboration, observable processes for measuring results and ways of communicating those results to students, parents, and communities.

Democratic values in secondary schools, student achievement, and effective citizenship are intrinsically linked: an intersection of superordinate goals, learning by doing, mistakes as building blocks, respect for minorities, distributed leadership, community connections, confluent education, ethical purpose, freedom and capacity to choose, collective responsibility, and finding common ground.

Michael Fullan and Joanne Quinn, in their book, *Coherence: The Right Drivers in Action for Schools, Districts, and Systems* (2016), recognize the importance of collaboration while building/maintaining trust. Relationships amongst students, teachers, families, and community, they assert, are the foundation for student learning ownership locally, nationally, and globally.

We need relationships that are both professional and personal. One is the mentor-mentee relationship between experienced teachers and those early in their careers. Positive relationships and social interactions at work keep us physically and mentally healthy. Working in an environment where you feel relaxed about yourself can provide you with inspiration to learn from and with others.

Barth (1990), deploring our history:

> The biggest problem besetting schools is the primitive quality of human relationships among students, parents, teachers, and administrators. Many schools perpetuate infantilism. School boards infantilize superintendents; superintendents, principals; principals, teachers; and teachers, students. This leads to students and adults who frequently behave like infants, complying with authority from fear or dependence waiting until someone's back is turned to do something 'naughty'. To the extent that teachers and principals together can make important school decisions, they become colleagues. They become grown-ups. They become professionals. (p. 36)

Present day Horsefly in British Columbia has a population of approximately 1000 people who enjoy a quiet, rural lifestyle where everyone knows their neighbour. One continuous event during my years as principal was community volleyball in the school's gym from 7–9 pm during the week—students, parents, teachers, and other community members.

Another opening for building school and community relationships was our school outdoor skating rink—mostly evening skating (the district provided lights). Pick up hockey games (a mix of adults, teachers, and students) on the weekends were attended by a good portion of the community. Another event organized by teachers was a Saturday family scavenger hunt where you had to solve puzzles/academic problems in order to gather clues along the route. Steps in the right direction.

A reminder of on-line comments from local citizens in Vancouver, British Columbia:

"[There is] poor utilization of valuable public facilities. Schools should be the centre of the community, but cannot be when the doors are locked…"

"[I hope for] a community of schools that are closely connected and feel like part of a whole group instead of separate schools."

"Schools set the tone for a neighbourhood. If the school is doing well, a lot of people will care about other aspects."

Language

Malcolm Gladwell (2011) submits ten thousand hours as the time required to develop high levels of proficiency in just about anything. Finding time to teach learning to learn capacities of reading, writing, and speaking is doable if it occurs in all subjects. Failing that, secondary students are severely handicapped at becoming self-directed learners. A comprehensive literacy program is not only one of the goals, it is a strong contributor for learning anything.

Biancarosa, C. & Snow, C., writers of "Reading Next—A Vision for Action and Research in Middle and High School Literacy: A Report to the Carnegie Corporation of New York" (2004):

Most older, struggling readers can read words accurately, but they do not comprehend what they read, for a variety of reasons. For some, the problem is that they do not yet read words with enough fluency to facilitate comprehension. Others can read accurately and quickly enough for comprehension to take place, but they lack the strategies to help them comprehend what they read. Such strategies include the ability to grasp the gist of a text, to notice and repair misinterpretations, and to change tactics based on the purposes of reading. Other struggling readers may have learned these strategies but have difficulty using them because they have only practiced using them with a limited range of texts and in a limited range of circumstances. (p. 8)

In order for students to learn these skills, they recommend all teachers incorporate reading, writing, speaking, and thinking as part of their instruction. They suggest the following fifteen elements within successful high school literary programs:

1. Direct, explicit comprehension instruction, which is instruction in the strategies and processes that proficient readers use to understand what they read, including summarizing, keeping track of one's own understanding, and a host of other practices.
2. Effective instructional principles embedded in content, including language arts teachers using content-area texts and content-area teachers providing instruction and practice in reading and writing skills specific to their subject area.
3. Motivation and self-directed learning, which includes building motivation to read and learn, as well as providing students with the instruction and supports needed for independent learning tasks they will face after graduation.
4. Text-based collaborative learning, which involves students interacting with one another around a variety of texts.
5. Strategic tutoring, which provides students with intense individualized reading, writing, and content instruction as needed.
6. Diverse texts, which are texts at a variety of difficulty levels and on a variety of topics.
7. Intensive writing, including instruction connected to the kinds of writing tasks students will have to perform well in high school and beyond.
8. A technology component, which includes technology as a tool for and a topic of literacy instruction.

9. Ongoing formative assessment of students, which is informal, often daily assessment of how students are progressing under current instructional practices.
10. Extended time for literacy, which includes approximately two to four hours of literacy instruction and practice that takes place in language arts and content-area classes.
11. Professional development that is both long-term and ongoing.
12. Ongoing summative assessment of students and programs, which is more formal and provides data that are reported for accountability and research purposes.
13. Teacher teams, which are interdisciplinary teams that meet regularly to discuss students and align instruction.
14. Leadership, which can come from principals and teachers who have a solid understanding of how to teach reading and writing to the full array of students present in schools.
15. A comprehensive and coordinated literacy program, which is interdisciplinary and interdepartmental and may even coordinate with out-of-school organizations and the local community. (pp. 4–5)

Recognizing a common approach to improving reading across all subjects, Kylene Beers et al. in their introduction to *Adolescent Literacy: Turning Promise into Practice* (2007) do not see literacy development as subject specific:

> In other words, we don't see cause-and-effect relationships one way in science and another way in history. Instead, we learn the syntactical cues that show us those relationships and use those cues across all subject areas…though the student in English class might read with an eye toward what a character will do next while the student in chemistry class wonders what will happen when two chemicals are combined, both are predicting. (p. xiv)

Stressing the importance of writing in *Change Leadership: A Practical Guide to Transforming Our Schools* (2006), Tony Wagner et al. had this to say:

> When they talk about good writing skills, for example, both groups (academics and learning leaders), are associating effective writing with a person's ability to reason, analyze, and hypothesize; find, assess, and apply relevant information to

the solution of new problems; and, of course, write and speak clearly and concisely. (p. 4)

Writing influences content retention, boosts acquisition of academic vocabulary, and enhances reasoning ability. Writing in response to read-alouds/think-alouds that includes math and science problem solving, social studies perspectives, and small-group formative assessments makes sense every part of the day.

As previously noted, the relationship between writing and speaking is rarely recognized in high schools. Each reinforcing the other. Tony Wagner and Ted Dintersmith (2015) paint a sobering picture:

> The ability to write and speak persuasively go hand in hand. Rarely can someone learn to present a coherent argument to an audience without having honed the skill through writing. Having spent more than fifteen years teaching writing to a wide range of high school students, as well as to college and graduate students, Tony came to discover the hard way what are, in fact, the key ingredients for learning to write.
> First, students need to be writing constantly. Learning to write well, like any other skill, takes many, many hours of practice. Second, students need to write for a real audience and to receive regular, structured feedback from their audiences. Other than looking for a grade on the front of the paper, students are usually totally indifferent to the teacher's opinions of their work. But when they are writing for or presenting to an authentic audience, which has been asked to assess the work being presented—whether it is their peers or someone outside of school—they work much harder to polish their work, and they seek and pay attention to feedback. Writing for a real audience, and writing about things they know and care about, are central to students' development of an authentic *voice* in their work. (p. 105)

Their concern for serious writing is reiterated in student speaking and presenting:

> So now let's talk about oral presentations in high school classes. We will be very brief because, essentially, there aren't any. Most students get through high school without ever having to practice and perform a single speech before a real audience. And one of the commonalities of nearly every

class that we've observed is students' stunning inability to clearly articulate a thought. We can barely make out anything students are saying when they answer a teacher's question. Their responses are often half-sentences, spoken in half-whispers that cannot be heard by half the people in the room. Students are sometimes required to give PowerPoint presentations to their inattentive classmates in a few classes, but the ones we've seen are almost always incoherent. (pp. 112–113)

One suggestion is for teachers to regard these students as second language learners—English being their second language (my sense of humour). We could start by banning the word, "like" since my grandchildren seem to think it belongs in each and every sentence regardless of its ability to confuse. "She was like you're not using that word right and I was like yes I am."

Wagner and Dintersmith describe debate classes:

"We've recently learned that most of the debate classes and competitions today bear absolutely no resemblance to the ones we remember from many years ago." They reference Greg Whiteley's 2007 film "Resolved":

Today, to compete as a debater, you are trained to speak at 200 percent or more of your normal speaking cadence in order to make more points in the allotted time. You speak so quickly that ordinary mortals cannot understand you. And what you talk about has come from the bins of research that you have dug up on often arcane topics that no one really cares about. Sadly, watching high school debate is like listening to two different podcasts being played at three times the normal speed and then having someone tell you in the end which podcast contained more sentences. (p. 114)

The effectiveness of collaborative output such as dictogloss, jigsaw, and reciprocal teaching is attributed to improved language awareness as students reconstruct text and notice links between form and meaning, largely credited to feedback from fellow students. The research again showing greater accuracy from collaborative tasks as compared to individual efforts.

Read Aloud-Think Aloud lessons, modeled by the teacher, followed by student paired practice, is an important part of this effort. Janet Giltrow et al. in *Academic Writing: An Introduction* (2005) make a significant point regarding its use: teachers, while reading aloud, should focus on showing students how grammar and punctuation are related to comprehension and how mistakes in both confound efforts to find meaning.

Improving writing is accelerated by direct feedback *as students write* as compared to written teacher feedback *after the fact*. Another is Giltrow's read-alouds, paralleled by students, replacing traditional written comments on grammar and form.

In the research she describes, Schriver (1994) divided senior writing students into an experimental group and a control group. The control group was given feedback through traditional commentary while the experimental group studied transcripts through read-aloud-think alouds. The result was that the control group did not improve their abilities to identify where readers would have trouble understanding the writing, while the experimental group improved by 62%.

Interestingly, her research also showed that writers can also learn from read-alouds when the read-aloud text is not their own: teacher modeling feedback on some students' writing benefits the rest of the class. The question then arises: *How does read-aloud-think aloud to improve reading skills differ from similar modeling designed to improve writing?*

Read alouds-think alouds improve reading by advancing connections, summaries, and inferences as reading skill outcomes. These mindful activities extend, deepen, and solidify textual information in both fiction and non-fiction material. The reader works to get the most out of what is there. Read-alouds designed to improve writing, on the other hand, are bent on analyzing words, phrases, sentences, and gist more critically, striving to highlight difficulties the reader faces in making meaning.

Unlike other authors, Janet Giltrow gets specific about how Read Aloud-Think Alouds to improve writing should be done. Her guidelines countermand the view of some teachers that whatever enters your head while reading is what you share.

Giltrow's Guidelines for Readers:

Do not make judgments. Sweeping editorial comments are not helpful. Remember that you are reading on behalf of other readers and although you might understand a particular phrase or sentence, others with less experience may not—that needs to be said and why. As an example, for international students, the teacher must keep in mind idioms, figures of speech, cultural/social contexts, and metaphors. You are not a marker. No grades. You do not praise; you are interested in what works and what doesn't, and specificity is everything. You report when you are understanding and getting new ideas of your own, also the gist or essence of the writing piece.

Janet's Guidelines for Authors during Read-Alouds: "You don't need to explain or justify what you've done. Instead, value the chance to watch someone making meaning from what you've written. Listen carefully to your reader's comments. Take notes. Your reader's response will guide your revision strategies" (p. 131).

These are not easy lessons. Teachers will need substantial practice with each other to get a good start. They model with the whole class, then volunteer students do Read-Alouds of others' work, finally work in pairs. Eventually authors need to be their own feedback. They must read as if it were brand new to them; that's why writers leave "final drafts" in a drawer for a week or so and then re-read them aloud carefully. So many surprises—so many opportunities for improvement.

In 1985, I taught a demonstration lesson with a class of grade 12 Indigenous and non-Indigenous students at Frontier Collegiate Institute in Cranberry Portage. This was shortly after Richard and Jo-Anne Vacca's first edition of *Content Area Reading* was available, the most comprehensive book of its time (still available in its tenth edition) on improving student literacy in all subjects.

I began by discussing examples of organizational patterns, leaving those on the chalkboard. These included cause and effect, comparison and contrast, sequence, general concepts and supporting ideas, and problem-solution. All from Vacca and Vacca.

Students then sorted themselves into groups of five then given five pieces of writing from various subject areas, each representing a different pattern. Their task to connect the right pattern with each piece of writing, then present, through their spokesperson, their reasoning to the class.

The students seemed interested, worked well together, and made notes to assist their spokesperson. I expected to hear the same answers from the groups along with the same evidence for their conclusions.

I was wrong. Although the main organizational patterns were largely agreed upon, I was surprised by the number of different observations across the groups that identified patterns beyond the few I had indicated. In what I had chosen for a comparison/contrast example, they not only found other patterns, but patterns within patterns. Attacking this assignment as a puzzle to be solved, they had gone beyond my expectations. Moreover, I later learned that the patterns had become filters through which they analyzed thinking in other texts.

In 2012, as a self-appointed Language Support Teacher, I took that experience into an adjunct English class at our BC High School in Shanghai. This time, the students worked with short stories. Groups of four or five students were given key words and phrases and asked to build a word map where position equals relationship. Again, a few organizational patterns were highlighted at the beginning. As in the lesson at FCI, each group's spokesperson presented their concept map to the rest of the class, followed by class feedback.

The richness/variety of their conclusions was apparent. The process allowed students to become aware of the author's thinking and choice of words, as well as the differing conclusions of their fellow students. This included reflection and sharing of their feelings in response to particular parts of the stories and why.

Sandra Fotos and Hossein Nassaji, editors of *Form-focused Instruction and Teacher Education, Studies in honor of Rod Ellis* (2009), provide another collaborative learning strategy. Dictogloss is more than a lesson plan; it suggests a teaching-learning structure that, with experience and proper detailing, is a vehicle for a range of outcomes.

Again, the process needs to be directly taught to students—part of a number of fundamental strategies/processes for which effectiveness grows from considered practice. Its simplicity, as well as its range are its strengths. It was originally designed for second language students, but there is no reason, I believe, for the strategy not to be effective with all students.

Dictogloss begins with choosing a piece of writing to be read to the class at a normal conversation pace. You will need to practice. You will also need to guess how many unfamiliar words are in the piece.

A sample: We are always looking for good friends. These days it is hard to find true friends whom we can trust. Certainly, it is important to be considerate of those who care for us. A true friend, however, is someone who is sincere and loyal and who is with us through tough times. We don't have to wonder if a friend, who has many other activities such as studying and practicing basketball, has time for us after a bad day. True friendship is like a bridge that is built with bricks of loyalty and held together with the mortar of sincerity. It is those kinds of connections that bind us together.

Before reading, you need to activate prior knowledge. There is nothing in this world that can be learned unless new knowledge is connected with old. It can't be done. The topic is friendship, so we start with a class discussion of the importance of friendship, ways someone can be a good friend, and asking students to predict what the writing piece will contain. Next, the teacher explains more difficult vocabulary such as *trust, loyalty, mortar, sincerity, and consideration.*

The teacher reads the text aloud once at normal speed as students listen but do not write. The teacher reads the text again at normal speed and students take notes. Students are not trying to write down every word spoken; they could not even if they tried, because the teacher is reading at normal speed.

Students work in groups of 2–4 to reconstruct the text in full sentences, not in point form. This reconstruction seeks to retain the meaning and form of the original text but is not a word for word copy of the text read by the teacher. They should be trying to reconstruct the text as closely as possible to the original—working together to create a cohesive text with correct grammar and other features of the relevant text type, such as factual (inform, instruct, or persuade) or literary (entertain, enlighten, or elicit emotion).

Groups then visit each other with the view of comparing and analyzing their versions. Teachers should be hovering over them like armed drones waiting to strike a blow for cohesion, coherence, and accuracy. Do not show learners the original text until after the students' texts have been compared and analyzed.

Students, with the teacher's help, identify similarities and differences in terms of meaning and form between their text reconstructions and the original, which is displayed on the projection screen. Dictogloss forces students to examine grammatical structures carefully and to discuss their effects with a specific goal in mind—constructing meaning.

Brownlie and Schnellert (2009) quote Richard Allington in *It's all About Thinking: Collaborating to Support All Learners* (2009). They begin with, "*How can you learn from texts you can't read?*" They contend that most texts in subject areas are written substantially beyond the independent reading level of many students.

Their suggestion is to use sets of lower reading level content books on curricular topics. They advocate *literature circles* (book clubs) for English courses and *informational circles* for content areas. The circles are organized within classes, with the added option of extending them via the internet to other classes within the school and beyond. This in keeping with their admonition not to *water-down* curricular expectations while providing scaffolding/ resources for those needing additional support.

Danling Fu, a second language specialist, concurs. In *Writing Between Languages* (2009), she observes, "*Most content area study in-*

volves reading textbooks that are written in condensed language and inundated with compact information. ELL's (English Language Learners) have a hard time digesting it all" (p. 78). According to Professor Fu, high school ELL students reported an understanding of about 30% of the content. Their teachers' estimate was closer to 10%.

Her experience in observing second language students in regular western high schools is that they mostly fill in the blanks, answer T & F questions, and answer one-word or short phrase questions from books they barely understand. They copy words from the text onto worksheets with little comprehension.

In *Rethinking High School: Best Practice in Teaching, Learning, and Leadership* (2001), Harvey Daniels et al. have the following advice on using textbooks:

> How much extra time and effort it takes to replace traditional textbooks with more balanced, richer, and more engaging materials. Workaday teachers cannot be expected to make such extraordinary out-of-school efforts every day; after all, who is going to coach softball and who is going to make dinner at home? It takes years of a career to assemble such materials, and it takes teams of colleagues working together inside of and across departments to gradually acquire books, articles, files, folders, documents, pages, shelves of better materials. (p. 214)

They go on: "Until all teachers possess these rich sets of hands-on materials, the traditional slick-covered, seven-pound textbooks will still have an important role to play in our high schools. How they are used makes a big difference. Here's what we've learned so far about using textbooks more wisely and effectively":

1. *Use textbooks less.* Dependence on single sources of information misrepresents the way scholars and experts in most fields actually operate. Real experts draw on a wide range of sources to understand their field, and we should start modeling this intellectual reality in school. Respect the enormous difficulty of typical textbook material by assigning short, critical passages only. Spend time on the truly important sections and omit chaff.
2. *Slow down.* If you're going to use textbook selections, allow enough time for students to build comprehension, not just skim.

Of course, slowing down necessarily goes with the idea of assigning selected chunks, not the whole book.
3. *Substitute with real, readable sources in place of content-overloaded textbooks.*
Build an inventory of other materials: magazine and newspaper articles, graphs and charts, historical novels, primary source documents and biographies of historical figures.
4. *Teach the kids the specific reading skills they need to cope with dense non-fiction text.* If you are in a situation where you must stick to a textbook, remember: students will learn and remember information best when they *act upon the material.* That means teachers must employ before-reading, during-reading, and after-reading activities that help kids activate prior knowledge, set purposes for reading, monitor their comprehension, and actively construct meaning.
5. *Jigsaw textbook assignments.* Everybody does not need to read everything! Have different kids read different sections and then put them together.
6. *Give students choices.* As you become more selective about what sections of a textbook you assign, invite students to follow your model by selecting their own readings when appropriate.
7. *Make reading more social and collaborative.* Use pairs, partners, groups, or teams at all stages of the reading process.
8. *Do more reading during class time.* If the text is really important, but kids can't dig out the meaning on their own, then we must provide time and support to make sure they succeed. Cover less material more thoroughly.
9. *Read aloud-think aloud to introduce selections.* This helps build interest and momentum.
10. *Provide for real applications.* Help students find meaningful connections in the real world—not just take quizzes on the information.
11. *Avoid the read-test trap.* Don't test only for factual recall. Let students approach textbooks like every day reading, seeking the main themes and the big ideas.
12. *Don't give lectures that duplicate the textbook.* Create activities that help students process and analyze information instead.
13. *Work to change your school's textbook-driven curriculum.* Lobby for one that includes a wide range of real literature—novels, autobiographies, essays, journalism, research reports, and primary sources in all content areas. In general, reading

and language arts instruction includes close reading with deliberate, systematic, and explicit teaching of word recognition while enhancing students' subject-matter knowledge, expanding vocabulary, comprehending sentences, and becoming increasingly familiar with the language of written texts. (pp. 214–215)

Not being able to read the material is not the only challenge; those who don't understand the concepts can't employ *writing as a learning aid*. You can't summarize, relate material to personal experience, compare and synthesize other sources of information, predict consequences, or engage in other higher-level thinking that accrue from writing if you haven't grasped the content.

Assisting with the above, Breanne Reinheimer, in her University of Victoria's Master of Education thesis entitled "Information Circles: Teaching Students to Read and Respond to Informational Texts" (2011), determined that informational texts have more difficult reading material than narrative texts. This occurs because of student inexperience with the text type and partly because students are unfamiliar with the organization and structure of informational texts. Comprehension strategies include peer-based assessment of background knowledge, making connections, questioning, inferring, and identifying main idea and details, summarizing, and synthesizing.

Strategies: Many reports, studies, and documents discuss best practices for adolescent literacy and identify what must happen in middle years' classrooms in order for our students to graduate with the necessary literacy skills to be active, productive, and successful citizens. This literature clearly identifies reading comprehension instruction through the explicit teaching of cognitive strategies as a best practice in adolescent literacy instruction.

Reinheimer:

> Some of these strategies are more applicable to informational texts than others (e.g., identifying main idea/details), and it is these strategies that students participating in information circles will use and practice while reading and responding to Informational texts. Further, research in strategy instruction identifies instruction in recognizing and using the internal and external features of informational texts as a means for increased comprehension.
> Research has examined the role of content area literacy skills on student success in school—*students need to know how to*

> *read to learn, and it is important for teachers to adopt best practices for reading instruction in specific content areas.* Finally, it is important to look at the research that identifies literature circles as an instructional technique worthy of use in our classrooms specifically to teach the reading of information texts.
> The research on literature circles suggests that this structure is motivating for students and provides students with opportunities *to* further develop their understanding of a variety of texts through peer-based discussions. (p. 12, [emphasis added])

Her summary of the value of information circles:

> The goal of instruction is often subject specific skill mastery and content recall, which are not the only abilities our students need to possess. *Successful citizenship in today's society requires a much more dynamic set of skills that includes critical thinking, problem solving and working collaboratively with others.* Therefore, it is necessary to take a much a broader view of content area literacy, one that moves away from a transmission model of teaching and learning and moves towards a participatory model where students are required to generate their own knowledge and make their own interpretations of texts. (p. 39, [emphasis added])

When a teacher, through the direct transfer of information to be memorized, makes it unnecessary for students to grapple with texts, they are actually eliminating what is needed for student growth *and* informed participation in a democracy. We need referenced books/readings at different reading levels to accommodate all students. Self-regulated learning is part of the process. Teacher-led lessons and direct instruction, complete with descriptions/modeling, is the first stage toward independent practice. Guided practice giving way to full responsibility as confidence improves.

Oakley B. et al. (2021) on using guided practice:

> Students generally have no idea about the differences between working memory and long-term memory. This is part of why they can be so easily fooled about whether

they've truly learned the material. The perfect way to address this is to do an active exercise with your students that teaches them the valuable learning technique of recall.

1. First, explain to your students the difference between working memory and long-term memory. Tell them that working memory is like an octopus that has to juggle the information to keep it in mind. An octopus can usually keep at most four pieces of information in mind—and that information can easily fall out. Long-term memory, on the other hand, is like a set of links in their brain that they can easily draw on—easily, that is, if they've made sure those links are solid and well-connected.
2. Next, ask the students to pair up and explain to each other what you have just taught them about the difference between working memory and long-term memory.
3. After students finish, explain that they have just used the *recall technique.* That is, they've just checked whether they have understood and can remember the key idea. In this case, they've performed the check by trying to explain the concept to their partner.
4. Explain to students that they can use the recall technique even when they are alone. To use this technique when they are by themselves, all they do is look away from what they've just learned and see if they can *recall* the key idea. Or they can test themselves to see whether they can remember a word or work a problem from scratch. (pp. 11–12)

Commenting on the need for improved language arts engagement, Patricia H. Hinchey in the book, *Students as Researchers: Creating Classrooms that Matter* (1998) had this to say:

And, while I will clarify difficult passages, I will *not* lecture on the textbook. In fact, I discourage my colleagues from such lecturing every chance I get, being sorely tempted to scream every time someone implies that the logical response to a lack of reading ability among students is to ask them to do *less* reading. Students can only become more skilled and more active readers by practicing active reading. When a faculty member makes it unnecessary for students to grapple with texts, they are actually eliminating practice essential for student growth—not to mention for informed participation in a democracy. (p. 42)

Active reading is enhanced by such routines as double-entry journals. Tomlinson and Strickland (2005):

> Double-entry journals ask students to react to classroom content in a two-column format. Students record information about content in the left-hand column (e.g., key ideas from the reading, brief summaries, lists of symbols, important vocabulary) and react to that information in the right-hand column (e.g., give a personal reaction to the reading, drawing on memories and emotions; ask questions; agree or disagree with a character's choices, compare and/or contrast the passage with another passage or another work of literature; make a prediction based on reading already accomplished; identify the theme; and/or explain and interpret figurative language and motif as a representation of theme). (p. 351)

Motivating high school students to read can be simplified. Deborah Appleman, in her chapter "Reading with Adolescents" within *Adolescent Literacy: Turning Promise into Practice* (2007), emphasizes the influence of reading the first chapter of a book on students:

> The language of literature is sometimes musical, sometimes soothing, and sometimes simply exhilarating. There is no better way to hook kids than to read them the first chapter of a book. I've seen it work with all kinds of texts, from the traditional—*Of Mice and Men* (Steinbeck), *The Old Man and the Sea* (Hemingway), *The Great Gatsby* (Fitzgerald), *To Kill a Mockingbird*, *A Separate Peace*, any Shakespeare play—*Their Eyes Were Watching God* (Hurtson), *The God of Small Things* (Roy), *The Things They Carried* (O'Brian), *The House on Mango Street* (Cisneros). This fascination with hearing the sound of literature is a lesson that all elementary teachers and most middle school teachers have learned well. It is one that high school teachers need to remember. (p. 146)

She followed up by emphasizing the importance of the environment:

> Hard brown desks, fluorescent lighting, the close press of peers—why would we think that school is a great place to

> experience the pleasures of reading? The lesson learned from observing students discussing their ideas in book clubs is that it's not just the actual *reading* of texts that is more enjoyable in comfortable surroundings. *Talking* about reading needs to be more comfortable as well.
>
> Of course, this lesson is not meant to insult the good work of English teachers everywhere who inspire great conversations about great and not-so-great books. But let's face it: students sometimes do a better job of asking each other questions about books than their teachers can, and they can sometimes have more fun talking about books without us. If we truly want students to regard literature not simply as a school subject but as a habit of mind and heart, as a practice essential to leading a literate life, then we need to be more willing to create spaces for students to read—without us. (pp 146–147)

In summary, enhancing communication capabilities through reading, writing, and speaking instruction in all high school courses is both a strategy for change and a goal; indispensable for achieving high academic achievement, improved creativity/choice in a variety of learning/career opportunities, collaboration with others, improved engagement with their learning, participation in the governance of our democracy, and a lifetime of learning.

Collaborative Learning/Citizenship

Boaler (2019):

> One of the goals for schools should be to produce citizens who treat each other with respect, who value the contributions of others with whom they interact, irrespective of race, class, or gender, and who act with a sense of justice, considering the needs of others in society. A first step toward producing citizens who act in such ways must be the creation of classrooms in which students learn to act in such ways. (p. 186)

> Many people believe that the essence of high-quality learning is working alone, studying hard… But thinking is inherently social. Even when we read a book alone, we are interacting with another person's thoughts. It is very important, perhaps the essence of learning, when we develop the capaci-

ty to connect with another person's ideas, to build them into our thinking, and to take them forward into new areas. (p. 198)

Resilience when we connect with other people: The thing that people who overcome hardship and do not become defeated by it have in common is that in times of need they all reached out to someone—a friend, a family member, or a colleague—and those connections helped them survive and develop strength. (p. 172)

Collaboration is vital for learning, for college success, for brain development, and for creating equitable outcomes. Beyond all of this, it is beneficial to establish interpersonal connections, especially in times of conflict and need. (p. 171)

This research reveals the potential of collaboration, not only for girls or students of color but for all learners and thinkers. When you connect with someone else's ideas, you enhance your brain, your understanding, and your perspective. (p. 170)

Non-immigrant students achieving at higher levels when they were in schools with larger numbers of 'immigrant' students—suggesting that diverse communities of learners help students become better collaborators. (p. 170)

Neuroscientists discovering that when people collaborate "our brains are charged with the complex task of making sense of another's thinking and learning to interact." (p. 171)

Halbert and Kaser (2016) on school-to-school collaboration:

A design challenge for inquiry teams is to ensure that professional learning is linked directly to real settings with real learners. We have seen effective use of video clips to illustrate new approaches—especially when the setting and the learners being filmed look and sound much like the ones in our own school. We also think that study tours are an underused strategy in BC even though they are commonplace in many others countries, especially Australia. Seeing what is taking place in other BC schools serving similar groups of learners can be motivating and encouraging for the unenthusiastic or reluctant.

Pam O'Connell, a New Zealand researcher, studied schools with records of sustained improvement in both teaching practices and student outcomes following whole school professional development. The transformed schools were those that had developed an evidence-informed inquiry focus for leaders and teachers that was coherent with their school goals. Individual teacher inquiries, connected to the specific needs of their own learners, were consistent with the overall school focus. (p. 67)

Chrona J. (2022): "Connect learning to the community. This includes creating opportunities for learning experiences outside the classroom and school, so that learners understand the connections between what they are learning and the broader community" (p. 126).

In chapter 7, the corona-19 example was students (with teacher support) extending school citizenship and student achievement inquiry to the local community *or communities*. Expanding the research means expanding the team. Indigenous, along with other at-risk minorities, as set out by Chrona, are to be consulted on a regular basis, along with formative assessments of achievement levels/needed support.

Based on local concerns, a mix of high school students, parents, teachers, school board members, business owners, local and regional government officials, minority leaders, politicians; and in fact, any community members, to carry out investigative inquiries into local community/provincial/national issues.

The time for such collaboration exists. Beyond regular school hours, the high school timetables previously described have meeting times available during advisories, internships, and activities periods. The products of such investigations are fed back to the local community or communities for response as in the covid-19 example.

One concern regarding community-based investigations is politicization and polarization of public education. Examples exist in the United States and Canada where concerns based on human rights are fought based on what teachers do or don't do in classrooms. Teaching, as emphasized throughout this book, is not about indoctrinating students but assisting them in making their own evaluations. Our responsibility to help them self-regulate, improve thinking abilities, carry out research, evaluate evidence, and determine their own conclusions. One example being the consideration of outrage based on outrage as a first response.

Teaching, again emphasized throughout this book, is not about indoctrinating students but assisting them in making their own evaluations. Our responsibility is to help them self-regulate, improve thinking abilities, carry out research, and compare evidence.

In no way, however, should we avoid the issues; addressing the fragility of our democracies, human rights concerns, and other democratic values, in and of themselves, is not the problem. Educators are free to share their own views, but not at the expense of our professional responsibility to allow students to determine, through evidence and a non-partisan approach, their own points of view, understandings, and choices. The job is not teaching students *what to think* but helping them learn *how to think.*

Comporting with the above, P. Freire, in *The Pedagogy of the Oppressed* (2018) emphasize the need for a problem-solving approach vs teacher-based knowledge of the past: "The students—no longer docile listeners—are now critical co-investigators in dialogue with the teacher. The teacher presents the material to the students for their consideration, and re-considers her earlier considerations as the students express their own" (p. 81).

Senge et al. in *Schools that Learn: A Fifth Discipline Fieldbook for Educators, Parents, and Everyone Who Cares About Education* (2012) summarize Paulo Freire and Myles Horton (1990):

> To them, education was not an end in itself or merely a means to employment. They saw schools as political sites that either engaged people in informed political participation for a stronger democracy and a better future or prevented them from becoming engaged. Both Freire and Horton believed in democracy and equality and didn't shy away from explaining how these were enabled or disabled by power and politics. (p. 255)

Hinchey P. H. and Konkol P.J. (2018) in *Getting to Where We Meant to Be: Working Toward the Educational World We Imagined*:

> Rather than avoiding political issues related to social problems that plague individual communities as well as the nation as a whole, the justice-oriented perspective encourages student analysis of structural causes of the problems and efforts to provoke change in them. Citizenship in this case involves ongoing critical analysis to determine where tenets of

democracy seem to have been violated or abandoned and working to get things back on course. (p. 106)

Similar concerns are set out by Josh Fullan, director of 'Maximum City', a national education and engagement organization. From his online article, "Canadians get a failing grade in civics" (April 14, 2022):

> In Ontario high schools, civics is a mandatory half course taught with varying degrees of expertise and enthusiasm, and there is no coherent approach to teaching the subject across provinces and territories. Effective courses in civics should go beyond the minutiae of parliamentary law-making and *teach how power works, our rights and responsibilities and how to make use of them for individual and collective good.* Yet, too often what students get in these classes is a slog through different levels and branches of government, and a stream of decontextualized information they can't wait to forget.
> If civic education is failing our students and the adults they become, it's logical to conclude that we need to beef up the curriculum. One approach could be to teach political systems starting in Grade 1, or have each province make civics a full-year course mandatory for high school graduation. We could also lower the voting age to 16 so young people can establish good participation habits.
>
> Some of these might be ideas worth pursuing, *but educators know from experience that simply adding more to the curriculum won't lead to student engagement and success. Doing more of the same thing that already isn't working is a pitfall of educational reform.*
>
> A better way might be to get rid of civics classes entirely *and incorporate the active-citizenship component into other classes.* The best civics lesson—the one that sticks—could actually take place in science or art class by giving students the autonomy to identify an issue they care about, then guiding them through the process of becoming informed advocates. Maybe the issue they want to champion is climate change; maybe it's graffiti murals.
>
> *As they delve into a topic, they are intrinsically motivated to pursue it deeply. They explore the institutions and examine the decisions responsible for the status quo. The social and*

> *political knowledge they gain and apply in this inquiry process is twinned to their emotional attachment and endures. Agents of change are developed. People power is restored.*
>
> Of course, this is already happening in schools across the country, but it isn't nearly widespread enough. *Infusing active citizenship across school subjects where students take control of their own learning will help to recharge Canadian democracy. It is our best defence against ignorance and disinformation.* (p. 2, [emphasis added])

Dalton B. Curtis Jr. in Chapter Six of *Thirteen Questions: Reframing Education's Conversation* 2nd edition (1996) entitled, "Education and Democracy: Should the fact that we live in a democratic society make a difference in what our schools are like?" agrees:

> Clearly, it is essential for the entire community to engage in education for public responsibility. The school must lay the intellectual foundations of citizenship and develop practical skills in the art of politics, and the citizenry must participate in public life. If excellence in politics were to become the highest practice for the citizen, then the moral stature of public responsibility would be demonstrated, the work of the school in educating citizens would be meaningful and effective, and the conditions most necessary for democracy to become a way of life would be achieved. (pp. 136–137)

Liu L. et al. (2021) in *Measuring and Evaluating the Effectiveness of Active Citizenship Education Programmes to Support Disadvantaged Youth recognize* the following:

> Two things are found to promote students' participation: (a) adopting a participatory practice method to extend students' civic learning and participation beyond the classroom into the local communities. Students, especially those of disadvantaged background will feel empowered by solving a real-world problem and enjoy their voice being heard by the public. This also helps students build up social and moral responsibility and realistic knowledge and skills to participate in real-life contexts; (b) developing a student-centred learning format brings positive civic and political learning outcomes. This does not only reflect on the teaching methodology itself but also somewhat stresses that the relationship between students, teachers, and schools is critical. A support-

ive, accessible, and trustworthy environment allows students to develop an identity and participate more in the activities held at schools. (p. 8)

I taught a summer school Indigenous history course in Grand Rapids, Manitoba for BUNTEP (Brandon University Northern Teachers Education Program)—the home of Ovide Mercredie, national chief of the Assembly of First Nations in Canada from 1991 to 1997 and with whom I worked as principal of Frontier Collegiate on a trip to Berens River early in our careers. Prior to the course, I had been the principal of Grand Rapids school. The dozen or so future teachers were from the community, including some of my former students.

The only academic qualification I had was a master's degree in administrative studies from the University of Manitoba. I had no other qualifications for the position, my teaching major was mathematics, and my history learning experience beyond high school limited to one course. As principal of Frontier Collegiate for five years, where a high percentage of our students were Indigenous, I had read a number of books written by Indigenous authors, one of which was Harold Cardinal's *The Unjust Society* in 1969. Not much to go on.

But I knew what I didn't know. Besides getting to work on my reading, I had one idea: "history is in you" as a resource for gathering personal information on the past. For example, my father, a history teacher, had experienced the Great Depression of the thirties; this and other of his personal experiences growing up made a deep impression on me and my brother.

To supplement classroom efforts, I asked the students to research Indigenous history in Grand Rapids through the eyes of their relatives. They were to interview parents, grandparents, as well as other community members for information that could help us with the course.

They did, and they did it well. Through their relatives and other community members' eyes, as set out in the students' reports/presentations, our readings were, to say the least, enriched. Not only did students bring their research—they brought history to life—one example was bringing artifacts from the early days of the Hudson Bay Company's fur trade to the class.

We learned of conflict between the Lakota nation south of Canada and the Salteaux people not so far from Grand Rapids—this information was not in our readings. I also learned that Grand Rapids' people who had lived through the nineteen thirties never knew there *was* a Great Depression—their lives were not part of that history—their ways of living were totally isolated from my father's experience. I received positive feedback from BUNTEP, but the real credit for our deepened learning goes to the students, their research, and the citizens of Grand Rapids who brought history to life and life to history.

Student Leadership

In the 'Students as Researchers Conference' Toronto, February 2012, one hundred and fifty teachers and students worked for two days to learn how to conduct collaborative inquiry research using student input for questions/ concerns about what might improve their school communities and their education.

One of the chief organizers, Mary Gallagher, Assistant Deputy Minister in the Ontario Ministry of Education at the time, summarized their efforts:

> By making students equal partners in collaborative inquiry, we can support active engagement of students in questions of interest to them. Students work alongside teachers, mobilizing student knowledge. Students become 'change agents' who affect school cultures and norms. *Students and teachers develop a sense of shared responsibility for the quality and conditions of teaching and learning, both within particular classrooms and more generally within the school community.* Online source

Examples include student engagement in class, the efficacy of teaching methods, barriers for minority groups, levels of peer support, critical feeling, guidelines on best practices for teaching and learning, role of student government; investigating diversity in student demonstration of success in subject outcomes, and other opportunities for both student and parent leadership. Teacher awareness in this regard means recognizing their need for professional learning on how to conduct investigative inquiries—not something that has historically been an integral part of their professional lives.

In grade nine, I did well. One of the years I combined my love of reading with effort. My friend sitting behind me in one of the rows of desks bolted to the floor, all facing the blackboard, was not. Charlie (not his real name) came from a home with few supports. At the end of June, we received report cards with short teacher comments. Charlie didn't come to school that day. I asked my teacher if Charlie had passed—he had. The next day, our first day of freedom for the summer, I saw him. He told me he probably failed, and I told him what our teacher said.

He never showed up for grade ten. Not so many years later, Charlie shot himself. I know I could have helped him do better in school—this may not have changed what later occurred, but the chance that I could have helped my friend troubles me still. I know if I had tried, I could have helped build his confidence somewhat, but I didn't. Perhaps showing I cared would have made a difference. I will never know.

I now reflect on how current school/student leadership can boost academic, social, and emotional supports for students like Charlie. The need for a democratized school support system is part of the answer. As a reminder, in Chapter One we were informed of the mental and social stresses of the cyber age as perceived by a student—stresses and concerns that people of my generation could not imagine.

Peer tutoring, then, along with a learning to learn curriculum and teacher advisor support, could be a life changer for disadvantaged students. They need extensive support (intellectually, emotionally, and socially). In the suggested timetable above, there are eight hours per week set aside for student-led activities/room for peer tutoring.

Van Der Meulen, K. et al. [online article] "Emotional Peer Support Interventions for Students with SEND (specific educational needs and disabilities): A Systematic Review", December 28, 2021, describe possibilities:

> Peer support is about social interactions that involve giving information, emotional, or practical help based on what peers have in common and many times with benefits for both. Various types of peer support systems exist, which can be broadly divided into two categories. The first involves methods related to education and information-giving, such as peer tutoring and mentoring. The contents of the support are mainly academic such as reading activities or mathematical problems.
>
> The second category involves emotional support given by peers to others who are in need, and refers to befriending, mediation/conflict resolution, and counseling-based approaches. Befriending implies support in various formats, such as offering companionship to students perceived as solitary or helping peers who are bullied or find it hard to make friends. Conflict resolution entails mediating between peers, or a peer and an adult, who are in disagreement.

Counseling-based interventions require more extended training in counseling skills. Students ask for help to one of the counselors directly or the student contacts the service and is referred to a counselor. All these types of emotional peer support systems share several aspects. For a start, they require a recruitment or selection process. *Students receive training focused on listening and communication skills, empathy for peers with social or emotional difficulties and problem-solving strategies.*

Adults are in charge of this training and maintain a supervisory but non-directive role during the intervention. The peers themselves fulfill the most important role and have the capacity to manage the helping practices. And finally, as it typically takes place outside the classroom, whether the support system succeeds or fails depends on the commitment of the students who volunteer for it.

The effectiveness of emotional peer support has been demonstrated in several general population studies in secondary schools, with respect to counseling-based systems. *Results showed these were efficient in terms of the helping process; students who were supported by peers reported feeling emotional relief and an increased ability to cope with problems. Benefits for peer supporters included increased self-esteem and communication skills.*

Peer support in schools is more effective when it is integrated into a whole school supportive ethos or policy. *This means that it is an integrated element among practices and attitudes related to the improvement of relationships and the well-being of the entire educational community.* Moreover, the degree to which students and teachers know about the peer support available in their school is important.

In addition, the active backing of the head teacher or those involved in the school's management contributes to the program's success. School staff as well as families are able to be positive influences by spreading the word and motivating participation. Finally, the extent to which students are able to have control over the intervention, properly contributing to it by themselves, needs to be taken into account. (pp. 1–2, [emphasis added])

Leadership requires resilience. Erik Vance's definition of resilience from a *New York Times* article, Sept 1, 2001: *The ability to engage with a challenge, risk, or impediment and come out the other side with some measure of success. A psychological principle blending optimism, flexibility, problem-solving, and motivation.*

Appreciating yourself for overcoming obstacles in the past, learning to ask the right questions, slowing everything down, developing positive relationships, accepting yourself as less than perfect, not ruminating over past mistakes and failures; and establishing achievable goals matter. One of the most appreciated appraisals I ever received after one hard setback was from my daughter: "I knew you would be OK, Dad. You're a survivor."

And then, once you start leading yourself, you will be tempted to team up with friends/fellow learners who need the same kind of support. All applicable to students *and* teachers. As specified in Chapter 6, opportunities for students to become collaborative partners with teachers and administrators range from setting up chairs for school assemblies to participating in teacher evaluations to having input into school decision making such as discipline policies, student evaluation, and school timetabling.

Others are participation in school management teams, representation in teacher hiring, monitoring the teaching of learning-to-learn through observations, student and teacher interviews, and attending staff and PLC meetings.

Online description of the "Students as Researchers Conference" (2012) in Toronto:

> This effort to involve students in research is not meant to exclude an adult presence. The goal is to combine the experiences and efforts of both adults and students for mutual benefit. The Students as Researchers Conference concept encourages young people to organize around issues of their choice, youth and adults to come together in intergenerational partnerships.

Spencer Izen and Jessica Kim, journalists for their high school newspaper, *The Griffens' Nest,* in Vancouver BC, are a striking example of student leadership. The online article "BC high school students draft student press freedom act to protect journalistic rights" (May 13, 2022) by Kyshia Osei summarizes the issue—freedom of the press as defined by the Canadian Charter of Rights and Freedoms.

The students had conducted an inquiry into "district policy making and the level of student-teacher input into that decision making"

(p. 3); then, after gathering views of over 100 students and 12 teachers, they concluded that neither students nor teachers "were being consulted meaningfully in any way" (p. 4).

They then forwarded their findings to the district's communications office along with a response request. The office did respond, but also sent their email to the school principal. The vice principal then told them the article needed to be approved by the principal.

After consulting with the teacher who worked with them on the paper, Izen and Kim wrote a letter to the British Columbia Civil Liberties Association (BCCLA). A day later, The Griffins' Nest was formally told to stop sending their paper to the printers and to cancel their orders.

Determined to do something, they worked with some pro-bono lawyers to draft a proposed law: the Student Press Freedom Act. It states that student journalists have rights to freedom of expression and freedom of the press, regardless of whether a school supports them in the creation of student media (Osei, 2022, p. 6).

According to Osei:

> "The students' proposed law does allow for oversight. It acknowledges several scenarios where teachers or school board administrators can prevent students from publishing, such as stories that include obscene or libellous material, or content that poses a threat to safety and security of the school". (p. 7)
> "Although the Student Press Freedom Act (SPFA) has been presented to BC's Attorney General for consideration, it is not currently a priority for the government. Izen and Kim are hopeful the act will be addressed in the 2023–2024 legislative calendar". (p. 9)

Democratic student government is pertinent to school/district culture change. Through whole school assemblies and newsletters, students' representatives report their contributions to the governance of the school/influence on the rest of the district and larger communities.

Daniels et al. (2001) provide a summary of the history of "choice theory." Back in 1986 William Glasser asserted that people's actions are guided by five basic needs: love/belonging, power, freedom, fun, and physical survival. He believed people develop mental images of what will fulfill those needs. Students with problems in school often do not see the classroom as a place where their needs will be met, and as a result, neither threats, nor punishments nor rewards are effective in changing behaviour. He recommended the schools centre learning on *collaboration, student choice, and support for gaining success, along with caring attention from adults.*

Alfie Kohn in *Choices for Children: Why and How to Let Students Decide* (1993) cites evidence for involving students in decision making in schools. People who self-determine are healthy physically and emotionally, learn responsibility and self-control, and improve academic achievement levels through deciding what and how to study. Teachers also find their work more exhilarating as students are deeply involved in their work.

Peter Senge from *Schools That Learn* (2012) summarizes the importance of students as change agents:

> One last comment on why schools seem remarkably difficult institutions to change and where the most significant source of leverage may lie. Industrial-age schools have a structural blind spot unlike almost any other contemporary institution. This blind spot arises because the only person who could in fact reflect on how the system as a whole is functioning is the one person who has no voice in the system and usually no power to provide feedback that could guide change. This person is the student.
>
> The student is the one person who sees the whole picture; all the classes, the challenges on the playground and streets, all the stress at home, the multiple conflicting messages from media—the total environment. Kids know when the overall workload is too big or small, when the stress level is too high or the level of respect too low. But they have no power or standing in the system. Their opinions are discounted. They are, after all, just kids—in a system run by adults supposedly for their benefit.
>
> To see the folly of this, imagine that we enforced a rule on a company's workers: under no circumstances are you to talk to customers. We would not expect that company to survive for long. If anything, silencing the voice of students is even more limiting. Unlike customers who passively purchase what a company produces, students co-produce the results achieved by schools. Where there is no student engagement, there is no learning.
>
> I then have come to believe that the real hope for deep and enduring processes of evolution in schools lies with stu-

dents. They have a deep passion for making schools work. They are connected to the future in ways no adult is—and in many ways more connected to the larger world and its challenges. They have imagination and ways of seeing things that have not yet been reshaped by the formal education process. And they are crying out to be involved, to become more responsible for their environment.

This does not mean that all that is needed is student leadership. But it does mean that without the leadership of students, there is little hope. The rest of us have been in the system of education for our entire lives. We are truly the fish in the water of industrial-age assumptions. Young people are acutely aware of how dramatically our world is evolving away from those assumptions. And young people are still new enough to the system that they can see the tacit rules and assumptions and help the rest of us see them as well. (pp. 68–69)

School Supports/Incentives

School initiated credit courses on leadership and research provide additional time/support for students to assess school achievement. Courses to include interviewing, fostering ownership, developing self-questionnaires, conducting focal groups, research ethics, and quality presentations. Other teacher supported initiatives are student government and student observation across classrooms. Herein lie opportunities for our "Future Teachers" to collaboratively lead/work with their teachers.

The physical nature of high schools could use a remake: teacher staffrooms, as we did in China, replaced by a common room for teachers, students, parents, and community members—a signal embracing them as partners. Another option could be a *community centre room*, again marking parents and other community members' rightful role within a collaborative culture—an open-door home base/lunchroom for parent/community support groups taking part in classroom observation/participation, supervision, attending advisories, auditing classes, activities period, leadership, and building relationships.

Student research capability not to be confined to classrooms, schools or districts. These skills, attitudes, and knowledge also useful in almost all employment/service organizations. Students' abilities to gather and evaluate quantitative and qualitative data are valuable in any career: all based on reciprocal learning, resilience, response-ability, reflection, and improved school supports.

Kuhlthau et al. (2007) see the early teens as an opportunity to combine community service projects that enrich curriculum goals with research such as: What conditions bring about the need for a food bank? What is needed to create transportation that fits the needs of the elderly? What oversight is required over senior centres, public or private, given our recent experience during the pandemic?

What would it take to lower the mortality rate for young people using drugs? How can high school students (individually and collectively) below the age of voting participate in local, state, provincial, and national elections? How do we recognize those who might resort to shootings? What immediate and long-range strategies will alleviate the plight of the homeless? How do we reduce the number of sidewalk traffic fatalities for people using bicycles, electric scooters, or simply walking in our community?

Having PLCs' subject teaching rooms adjacent to each other would be a plus. Especially helpful in larger high schools is having the same course taught next door. This goes back to the suggestion in Chapter 2 of distributing the teaching load, not by grade level, but over all grades. This improves collaboration opportunities and builds expertise for inexperienced teachers through common goals, while endorsing a more complete learning sequence. Some student choice, however, on which teacher they get, is crucial; teachers gaining experience over all grades does not necessarily mean students restricted to the same subject teacher for their high school careers.

When we self-regulate learning along with accelerated parent and student participation and leadership, we also free up teachers to visit other professional learning communities in other schools and other districts. Students do not need to be in the same room as their teachers all the time. Gradual release of responsibility, as discussed in Chapter 4, providing increased opportunities for students to organize their own learning while doing the same for teachers.
Another option for empowering teachers is recommended by Barth (1990):

> Money can be an antidote to a feeling of powerlessness. A little money is a large antidote. Each year our school was allocated about $30 per child for all instructional purposes. I allocated a 'fair share' to each teacher—about $750 a year. How this money was spent was up to each teacher; it could

go for texts, games, food, teacher courses, field trips, or testing materials.

Seven hundred and fifty dollars is not much, but it is more than many teachers have to spend. It is meaningless to give people responsibility without giving them the resources to exercise that responsibility. In that sense, the money is almost as important as a symbol as it is a means for teachers to buy materials and supplies. It is a vote of confidence. What teachers do with limited funds is what most people do with their budgets; they become responsible and resourceful; they feel empowered. And what most teachers do is pool their precious resources in order to stretch them further. Joint purchases of books, science materials, and field trips led to joint discussion about these materials, their use and benefit to youngsters. A simple budget and the occasion to make decisions helped generate complex forms of collegiality. (pp. 34–35)

John Goodlad (2004) concurs:

Teachers should have a say in how the money allocated for materials is to be spent in their school. Indeed, they should have some funds to spend as they see fit. It should be acceptable, for instance, for a teacher to request and obtain six copies of each of five books rather than 30 of a single book for a particular class. (p. 278)

Collaborative team efforts allow peer coaching from students in other grades, parent coaches, and "Future Teachers in Training." An internship process of leadership skills, organizational development expertise, community involvement, voluntary contributions, collaborative experience, and gradual release of support encompassing elementary students, research skills, and ethical, democratic standards.

It is time to ensure all students have computers with plug-in access everywhere—if we want writing to be an important learning asset in every subject, we cannot be dependent on computer rooms. Nobody in their right mind writes with pen and paper anymore. Students having access to a computer is a must in flipped classrooms—students able to access teacher-made videos at any time. Just think of the printer access, close computer use, books, highlighting pens, and anything else you need as a writer.

Carol C. Kuhlthau et al. in *Guided Inquiry: Learning in the 21st Century* (2015) describe studies where school librarians and teachers attempted to identify elements that contribute to problems or success in bringing about guided inquiry. They looked at their first-hand experience, reflection on that experience, and worked with colleagues to analyze the results. The follow-up identified inhibitors to success as 1) lack of time, 2) confusion about roles, and 3) poorly designed assignments.

The lack of time was for students on task *and* for teachers/teams to plan assignments. Teachers exclusively setting inquiry assignments is *not* what is being suggested here. *Students need help, as noted previously, with finding questions that they care about and that advance quality thinking. Questions where the interests of students and teachers, based on life experiences and community concerns, become the norm.*

Within the timetable suggested in Chapter 7, professional learning communities have three, one-hour scheduled sessions per week when all students are free. This provides collaborative time for teacher groups and students to work on learning research. Time for students is also available at forty minutes per day in advisories, as well as the eight hours per week after school activities period—with or without adult leadership. Opportunities in the Best Practices High School edition, as described, are flex time and internships with one-half day per week for student choice/research.

Daniels et al. (2001):

> Of all the program elements we've developed or stolen for BPHS (Best Practice High School), we consider the internship program the 'jewel in the crown'. This program has two goals: first, to provide students with opportunities to experience the worlds of work and service and, second, to give teachers time to meet together. Teacher teams meet while the students are out of the building, and the internships have enabled students to operate outside the school as responsible young adults, exposing them to a rich range of employment opportunities of which few teenagers are aware. Our program has been named an exemplary site by the Corporation for National Service Learning. (p. 154)

There is no reason for schools to be closed to students during professional development days. Over time, a high percentage of the student body could use these days to work collaboratively with other students or learn with teachers. In Chapter 1, I shared the success of a student's suggestion: expanding the length of one course to six months rather than five and shortening another from five months to four. This should not be an isolated instance. We need to get rid of the antiquated idea that all credit courses should have the same length of time. This is for teachers and students in those classes to decide.

Students taking online courses at universities across Canada have no forced timeline for completing each course. Nor do students opting for online ministry high school credit courses. The BC ministry of education, according to their online information, states that in general, students are allowed "flexible timetable and course options to meet their individual needs."

Should this be true, many courses could be completed in less than five months or more if students desired. In addition, as we gain momentum toward self-differentiated learning and its freedom with responsibility, students will have time to work on improving education for all students. No student should be time-bound in any class—self-differentiated and self-regulated learning allowing course completion based on individual success/choice.

When I recall teaching mathematics in Minitonas, there was a significant percentage of students in every class who didn't need to be there every period, or could have completed the math courses in far less than the mandatory time. They would have made great peer tutors/educational assistants both in their high school and the elementary school occupying the same building.

This observation is backed by Halbert and Kaser (2013). They report on reciprocal teaching where Vicki Chapman, the learning support teacher at Port Kells Elementary, a school in Surrey, BC "decided to train intermediate students as reading coaches for younger learners. By coaching the older students on the use of performance standards to provide feedback to their younger partners, she saw improvements in reading comprehension for both groups of students." (p. 23).

Student Achievement/Accountability

Guy Claxton et al. (2013) report student success in applying self-regulating principles in the British rural community of Solihull after two years:

> Pupils' perseverance in the face of difficulty has improved markedly. They are more likely to see mistakes as a natural

part of learning and not to worry if they get things wrong to start with. One secondary student remarked, "If learning is hard, that means it's at your level". A younger child said, "I used to cry when I couldn't do my work. I don't anymore."

Pupils show greater interest in the process of learning, and in how their capacities can help them in out-of-school activities, and—especially in secondary schools—in their lives after they leave school. One said the 4R's (resourcefulness, reciprocity, resilience, and reflection), will help us when we leave school'. Another said, "As we get older, we'll depend on learning to learn more".

Students show greater collaboration and have learned naturally to coach each other. The lower-achieving students particularly have seemed to benefit in terms of confidence, perseverance and their interest in "how to get better."

Classroom environments have changed to stimulate students' resourcefulness and independence. Resources are more available and pupils encouraged to make use of them as needed. Staff conversation and planning has shown a shift from "teaching' and 'behaviour" to a greater focus on pupils' learning. (pp. 257–258)

Claxton et al. also describe the resilience of students from Park View Community School in Chester-Le-Street, County Durham based on self-regulation/ building learning principles:

On 25th January, 2010, England's biology A-level students sat for the first of their two exam papers. The following day thousands of these students launched an online protest saying that the exam was unfair, and over 3,000 students sent furious messages to a Facebook group about the exam set by AQA. Pupils described the exam as a disgrace, saying it bore no resemblance to specimen papers and feared it would jeopardise their chances of a university place. One student said: *'I'm actually more upset than angry, I've worked so hard and need an A to get into the university I've applied for, no chance of that now, thanks AQA for potentially ruining my life with your ridiculous paper!'*
But interestingly there were no complaints from the A-level biology students at Park View, who wondered what all the fuss was about! They had studied and prepared for the exam using BLP (Building Learning Power) princi-

ples. They understood deeply the need to persist in the face of difficulty, to try another tack if the first one failed, to take time to reflect on their learning, and to stay calm and make the best use of whatever they already knew. The biology staff at the school had ensured that their students were able to apply their subject knowledge and understanding to any possible set of exam questions.

The students acknowledged that the paper was challenging, with many unfamiliar elements, but they had made intelligent attempts at all the questions; demonstrating, according to all their teachers, remarkable resilience and resourcefulness under difficult circumstances. When the exam results were published, the students found that they achieved among the highest marks in the country. 42% of Park View pupils obtained an A grade on this paper compared to 22% of similar schools and 27% of students nationally. (p. 250)

One function of the suggested District Learning Support Committee is to monitor such achievement: providing information on how well goals are met, what is working, and what changes or additional incentives will help. We also need to learn *how* schools/districts support ongoing summative and formative investigations. How and *by whom*. Again, seeking to relate the parts and the whole.

Co-investigation begins by gathering information from students. George H Wood (2005) as principal of Federal Hocking High School in Stewart, Ohio:

> We must start where any honest discussion of schools must start—with the experience of the students. For all our talk about improving schools, this is the only issue that matters: What is the daily experience of high school like for our kids? Does that experience allow young people to do their best work possible? Does it prepare them for a life of engaged and productive citizenship? (p. 9)

He goes on:

> High school should be, most fundamentally, about the work of students. The quality of papers they write, the clearness of the explanations they offer, the persuasiveness of their speeches, the precision of their drawings, the creativity of

their art, the skills of their play, and the integrity of their character should be our primary concerns.

Start with what we teach. We should begin, not with lists of courses and objectives, but with actual examples of the type of work we want our students to do. Next, we should look carefully at the type of work students *can* produce upon entering high school. Only then, knowing what we want them to do and how we want them to do it, would we be able to set forth a curriculum for students to follow. The 'stuff' we want to teach would be whatever is needed to get kids from where they are to where we want them to be. (p. 79)

What outcomes are easily recognized? What are the criteria for these outcomes? How will the perceptions of the parents/community be assessed? How will the students help? What incentives will they have? How will student leadership/research assist in these determinations? How do we learn from our failures? Is *our* learning different from what we propose for students in our high schools?

In Concept Map 3, improved student achievement provides pressure for additional supports—financial and social. Recognition of success from parents, school boards, community leadership, minority groups, the business community, and other community support ventures is critical for increasing capacity to meet the needs of all learners.

Students, with support and encouragement from their teachers, conduct and publish research that includes gathering qualitative and quantitative data from board members, principals, teachers, students, and superintendents. All providing needed information for improvement. Parents and communities have every right to better information for judging how well our schools serve their children.

Summative student achievement is still an important part of the process. At some point, we may replace standardized examinations with personal/ comprehensive evaluations of both students' thinking/academic achievements. But we aren't there yet. Therefore, we still have, as one of our goals, a high percentage of our students doing well on external, standardized examinations.

The evidence is that self-differentiated learning results in improved test scores for students seeking entrance to universities, community colleges, and career opportunities. Deeper thinking people remember more. There are, as stated, two reasons for this: the first, as emphasized by Hattie, is that surface information, vocabulary, and related concepts are required for advanced thinking, and the second is factual knowledge and processes over-learned *while* students are engaged in deeper thinking. Both dependent on improved student motivation founded on choice, gradual release of responsibility, and collaborative learning.

This is especially true, according to Mike Anderson (2016), for highly advanced students as well as those who start from a different place. His experience sees choice as one of the most powerful vehicles for creating inclusive classrooms. When we share power and control of learning with students; when we teach them how to self-direct and nurture their sense of ownership and agency, students progressively invest in their learning. Self-differentiation is impactful because students will increasingly learn to choose learning opportunities that fit their needs.

Results are student/ staff engagement and satisfaction, demonstrated success of Indigenous learners, other minority groups, second language students, children with special needs, of poverty, and academically advanced students; citizen readiness, communication capabilities, working collaboratively with others, confidence, improved motivation, resilience when encountering stringencies, love of learning, seeing alternate points of view, and increased ownership for their own learning.

These will differ from school to school and district to district. To over-generalize student achievement (such as comparing nations on international tests) as some ministry and government officials are wont to do, would be laughable except for its sad influence. Oversimplification of education in the interest of self-promotion is the wrong path. I have, unfortunately, met some of these bureaucrats from never-never land masquerading as educators.

All of these goals are related, intertwined, dependent on each other, and cannot be attained in isolation. Nothing is simple but all are achievable. A sub-heading: How can we support students demonstrating their progress in achieving these goals? Not at the end of some predetermined time, but by continually making their learning visible through choice.

Faye Brownlie and Leyton Schnellert in *It's all about thinking: Collaborating to Support All Learners* (2009) bring us back to earth: Their key questions: "What is working? What can these students do? What is not yet working? What do these students need? What is my plan to address this need? Is our teaching making a difference?" (p. 31).

These questions not only apply to classroom teaching but to schools and school districts: What are the indicators? What constitutes high academic results? What kind of school/district-wide formative and summative assessment would provide answers? How do we assess such elements as writing, deeper thinking, research capabilities, transfer of knowledge, deductive reasoning, analytical thinking, delineating evidence, making new connections, and seeing alternative points of view?

Where is the collective accountability for teachers, professional learning communities, schools, districts, and ministries of education? Historically, individual teacher *and* school accountability have been missing in action; freedom to teach disconnected from our responsibility for teaching well. What qualitative data beyond numbers are students, parents, school boards, and communities entitled to? How will we collectively know how well we are succeeding with our goals/shared vision of success?

Wagner et al. (2006) describe schools and districts as overwhelmed and confused about their meaning or priorities. He recommends schools and districts track and publicize only some quantitative data as a first step in establishing better understandings. He provides an example where almost no one in a district was aware that one in five high school students had dropped out between grade nine and grade twelve.

Other possible data reports (overall as well as for at-risk minorities): (1) percentage of students reading at grade level (2) reading levels for each high school grade at the end of each semester (3) number/quality of published writing pieces (4) number of books read by grade as determined by student research that includes community libraries (5) grade level improvement through one on one interventions (6) number/quality of student research presentations at town councils, local service groups such as Lions, and (7) assessments of graduates in occupations/community colleges/universities in summarizing their high school experience.

Chrona (2022):

> As a system, I think we can do better in terms of not creating high-anxiety situations for learners when implementing large-scale assessments. I also think we can create large-scale assessments that are more responsive to finding out what learners *do* know and *can* do, rather than what they do not know and cannot do.
>
> However, we need to continue to carefully use low-stakes large-scale assessments that reflect the common learning goals in an education jurisdiction (i.e., the skills, knowledge, and understanding that are considered vital for all learners) at specific points in a learner's K-12 experience. There is a danger in not paying close attention to the system's quantita-

tive data, such as graduation rates or achievement on standardized assessments. Yes, they tell only part of the story and do not reflect all there is to know about a learner. But if we do not look at parity or disparity in all data sets, we lose the opportunity to learn about, and systemically address, gaps in how well we respond (or do not respond) to groups of learners. If we see that the data, even in standardized assessments, show inequity (based on race, ethnicity, or culture), then we have evidence of something we need to act on. (pp. 97–98)

Brownlie and Schnellert (2009) advocate a formative assessment grand event such as that described in *Student Diversity (*1998; 2006*)*. This performance-based reading assessment is used to 'target specific areas of instruction'. Repeating the assessment helps teachers, "monitor the effectiveness of their instruction, get feedback, and make new teaching plans" (p. 29).

In the assessment, teachers choose a passage from a textbook, build background knowledge with their students, set a purpose for the reading, pose several open-ended questions, listen to students read, and have a short interview where each student receives descriptive feedback.

Rubrics/descriptors are used to code individual responses, find common patterns, and set class goals based on strengths and needs. Shared with each class, the teacher and students develop ways to address concerns. These assessments are carried out five times throughout the year.

They report Johnston Heights School's efforts in Surrey BC to design and assess learning in English. This is a two-week project for students connected to ongoing learning in class. Their guidelines allow five to eight 90-minute classes for project work, two more 90-minute classes for self-assessment/peer assessment, English-language support, resource support, additional time, technological support, and encouragement for gathering short stories/poems outside class time.

The difference between quantitative and qualitative information deserves emphasis. Data refers to them both. Too often it is the qualitative data that is missing. Wagner (2006):

> But often we have found that qualitative data (such as that generated from interviewing students and adults in focus groups about their experiences with school) are particularly powerful in illuminating and communicating key insights. *Seeing the faces, and hearing the stories, hopes, and opin-*

> *ions of those in our own community moves us emotionally, reminds us of the moral imperative behind our work, and enables us to see the information in three dimensions instead of just one.* (pp. 134–135, [emphasis added])

Starr Sackstein (2015) in "Teaching Students to Self-Assess: How do I help students reflect and grow as learners?" believes quantifying a particular task or curriculum outcome should be supplanted with consistent demonstration of proficiency of a task in different settings along with teaching it to a peer. That would be the evidence of achieved mastery. So far above impersonal conclusions of written tests and tiny samples. Teachers to spend less time determining mean scores and more on evaluating real time student behaviour.

Admonitions from Andy Hargreaves and Michael Fullan in *Professional Capital: Transforming Teaching in Every School* (2012):

> Performance data and professional learning communities can narrow your focus excessively to what the data is about—usually tested literacy, mathematics, and science. The data on these basics and the discussions in PLCs that arise from them therefore need to be *supplemented by other kinds of data, on other aspects of learning, and by knowledge of children and learning that is also based on shrewd experience and not easily quantifiable at all.* (p. 173)
> Often in the past there has been too little or too much information delivered to the public. In "Change Leadership: A Practical Guide to Transforming Our Schools," Tony Wagner et al. believe *"data must be persuasive on logical and emotional levels, touching individuals about the humanity of the effort so as to create and sustain energy."* (p. 139)

Again, superordinate goals are impossible to attach numbers to, but they, not content objectives, are what stimulate teachers to transform the system. The answers then combine 1) wide ranging teacher, student, parent and community ownership 2) a common agenda, and 3) expertise developed through collaboration.

George H. Wood (2005):

> While we don't need recipes, we do need models to help us overcome our fears of school change. Knowing that other schools have restructured helps overcome the fear of being

> alone. Knowing that, in a place similar to ours, restructuring has led to success and has been worth the discomfort helps overcome the fear of failure. Knowing that other communities have embraced change and, if skeptical at first, have become supportive helps overcome the fear of rejection. It is important to know these things cannot come from a book, a lecture, or a film; such knowledge can only come from direct experience with a school or schools that have ventured beyond the status quo in how they are organized. (p. 161)

Change is achievable, but we need to be constantly aware of critical determiners. First, as previously discussed, is relationships, second is common ground for superordinate goals such as democratic citizenry, third is recognizing the language arts as prominent change tools, and fourth is gradual release of responsibility.

John Goodlad (2004):

> We would be well advised to view parents, teachers, and students as an extended family and their school as a part-time home joined with other families and homes in a democratic educational mission. In my book I have summarized conditions that appear to correlate with the good health of individual schools as evidenced by high satisfaction of parents, teachers, and students. These conditions correlate, also, I believe, with the health of our democracy. (p. 378)

This book discusses *how* change in high schools might be realized, but the solutions are never-ending and can only come, as John Holt advised, from teams of local teachers, students, principals, superintendents, parents, district personnel, and community members who see beyond themselves, gather inside and outside resources, and plan to win.

The lessons for educators model those for local communities, states, territories, provinces, our nation, and the world. Considering what is happening around the world, finding *common ground* is not a luxury but a necessity. The need for balancing both conservative and progressive perspectives in democracies is paralleled by the need for compromise in our schools.

I close with three understandings. First: Leaders (inside or outside) to be sensitive to teachers' attitudes/awareness when introducing change.

Seymour Sarason, *The Culture of the School and the Problem of Change*, 2nd edition (1982):

> The more I have read about and personally observed efforts to introduce change in the classroom, the clearer several things have become. First, those who attempt to introduce a change rarely, if ever, begin the process by being clear as to where the teachers *are*; that is, how and why they think as they do. In short, they are guilty of the very criticism they make of teachers: *not being sensitive to what and how and why children think as they do.*
>
> As a result, teachers react in much the same way that many children do, and that is with the feeling they are both wrong and stupid. Holt (1964). Second, those who attempt to introduce a change seem unaware that they are asking teachers to unlearn and learn. Third, if there is any one principle common to efforts at change, it is that one effects change by telling people what is the 'right' way to act and think. Here too, those who want change do exactly that for which they criticize teachers. (p. 232, [emphasis added])

Evans R. (1996) (p. 16):

> At the core of traditional approaches to change lies an arrogance that invites failure and plays a key role in the inability of those approaches to overcome resistance. Innovation is almost certain to encounter problems when its implementation is defined according to only one reality (its creator's). The reason is straight-forward: the subjective reality of the implementer (in schools, the personal experience of the teacher) is crucial to successful innovation; transforming this subjective reality is a key task of change. When change agents assume they have "the right answer" and ignore the processes that foster this transformation, they can be "as authoritarian as the staunchest defenders of the status quo" (Fullan. 1991, p. 36).

Second: The power of goals. Sedlak et al. (1986):

> Families deserve schools that will empower their children *through the learning they offer rather than through the credentials that they award...* Empowered learning is foreign to most all of our schools, but it is not a difficult concept to un-

derstand. It consists of *intellectual and character traits: the ability to act independently and responsibly based an accurate assessment of the consequences of one's actions; the possession of values and the ability to exercise sound judgment that encourages the fair treatment of others; personal autonomy and control; problem-solving, critical thinking, and higher-order reasoning skills; and the ability to make informed decisions.* (p. 189, [emphasis added])

Third: The importance of school accountability as applicable to all Western democracies as evinced by commonly espoused concerns, research, and reforms. These indicators exposing greater differences within each country than between them.

Accordingly, the following comments by Ken Jones (2006) are as relevant to the United Kingdom, Japan, Finland, Canada, Austria, New Zealand, Germany, the Netherlands, Australia, and other democracies as they are to the United States:

> We must initiate and follow through with efforts to build a more comprehensive, coherent, and democratic system of school accountability. States need to transform their present regulatory roles into collaborative ones and convene the public to inform and gather information for developing the new system. Districts and schools need to develop internal accountability cultures and structures that can provide a firm foundation for a localized system of school accountability. Parent and community organizations need to be included in local school accountability systems. Local and classroom assessment systems need to be developed and implemented. Teacher organizations need to continue reforming themselves to engage more fully with professionalization efforts, including mentoring, peer review, and *advancement within the ranks based on performance.*
> Work of this magnitude speaks of the need for leadership at all levels. One can only imagine what might happen if the president of this country and the governors of our states devoted themselves and our tax dollars as much to a better model of school accountability as they have to the one that is now proving to be so debilitating. (p. 239–240, [emphasis added])

Parts of this book can be viewed as pessimistic, optimistic, or realistic. Taken as pessimistic, it sees opposition from communities, administrators, bureaucrats, teachers, students, families, and anti-democratic interests as powerful and inevitable. But it is also optimistic—instigating change based on appreciation for those who believe in our students while empowering learning for all.

Realism is also there; in-your-face learning that motivates everyone. Overdone cynicism is the enemy of success, while poorly thought-out optimism is just as damaging. This is democracy at work—increased group capacity to overcome obstacles while maintaining freedom and responsibility. The way forward for classrooms, schools, districts, counties, provinces, states, territories, nations, and the world.

The End

References

Abeles, V., & Congdon, J. (Directors). (2010). *Race to nowhere* [Documentary]. Lafayette, CA: Reel Link Films.

Abrami, P. C., Bernard, R. M., Borokhovski, E., Wade, A., Surkes, M. A., Tamim, R., & Zhang, D. (2008). Instructional interventions affecting critical thinking skills and dispositions: A stage 1 meta-analysis. *Review of Educational Research, 78*(4), 1102–1134. https://doi.org/10.3102/0034654308326084

Abrams, J. (2016). *Hard conversations unpacked: The whos, the whens, and the what-ifs*. Corwin Press.

Adams, J. (2019, August 28). *JEREMY ADAMS: My high school students don't read any more. I think I know why*. Arkansasonline.com. https://www.arkansasonline.com/news/2019/aug/28/columnists-my-high-school-students-don-/

Adey, P., & Shayer, M. (1997). *Really raising standards: Cognitive intervention and academic achievement*. Routledge.

Ancess, J. (2003). *Beating the odds: high schools as communities of commitment*. Teachers College Press.

Anderson, M. (2016). *Learning to choose, choosing to learn*. ASCD.

Anderson, S. E. (2006 Winter). The school district's role in educational change. *International Journal of Educational Reform, 15*(1), 13–37. https://eric.ed.gov/?id=EJ843386no

Atwell, N. (1987). *In the Middle*. Heinemann Educational Books.

Aylsworth, A.J. (2012). Professional learning communities: An analysis of teacher participation in a PLC and the relationship with student academic achievement.

Bailey, A. L., & Heritage, M. (2018). *Self-regulation in learning: the role of language and formative assessment*. Harvard Education Press.

Bambrick-Santoyo, P. (2010). *Driven by data: a practical guide to improve instruction*. Jossey-Bass.

Barth, R. S. (1990). *Improving schools from within: teachers, parents, and principals can make the difference*. Jossey-Bass.

Beers, G K., Probst, R. E., & Rief, L. (2007). *Adolescent literacy: turning promise into practice*. Heinemann.

Bennett, P. W. (2020). *The state of the system: a reality check on Canada's schools*. McGill-Queen's University Press.

Bergmann, J., & Sams, A. (2012). *Flip Your Classroom: Reach Every Student in Every Class Every Day*. International Society for Technology in Education. https://www.rcboe.org/cms/lib/GA01903614/Centricity/Domain/15451/Flip_Your_Classroom.pdf

Biancarosa, G. (2006). *Reading next—A vision for action and research in middle and high school literacy: A report to Carnegie Corporation of New York*. Alliance for Excellent Education.

Bickmore, K. (2014). Citizenship education in Canada: 'Democratic' engagement with differences, conflicts and equity issues?. *Citizenship Teaching & Learning, 9*(3), 257–278. https://doi.org/10.1386/ctl.9.3.257_1

Maeve Binchy. (1996). *Evening Class*. Little Brown and Company.

Boaler, J. (2019). *LIMITLESS MIND: learn, lead and live without barriers*. Thorsons.

Boaler, J., & Dweck, C. S. (2016). *Mathematical mindsets: Unleashing students' potential through creative math, inspiring messages and innovative teaching*. John Wiley & Sons, Incorporated.

Boushey G. and Moser J. . (2014) *The daily 5: Fostering literacy independence in the elementary grades.* Stenhouse Publishers/Pembroke Publishers

Brock A. and Hundley H. (2016). *The growth mindset coach: A teacher's month–by-month handbook for empowering students to achieve.* Ulysses Press

Brookfield S.D (1995). *Becoming a critically reflective teacher.* Jossey-Bass

Brookhart, S. M. (2013). *How to create and use rubrics for formative assessment and grading.* Association for Supervision & Curriculum Development. https://ebookcentral.proquest.com/lib/curtin/reader.action?docID=1123215

Brookhart, S. M. (2013). *Grading and group work: How do I assess individual learning when students work together?* ASCD

Brown, C., & Poortman, C. L. (2018). *Networks for learning: Effective collaboration for teacher, school and system improvement.* Routledge.

Brown G. (1971) *Human Teaching for Human Learning: An Introduction to Confluent Education.* Viking Books

Brownlie F. and Schnellert L. (2009). *It's all about thinking: Collaborating to support all learners"* Portage and Main Press

Bryk A.S and Barbara Schneider B. (2002). *Trust in schools: A core resource for improvement.* Russell Sage Foundation

Butler, R. (1988). Enhancing and undermining intrinsic motivation: The effects of task-involving and ego-involving evaluation of interest and performance. *British Journal of Educational Psychology, 58*(1), 1–14. https://doi.org/10.1111/j.2044-8279.1988.tb00874.x

Canadian Journal for Educational Administration and Policy (CJEAP) (1995). University of Manitoba

Carr N. (2020) *In the Shallows: What the internet is doing to our brains.* Norton

Castillo. G. A. (1974). *Left-Handed teaching*. Praeger

Christensen, L. (2004). Moving Beyond Judgment. *Rethinking Schools*, Volume 19(2). https://rethinkingschools.org/articles/moving-beyond-judgment-my-dirty-little-secret/
Winter 2004-2005

Christison, C. (2013). The benefits of participating in extracurricular activities. *BU Journal of Graduate Studies in Education*, 5(2), 17–20. chrome-extension://efaidnbmnnnibpcajpcglclefindmkaj/https://files.eric.ed.gov/fulltext/EJ1230758.pdf

Chrona, J. (2022). *Wayi wah! Indigenous pedagogies*. Portage & Main Press.

Claxton, G., Maryl Chambers, Powell, G., & Lucas, B. (2013). *The learning powered school: Pioneering 21st Century Education*. Tlo.

Claxton, G. (2015). *Intelligence in the Flesh: Why Bodies Are Smarter Than Thought*. Yale University Press.

Coleman, P., & LaRocque, L. (1990). *Struggling to be 'good enough'*. Psychology Press.

Colvin G. (2008) *Talent is overrated: What really separates world-class performance from everybody else.* Portfolio

Crowther, F., & Hargreaves, A. (2009). *Developing teacher leaders: how teacher leadership enhances school success*. Hawker Brownlow Education.

Cuttance, P. (2001). *School innovation: pathway to the knowledge society.* Commonwealth Of Australia.

Daniels, H., Zemelman, S., & Bizar, M. (2001). *Rethinking high school: Best practice in teaching, learning, and leadership*. Heinemann, Portsmouth, NH

Darling-Hammond, L., Wei, R. C., Andree, A., Richardson, N., & Orphanos, S. (2009). Professional learning in the learning profession: A status report on teacher development in the United States and abroad. In *ERIC*. National Staff Development Council. https://eric.ed.gov/?id=ED536383

Dauber, S. L., & Epstein, J. L. (1993). *Parent attitudes and practices of parent involvement in inner-city elementary and middle schools.* State University of New York Press.

Dean, S. (2023) *Beyond Civics: The Education Democracy Needs.* Sandra Every Dean

Dintersmith, T. (2018). *What school could be: Insights and inspiration from teachers across America.* Princeton University Press

Dominici, P. (2023). The weak link of democracy and the challenges of educating toward global citizenship. *PROSPECTS, 53,* 265–285. https://doi.org/10.1007/s11125-022-09607-8

Donohoo, J, Hattie, J. and Eells, R. (2018). The power of collective efficacy. *Educational Leadership, 75(6).*

Duckworth, A. (2016). *Grit: The power of passion and perseverance.* HarperCollins, Toronto, Ontario

Dufour, R., Dufour, R., Eaker, R., & Many, T. (2006). *Learning by doing: A handbook for professional learning communities at work.* Bloomington, IN: National Education Service

DuFour, R. and Fullan M. (2013). *Cultures built to last: systemic PLCs at work.* Solution Tree Press

Dynarski, S. (2018, January 19). Online courses are harming the students who need the most help. *The New York Times.* https://www.nytimes.com/2018/01/19/business/online-courses-are-harming-the-students-who-need-the-most-help.html

Ellis R. (2015). *Understanding second language acquisition"* 2nd edition. Oxford University Press

Elmore R.F. (2008) *School reform from the inside out: Policy, practice and performance.* Harvard Education

Emig, J. A. (1983). *The web of meaning.* Boynton/Cook.
Eva, A. (2017, November 28). *Why we should embrace mistakes in school.* Greater Good. https://greatergood.berkeley.edu/article/item/why_we_should_embrace_mistakes_in_school

Evans R. (2003). *The human side of school change: Reform, resistance, and the real-life problems of innovation.* Jossey-Bass

Feixas, M. & Zellweger, F. (2010): Faculty development in context: Changing learning cultures in higher education. In Ehlers, U. & Schneckenberg, D. (Eds.) *Changing cultures in higher education- Moving ahead to future learning. A handbook for strategic change.* Springer.

Fisher, D., Frey, N., & Hattie, J. (2016b). *Visible learning for literacy, grades K-12: Implementing the practices that work best to accelerate student learning.* Corwin Literacy.

Flink, C., Boggiano, A. K., & Barrett, M. (1990). "Controlling teaching strategies: Undermining children's self-determination and performance": Correction to flink et al. *Journal of Personality and Social Psychology, 59*(6), 1118–1118. https://doi.org/10.1037/h0090387

Fotos, S., & Nassaji, H. (Eds.). (2009). *Form-Focused instruction and teacher education - oxford applied linguistics.* Oxford University Press.

Freire, P. (1968). *The pedagogy of the oppressed.* (Ramos, M.B. Trans.). Continuum

French W.L. and Bell Jr. C.H. (1973). *Organization development: Behavioural science interventions for organization improvement.* Prentice-Hall Inc.

Fried R. L. (2005). *The game of school.* Jossey-Bass

Danling Fu. (2009). *Writing between languages: How English language learners make the transition to fluency, grades 4-12*. Heinemann.

Fullan, J. (2022, April 4). Opinion: Canadians get a failing grade in civics. *The Globe and Mail*. https://www.theglobeandmail.com/opinion/article-canadians-get-a-failing-grade-in-civics/

Fullan M. (1982). *The meaning of educational change*. OISE Press

Fullan M. & Stiegelbauer S. (1991). *The new meaning of educational change*. Teachers College Press

Fullan M. (2011). *Change leader: Learning to go what matters most*. Jossey-Bass

Fullan M. and Quinn J. (2016). *Coherence: The right drivers in action for schools, districts, and systems*. Corwin

Fullan, M. (2001). *Leading in a culture of change*. Jossey-Bass.

Fullan, M. (2014). *The principal: Three keys to maximizing impact*. Jossey-Bass

Fullan, M., & Mary Jean Gallagher. (2020). *The devil is in the details*. Corwin Press.

Fullan M. (2013). *Motion leadership in action: More skinny on becoming change savvy*. Corwin, Ontario Principals Council, learning forward

Gamoran, A. (2024a). *Synthesis of research / Is ability grouping equitable?* ASCD. https://ascd.org/el/articles/synthesis-of-research---is-ability-grouping-equitable

Gamoran, A. (2024). The variable effects of high school tracking. *American Sociological Review, 57*(6), 812–828. https://eric.ed.gov/?id=EJ456685

Glanz, J. (2016). Action research by practitioners: A case study of a high school's attempt to create transformational change. *Journal of*

Practitioner Research, *1*(1). https://doi.org/10.5038/2379-9951.1.1.1027

Gardner H. (2011). *The unschooled mind: How children think and how schools should teach.* Basic Books of Perseus Books Group

Gardner, M., Browning, C., & Brooks-Gunn, J. (2012). Can Organized Youth Activities Protect Against Internalizing Problems Among Adolescents Living in Violent Homes? *Journal of Research on Adolescence*, *22*(4), 662–677. https://doi.org/10.1111/j.1532-7795.2012.00811.x

Gavel, L. (2017). *Dropout: How school is failing our kids (and what we can do about it)*. Stray Dog Press.

Gill R.T. (2011) *A school as a living entity*. Association of Waldorf Schools of North America

Giltrow J. (2002). *Academic writing: Writing & reading in the disciplines* 3rd edition. Broadview Press Ltd

Giltrow J. (Ed.) (2002). *Academic reading: Reading and writing in the disciplines* 2nd edition Broadview Press Ltd

Giltrow et al. "ACADEMIC WRITING: An Introduction" (2005) Broadview Press Ltd

Gladwell, M. (2011). *Outliers: The story of success.* Penguin Books Random House

Glaze A. et al. "High School Graduation: K-12 Strategies that Work" (2013) Corwin and Ontario Principals' Council

Good, T. and Brophy J. "Looking in Classrooms" (1978) University of Michigan

Goodlad, J. I., & National Society For The Study Of Education. (1987). *The Ecology of school renewal*. National Society For The Study Of Education.

Goodlad, J. I. (2004). *A place called school*. Mcgraw-Hill.

Sinclair Goodlad, & Hirst, B. (1989). *Peer tutoring: A guide to learning by teaching*. New York.

Graham, P., & Ferriter, W. (2010). *Building a professional learning community at work: A guide to the first year*. Solution Tree Press.

Graves, D. H. (1980). Research update: A new look at writing research. *Language Arts*, *57*(8), 913–919. http://www.jstor.org/stable/41405057

Greany T. and Rodd J. (2003). *Creating a learning to learn school.* Network Educational Press Ltd, Stafford

Green, E. (2014). *Building a better teacher: How teaching works (and how to teach it to everyone)*. W.W. Norton & Company.

Hafner, J., & Hafner, P. (2003). Quantitative analysis of the rubric as an assessment tool: an empirical study of student peer-group rating. *International Journal of Science Education*, *25*(12), 1509–1528. https://doi.org/10.1080/0950069022000038268

Halbert, J., Kaser, L., & Bc Principals' & Vice-Principals' Association. (2013). *Spirals of inquiry: For equity and quality*. BC Principals' & Vice-Principals' Association.

Hargreaves, A., & Fullan, M. (2012). *Professional capital: Transforming teaching in every school*. Teachers College Press.

Hargreaves, A., Boyle, A., & Harris, A. (2014). *Uplifting leadership: How organizations, teams, and communities raise performance.* Jossey-Bass, A Wileybrand.

Hargreaves A. (2013). Push, Pull and Nudge: The Future of Teaching and Educational Change In X. Zhu and K. Zeichner (Eds.) *Preparing Teachers for the 21st Century.* (pp 119-142). Heidelberg Springer.

Harris A. (2014) *Distributed Leadership Matters: Perspectives, Practicalities, and Potential.* Corwin, A Sage Company

Hattie, J. (2012). *Visible learning for teachers: Maximizing impact on learning*. Routledge.

Hattie, J. (2009). *Visible learning: A synthesis of over 800 meta-analyses relating to achievement*. Routledge.

Hinchey, P. H., & Konkol, P. J. (2018). *Getting to where we meant to be: Working toward the educational world we imagined*. Myers Education Press.

Hinkel E. (2004). *Teaching academic ESL writing: Practical techniques in vocabulary and grammar*. Routledge

Holt J. (1964). *How Children Fail*. Persus Books

Hord, S. M., & Sommers, W. A. (Eds.). (2008). *Leading professional learning communities: voices from research and practice*. Corwin Press & National Association of Secondary School Principals.

Horton M. and Freire P. (1990) Education and Social Change. In *We make the road by walking: Conversations on Education and Social Change*. (Eds. Bell B., Gaventa G. and Peters J.) Temple University Press

Hu, W., Wu, B., Jia, X., Yi, X., Duan, C., Meyer, W., & Kaufman, J. C. (2013). Increasing students' scientific creativity: The "learn to think" intervention program. *The Journal of Creative Behavior, 47*(1), 3–21. https://doi.org/10.1002/jocb.20

Huberman A.M. and Miles M. (1984). *Innovation Up Close: How School Improvement Works*. Springer Publishing

Jones, K. (Ed.). (2006). *Democratic school accountability*. Rowman & Littlefield Education.

Kaner, S. (2014). *Facilitator's guide to participatory decision-making* (3rd ed.). Jossey-Bass.

Katz, J. (2012). *Teaching to diversity: The three-block model of universal design for learning*. Portage & Main Press.

Kaufman, S. B., & Tsay, C.-J. (2016, May 19). *People favor naturals over strivers — even though they say otherwise*. Harvard Business Review. https://hbr.org/2016/05/people-favor-naturals-over-strivers-even-though-they-say-otherwise

Fisher, R., Ury, W., & Patton, B. (2011). *Getting to yes: Negotiating agreement without giving in.* Pearson.

Kelly, G. A. (1963). *Theory of personality: The psychology of personal constructs.* Norton.

Kiley, D. (2011). *Differentiated instruction in the secondary classroom: Analysis of the level of implementation and factors that influence practice.* Scholar Works at WMU. https://scholarworks.wmich.edu/dissertations/427/

Kise, J. A. G. (2014). *Unleashing the positive power of differences: Polarity thinking in our schools.* Corwin/Learning forward.

Kincheloe, J. & Steinberg, S. (Eds.). (1996). *Thirteen questions: reframing Education's conversation*, 2nd edition. Peter Lang Publishing,

Kohn. A. (2011). *Feel-bad education and other contrarian essays on children and schooling.* Boston, Mass. Beacon Press.

Kohn, A. (1999). *Punished by rewards : The trouble with gold stars, incentive plans, A's, praise, and other bribes.* Mariner Books/Houghton Mifflin Harcourt.

Krapp, A. (1999). Interest, motivation and learning: An educational-psychological perspective. *European Journal of Psychology of Education, 14*(1), 23–40. https://doi.org/10.1007/bf03173109

Kristof, N. (2023, May 31). Mississippi Is Offering Lessons for America on Education. *The New York Times.* https://www.nytimes.com/2023/05/31/opinion/mississippi-education-poverty.html

Kuhlthau, C. C., Maniotas, L. K., & Caspari, A. K. (2007). *Guided inquiry: Learning in the 21st century* (Vol. 8). Libraries Unlimited.

Leana C. (2017). Social capital: An untapped resource for educational improvement. In E. Quintero (ed.) *Teaching in context: How social aspects of schools and school systems shape teachers' development and effectiveness.* Harvard University Press.

Lee, V. E., & Smith, J. B. (1996). Collective Responsibility for Learning and Its Effects on Gains in Achievement for Early Secondary School Students. *American Journal of Education,* 104(2), 103–147. https://doi.org/10.1086/444122

Leithwood, K. A., & Montgomery, D. J. (1986). *Improving principal effectiveness: The principal profile.* OISE Press, The Ontario Institute for Studies in Education.

Levin, S., & Engel, S. (2008). *A school of our own: The story of the first student-run high school and a new vision for American education.* New Press.

Lichtman, G. (2014a). *#EdJourney: A roadmap to the future of education.* Jossey-Bass, A Wiley Brand.

Little, W. J. (2002). Locating learning in teachers' communities of practice: Opening up problems of analysis in records of everyday work. *Teaching and Teacher Education, 18*(8), 917–946. https://doi.org/10.1016/s0742-051x(02)00052-5

Liu, L., Donbavand, S., Hoskins, B., Janmaat, J. G., & Kavadias, D. (2021). *Measuring and evaluating the effectiveness of active citizenship education programmes to support disadvantaged youth.* MDPI - Multidisciplinary Digital Publishing Institute.

Malatest, R. & Associates Limited. (2011). *National Youth Survey Report Prepared for: Elections Canada* (pp. 1–64). https://www.elections.ca/res/rec/part/nysr/nysr-e.pdf

Manson, M. (2016). *The subtle art of not giving a f*ck: a counterintuitive approach to living a good life.* Harper One, an imprint of HarperCollins Publishers.

Marshak, R. J. (2006). *Covert processes at work: Managing the five hidden dimensions of organizational change.* Berrett-Koehler Publishers.

Marshall, K. (2013). *Rethinking teacher supervision and evaluation: How to work smart, build collaboration, and close the achievement gap* (2nd ed.). Jossey-Bass.

Marzano, R. J., Waters, T., & Mcnulty, B. A. (2005). *School leadership that works: From research to results*. Hawker Brownlow Education.

Marzano, R. J. (2003). *What works in schools: Translating research into action*. Association For Supervision and Curriculum Development.

Milbrey Wallin Mclaughlin, & Talbert, J. E. (2006). *Building school-based teacher learning communities: Professional strategies to improve student achievement*. Teachers College Press.

McLaughlin and Talbert J. (2001). *Professional communities and the work of high school teaching*. University of Chicago Press

Miller D. (2009). *The book whisperer: Awakening the inner reader in every child*. Jossey-Bass Inc.

Mitchell, R., & Myles, F. (2004). *Second language learning theories,* (2nd ed.). Hodder Arnold.

Morrish, R. G. (2004). *With all due respect: Keys for building effective school discipline*. Woodstream Publishing.

Morrison, T. (2004). *Remember: The journey to school integration*. Houghton Mifflin Co.

Moseley, D., Baumfield, V., Higgins, S., Lin, M., Miller, J., Newton, D., Robson, S., Elliott, J., & Gregson, M. (2004). Thinking skill frameworks for post-16 learners: an evaluation A research report for the Learning and Skills Research Centre. In *US Department of Education* (pp. 1–158). University of Newcastle. https://files.eric.ed.gov/fulltext/ED508442.pdf

Mourshed, M., Chijioke, C., & Barber, M. (2010). *How the world's most improved school systems keep getting better*. Mckinsey & Company.

Mulford, B. (2004). Congruence between the democratic purposes of schools and school principal training in Australia. *Journal of Educational Administration, Australia, 42*. https://doi.org/10.1108/09578230410563638

Newman, F. M., Bryk, A. S., & Nagaoka, J. (2001, January). *Authentic Intellectual Work and Standardized Tests*. UChicago Consortium on School Research. https://consortium.uchicago.edu/publications/authentic-intellectual-work-and-standardized-tests-conflict-or-coexistence

Newmann F. and Rutter R. et al. "Organizational factors that affect schools' sense of efficacy, community, and expectations." (1989) *Sociology of Education*, 62, p 221–238.

Newport, C. (2016). *Deep work: Rules for focused success in a distracted world*. Grand Central Publishing.

Nielsen, J. (2006b). *F-Shaped pattern for reading web content.* from http://www.useit.com/alertbox/reading_pattern.html.

November A. (2012). *Who owns the learning? Preparing students for success in the digital age* solution. Tree Press

Nussbaum E. (2010) *Not for profit: Why democracy needs the humanities*. Princeton University Press

Oakley, B. A., Rogowsky, B., & Sejnowski, T. J. (2021). *Uncommon sense teaching: practical insights in brain science to help students learn*. Tarcherperigee, An Imprint of Penguin Random House

O'Connor K. (2002). *How to grade for learning: Linking grades to standards*. Pearson Education Inc.

Osei, K. (2022, May 13). *BC high school students draft student press freedom act to protect journalistic rights | Humber News*. Humbernews.ca; Humber News- Faculty of Media, Creative Arts, and Design. https://humbernews.ca/2022/05/bc-high-school-students-draft-student-press-freedom-act-to-protect-journalistic-rights/

Pearson P. & Gallager M. (1983). *The instruction of reading comprehension*. Contemporary *Educational Psychology*

Poliner, R. A., & Lieber, C. M. (2004). *The advisory guide: designing and implementing effective advisory programs in secondary schools*. Educators For Social Responsibility.

Postman N. (1993). *Technopoly: The surrender of culture to technology*. Vintage Books

Reinheimer, B. (2011). *Information Circles: Teaching Students to Read and Respond to Informational Texts* (pp. 1–153) [Master of Education Thesis]. University of Victoria

Ritchhart, R. (2015). *Creating cultures of thinking: The 8 forces we must master to truly transform our schools*. Jossey-Bass & Pfeiffer Imprints, Wiley. https://ebookcentral.proquest.com/lib/acu/reader.action?docID=1895847

Ritchhart, R., Church, M., Morrison, K., & Perkins, D. N. (2011). *Making thinking visible: How to promote engagement, understanding, and independence for all learners*. Jossey-Bass.

Ritchhart R. (2020) *The power of making thinking visible: Practices to engage and empower all learners*. Jossey-Bass Inc. Hoboken

Robinson, V. M. (Viviane M.). (2007). *School leadership and student outcomes: identifying what works and why / Viviane M. J. Robinson*. Winmalee, N.S.W.: Australian Council for Educational Leaders

Roberts T. and Billings L. (1997). *The Paideia Classroom: Teaching for Understanding*. Routledge

Robson, K. (2018, December 12). *Why won't Canada collect data on race and student success?* McMaster University: Business and the Economy; McMaster University. https://brighterworld.mcmaster.ca/articles/why-wont-canada-collect-data-on-race-and-student-success/

Roth, M. S. (2021, March 17). *A focus on critical thinking*. Inside Higher Ed | Higher Education News, Events and Jobs; Times Higher Education. https://www.insidehighered.com/views/2021/03/18/colleges-should-teach-critical-feeling-well-critical-thinking-opinion

Sackstein, S. (2015b). *Teaching students to self-assess*. ASCD.

Sackstein, S. (2015). *Hacking assessment: 10 ways to go gradeless in a traditional grades school*. Times 10 Publications.

Sapolsky, R. M. (2017). *Behave: The biology of humans at our best and worst*. Penguin Books.

Sarason, S. B. (1982). *The culture of the school and the problem of change*. Allyn and Bacon.

Sarason, S.B. [article] "The Predictable Failure of Educational Sarason, S. B. (1990). The predictable failure of educational reform: Can we change course before it's too late? The jossey-bass education series and the jossey-bass social and behavioral science series. In *ERIC*. Jossey-Bass, Inc. https://eric.ed.gov/?id=ED354587

Sarason, S. B. (1996). *Revisiting "the culture of the school and the problem of change."* Teachers College Press.

Sayer, M., & Adey, P. (2002). *Learning intelligence: Cognitive acceleration across the curriculum from 5 to 15 years*. Open University Press.

Schachter, H. (2023, December 7). *"Success is not one big event that changes your life": The benefits of micro-actions*. The Globe and Mail. https://www.theglobeandmail.com/business/careers/management/article-success-is-not-one-big-event-that-changes-your-life-the-benefits-of/

Schriver, K. A. (1994). What can document designers learn from usability testing? *Technostyle, 11*(3/4), 17–35. https://doi.org/10.31468/cjsdwr.364

Sedlak, M. W., Wheeler, C. W., Pullin, D. C., & Cussick, P. A. (1986). *Selling students short: Classroom bargains and academic reforms in American high school*. New York: Teachers College Press.

Seixas, P. (2015). A model of historical thinking. *Educational Philosophy and Theory, 49*(6), 593–605. https://doi.org/10.1080/00131857.2015.1101363

Senge, P. M., Lucas, T., Cambron-Mccabe, N., Dutton, J., Smith, B., & Kliener, A. (2012). *A fifth discipline fieldbook for educators, parents, and everyone who cares about education*. Crown Business.

Sharma, R. (2010). *The leader who had no title: A modern fable on real success in business and in life*. Free Press.

Shulkind, S. B., & Foote, J. (2009). Creating a culture of connectedness through middle school advisory programs. *Middle School Journal*, *41*(1), 20–27. https://doi.org/10.1080/00940771.2009.11461700

Siegel, D. J. MD. (2020). *Aware: The science and practice of presence: The ground breaking meditation practice*. Penguin Random House

Sizer, T. R. (1984). *Horace's compromise: The dilemma of the American high school*. Houghton Mifflin.

Storie J. (2015) *Becoming family: Living and learning at Frontier Collegiate.* McNally Robinson Booksellers

Strahan, D. (2003). Promoting a collaborative professional culture in three elementary schools that have beaten the odds. *The Elementary School Journal*, *104*(2), 127–146. https://doi.org/10.1086/499746

Strang, J., Masterson, P., & Button, O. (2006). *Attitudes skills knowledge: How to teach learning to learn in the secondary school* (B. Lucas, Ed.). Crown House Publishing Ltd.

Steinberg S. and Kincheloe J. (1998). *Students as researchers: Creating classrooms that matter*. Falmer Press, Taylor & Francis Inc.

Tieso, C. (2005). The effects of grouping practices and curricular adjustments on achievement. *Journal for the Education of the Gifted*, *29*(1), 60–89. https://doi.org/10.1177/016235320502900104

Timperley, H. (2011). *Realizing the power of professional learning*. Open University Press.

Tomlinson, C. A. & Strickland, C. A. (2005). *Differentiation in practice: A resource guide for differentiating curriculum grades 9-12*. ASCD.

Tsay C and Kaufman S. [study] "People Favor Naturals over Strivers – Even Though They Say Otherwise" (2016)

Kaufman, S. B., & Tsay, C.-J. (2016, May 19). *People favor naturals over strivers — even though they say otherwise*. Harvard Business Review. https://hbr.org/2016/05/people-favor-naturals-over-strivers-even-though-they-say-otherwise

Ungerleider C. "FAILING OUR KIDS: How We Are Ruining Our Public Schools" (2003). McClelland & Stewart Ltd, Toronto, Ontario Ungerleider, C. (2016, August 16). *Charles Ungerleider: The more things change, the more they stay the same.* Vancouver Sun. https://vancouversun.com/opinion/charles-ungerleider-the-more-things-change-the-more-they-stay-the-same

Vacca R. Vacca J. and Mraz M. (2011) *Content area reading; Literacy and learning across the curriculum.* tenth edition Pearson Education Inc.

Vance, E. (2021, September 1). *The secret to raising a resilient kid.* Nytimes.com; The New York Times. https://www.nytimes.com/2021/09/01/parenting/raising-resilient-kids.html

Van der Meulen, K., Granizo, L., & del Barrio, C. (2021). Emotional peer support interventions for students with SEND: A systematic review. *Frontiers in Psychology, 12*(1). https://doi.org/10.3389/fpsyg.2021.797913

Wagner, R.B. (1989) *Accountability in education: A philosophic inquiry.* Routledge

Wagner, T., & Kegan, R. (2006). *Change leadership: A practical guide to transforming our schools.* Jossey-Bass.

Wagner, T., & Dintersmith, T. (2015). *Most likely to succeed: Preparing our kids for the innovation era.* Scribner.

Westfall-Greiter, T. (2013). Austria's lerndesigner network: The dynamics of virtual professional learning and inter-school networks. In Brown, C., & Poortman, C. L. (2018). *Networks for learning: Effective collaboration for teacher, school and system improvement.* (pp. 92-113). Routledge.

Westover, S. (2021, August 22). *I found comfort in exercising – The one thing I used to hate.* The Globe and Mail.

https://www.theglobeandmail.com/life/first-person/article-i-found-comfort-in-exercising-the-one-thing-i-used-to-hate/

Wheelock, A., and Lynne L. (1997). "Making detracking work." *Harvard Education Letter 13*. January-February

White, E. B., White, M., & Meacham, J. (2019). *On democracy*. Harper.

Wiliam, D., & Leahy, S. (2015). *Embedding formative assessment: practical techniques for K-12 classrooms*. Learning Sciences.

Jon Douglas Willms, & Canada. Développement Des Ressources Humaines Canada. Direction Générale De La Recherche Appliquée. (2002). *Vulnerable children: findings from Canada's National Longitudinal Survey of Children and Youth*. University Of Alberta Press.

Wilson, M. (2006). *Rethinking rubrics in writing assessment*. Heinemann.

Wood, D. R. (2007). Professional Learning Communities: Teachers, Knowledge, and Knowing. *Theory into Practice, 46*(4), 281–290. https://doi.org/10.1080/00405840701593865

Wood, G.H. (2005). *Time to learn: How to create high schools that serve all students,* 2nd edition. Heinemann, Portsmouth NH

Wright, L. L. (2008). Merits and Limitations of Distributed Leadership: Experiences and Understandings of School Principals. *Canadian Journal of Educational Administration and Policy, 69*.

Zeichner and Liston. (1990). *Traditions of reform in U.S. teacher education*. International Centre for Educational Change Ontario Institute for Studies in Education

Zhao, Y. (2006, May 9). *A pause before plunging through the China looking glass (opinion)*. Education Week. https://www.edweek.org/policy-politics/opinion-a-pause-before-plunging-through-the-china-looking-glass/2006/05

Zins, J. Bloodworth M. Weissberg R. and Walberg J. (2004). "The scientific base linking social and emotional learning to school success."

Chapter published in *Building academic success on social and emotional learning: What does the research say?* Teachers College, Columbia University.

Zohar, A., David, A.B. Explicit teaching of meta-strategic knowledge in authentic classroom situations. *Metacognition Learning.* **3**, 59–82 (2008). https://doi.org/10.1007/s11409-007-9019-4